The Violence of Emotions

In *The Violence of Emotions* the author marries an ability to introduce the reader to the intimate climate of an analytic session with a passionate re-reading of Bion. To emphasize both the empirical nature of psychoanalysis and its extraordinary capacity to engender illuminating hypotheses concerning the functioning of the mind, clinical examples alternate with theoretical argument. The psychoanalytic model espoused by Giuseppe Civitarese in his approach to both is analytic field theory. Developed by various authors, including Ferro, commencing with Bion and continued with contributions from the Barangers, Grotstein and Ogden, the theory of the analytic field highlights the social nature of subjectivity and, in clinical work, the intersubjective and dreamlike climate in which a psychoanalytic session unfolds. This leads to a new way of interpreting the facts of analysis. As such, topics of discussion include:

- transcending the caesura as Bion's theoretical method
- hypochondria as de-subjectivation and narrative genre in analysis
- the aesthetic conflict and alpha function
- Bion's search for ambiguity
- the casting of characters in the analytic dialogue
- metaphors of text and translation in Freud and Bion.

Yet the book has an even more specific objective, focusing attention as it does on the central importance of emotions in mental life and of aesthetic experience as the model of what truly happens in analysis. This is an aspect which the author rediscovers and explores in the thought of Bion and his successors, and which he regards as a way of investigating the deepest and most primitive levels of mental life. This book will be of great interest to psychiatrists, psychoanalysts, and psychotherapists.

Giuseppe Civitarese is a psychiatrist with a PhD in psychiatry and relational sciences. He is a member of the Italian Psychoanalytic Society (SPI) and of the American Psychoanalytic Association (APsaA), both affiliated to the International Psychoanalytic Association (IPA). His previous publications include *The Intimate Room: Theory and Technique of the Analytic Field.*

THE NEW LIBRARY OF PSYCHOANALYSIS

General Editor: Alessandra Lemma

The New Library of Psychoanalysis was launched in 1987 in association with the Institute of Psychoanalysis, London. It took over from the International Psychoanalytical Library which published many of the early translations of the works of Freud and the writings of most of the leading British and Continental psychoanalysts.

The purpose of the New Library of Psychoanalysis is to facilitate a greater and more widespread appreciation of psychoanalysis and to provide a forum for increasing mutual understanding between psychoanalysts and those working in other disciplines such as the social sciences, medicine, philosophy, history, linguistics, literature and the arts. It aims to represent different trends both in British psychoanalysis and in psychoanalysis generally. The New Library of Psychoanalysis is well placed to make available to the English-speaking world psychoanalytic writings from other European countries and to increase the interchange of ideas between British and American psychoanalysts. Through the *Teaching Series*, the New Library of Psychoanalysis now also publishes books that provide comprehensive, yet accessible, overviews of selected subject areas aimed at those studying psychoanalysis and related fields such as the social sciences, philosophy, literature and the arts.

The Institute, together with the British Psychoanalytical Society, runs a low-fee psychoanalytic clinic, organizes lectures and scientific events concerned with psychoanalysis and publishes the *International Journal of Psychoanalysis*. It runs the training course in psychoanalysis which leads to membership of the International Psychoanalytical Association – the body which preserves internationally agreed standards of training, of professional entry, and of professional ethics and practice for psychoanalysis as initiated and developed by Sigmund Freud. Distinguished members of the Institute have included Michael Balint, Wilfred Bion, Ronald Fairbairn, Anna Freud, Ernest Jones, Melanie Klein, John Rickman and Donald Winnicott.

Previous general editors have included David Tuckett, who played a very active role in the establishment of the New Library. He was followed as general editor by Elizabeth Bott Spillius, who was in turn followed by Susan Budd and then by Dana Birksted-Breen.

ALSO IN THIS SERIES

Impasse and Interpretation Herbert Rosenfeld
Psychoanalysis and Discourse Patrick Mahony
The Suppressed Madness of Sane Men Marion Milner
The Riddle of Freud Estelle Roith
Thinking, Feeling, and Being Ignacio Matte Blanco
The Theatre of the Dream Salomon Resnik
Melanie Klein Today: Volume 1, Mainly Theory Edited by Elizabeth Bott Spillius
Melanie Klein Today: Volume 2, Mainly Practice Edited by Elizabeth Bott Spillius
Psychic Equilibrium and Psychic Change: Selected Papers of Betty Joseph Edited by Michael Feldman and Elizabeth Bott Spillius
About Children and Children-No-Longer: Collected Papers 1942–80 Paula Heimann. Edited by Margret Tonnesmann
The Freud–Klein Controversies 1941–45 Edited by Pearl King and Riccardo Steiner
Dream, Phantasy and Art Hanna Segal
Psychic Experience and Problems of Technique Harold Stewart
Clinical Lectures on Klein & Bion Edited by Robin Anderson
From Fetus to Child Alessandra Piontelli
A Psychoanalytic Theory of Infantile Experience: Conceptual and Clinical Reflections Eugenio Gaddini. Edited by Adam Limentani
The Dream Discourse Today Edited and introduced by Sara Flanders
The Gender Conundrum: Contemporary Psychoanalytic Perspectives on Feminitity and Masculinity Edited and introduced by Dana Breen
Psychic Retreats John Steiner
The Taming of Solitude: Separation Anxiety in Psychoanalysis Jean-Michel Quinodoz
Unconscious Logic: An Introduction to Matte-Blanco's Bi-logic and its Uses Eric Rayner
Understanding Mental Objects Meir Perlow
Life, Sex and Death: Selected Writings of William Gillespie Edited and introduced by Michael Sinason
What Do Psychoanalysts Want?: The Problem of Aims in Psychoanalytic Therapy Joseph Sandler and Anna Ursula Dreher
Michael Balint: Object Relations, Pure and Applied Harold Stewart
Hope: A Shield in the Economy of Borderline States Anna Potamianou
Psychoanalysis, Literature & War: Papers 1972–1995 Hanna Segal

Emotional Vertigo: Between Anxiety and Pleasure Danielle Quinodoz
Early Freud and Late Freud Ilse Grubrich-Simitis
A History of Child Psychoanalysis Claudine and Pierre Geissmann
Belief and Imagination: Explorations in Psychoanalysis Ronald Britton
A Mind of One's Own: A Psychoanalytic View of Self and Object Robert A Caper
Psychoanalytic Understanding of Violence and Suicide Edited by Rosine Jozef Perelberg
On Bearing Unbearable States of Mind Ruth Riesenberg-Malcolm
Psychoanalysis on the Move: The Work of Joseph Sandler Edited by Peter Fonagy, Arnold M. Cooper and Robert S. Wallerstein
The Dead Mother: The Work of André Green Edited by Gregorio Kohon
The Fabric of Affect in the Psychoanalytic Discourse André Green
The Bi-Personal Field: Experiences of Child Analysis Antonino Ferro
The Dove that Returns, the Dove that Vanishes: Paradox and Creativity in Psychoanalysis Michael Parsons
Ordinary People, Extra-ordinary Protections: A Post Kleinian Approach to the Treatment of Primitive Mental States Judith Mitrani
The Violence of Interpretation: From Pictogram to Statement Piera Aulagnier
The Importance of Fathers: A Psychoanalytic Re-Evaluation Judith Trowell and Alicia Etchegoyen
Dreams That Turn Over a Page: Paradoxical Dreams in Psychoanalysis Jean-Michel Quinodoz
The Couch and the Silver Screen: Psychoanalytic Reflections on European Cinema Andrea Sabbadini
In Pursuit of Psychic Change: The Betty Joseph Workshop Edited by Edith Hargreaves and Arturo Varchevker
The Quiet Revolution in American Psychoanalysis: Selected Papers of Arnold M. Cooper Arnold M. Cooper, Edited and Introduced by Elizabeth L. Auchincloss
Seeds of Illness and Seeds of Recovery: The genesis of suffering and the role of psychoanalysis Antonino Ferro
The Work of Psychic Figurability: Mental States Without Representation César Botella and Sára Botella
Key Ideas for a Contemporary Psychoanalysis: Misrecognition and Recognition of the Unconscious André Green

The Telescoping of Generations: Listening to the Narcissistic Links Between Generations Haydée Faimberg
Glacial Times: A Journey through the World of Madness Salomon Resnik
This Art of Psychoanalysis: Dreaming Undreamt Dreams and Interrupted Cries Thomas H Ogden
Psychoanalysis and Religion in the 21st Century: Competitors or Collaborators? David M. Black
Recovery of the Lost Good Object Eric Brenman
The Many Voices of Psychoanalysis Roger Kennedy
Feeling the Words: Neuropsychoanalytic Understanding of Memory and the Unconscious Mauro Mancia
Constructions and the Analytic Field: History, Scenes and Destiny Domenico Chianese
Projected Shadows: Psychoanalytic Reflections on the Representation of Loss in European Cinema Edited by Andrea Sabbadini
Encounters with Melanie Klein: Selected Papers of Elizabeth Spillius Elizabeth Spillius
Yesterday, Today and Tomorrow Hanna Segal
Psychoanalysis Comparable and Incomparable: The Evolution of a Method to Describe and Compare Psychoanalytic Approaches David Tuckett, Roberto Basile, Dana Birksted-Breen, Tomas Böhm, Paul Denis, Antonino Ferro, Helmut Hinz, Arne Jemstedt, Paola Mariotti and Johan Schubert
Time, Space and Phantasy Rosine Jozef Perelberg
Rediscovering Psychoanalysis: Thinking and Dreaming, Learning and Forgetting Thomas H. Ogden
Mind Works: Techniques and Creativity in Psychoanalysis Antonino Ferro
Doubt Conviction and the Analytic Process: Selected Papers of Michael Feldman Michael Feldman
Melanie Klein in Berlin: Her First Psychoanalyses of Children Claudia Frank
The Psychotic Wavelength: A Psychoanalytic Perspective for Psychiatry Richard Lucas
Betweenity: A Discussion of the Concept of Borderline Judy Gammelgaard
The Intimate Room: Theory and Technique of the Analytic Field Giuseppe Civitarese
Bion Today Edited by Chris Mawson
Secret Passages: The Theory and Technique of Interpsychic Relations Stefano Bolognini

Intersubjective Processes and the Unconscious: An Integration of Freudian, Kleinian and Bionian Perspectives Lawrence J. Brown
Seeing and Being Seen: Emerging from a Psychic Retreat John Steiner
Avoiding Emotions, Living Emotions Antonino Ferro
Projective Identification: The Fate of a Concept Edited by Elizabeth Spillius and Edna O'Shaughnessy
Creative Readings: Essays on Seminal Analytic Works Thomas Ogden
The Maternal Lineage Edited by Paola Mariotti
Donald Winnicott Today Edited by Jan Abram
Symbiosis and Ambiguity: A Psychoanalytic Study Edited by John Churcher, José Bleger and Leopoldo Bleger
Psychotic Temptation Liliane Abensour
The Theory and Technique of Psychoanalytic Supervision: The Sao Paulo Clinical Seminars Antonino Ferro

TITLES IN THE NEW LIBRARY OF PSYCHOANALYSIS TEACHING SERIES

Reading Freud: A Chronological Exploration of Freud's Writings Jean-Michel Quinodoz
Listening to Hanna Segal: Her Contribution to Psychoanalysis Jean-Michel Quinodoz
Reading French Psychoanalysis Edited by Dana Birksted-Breen, Sara Flanders and Alain Gibeault
Reading Winnicott Lesley Caldwell and Angela Joyce
Initiating Psychoanalysis: Perspectives Bernard Reith, Sven Lagerlöf, Penelope Crick, Mette Møller and Elisabeth Skale
Infant Observation Frances Salo
Reading Anna Freud Nick Midgley

TITLES IN THE NEW LIBRARY OF PSYCHOANALYSIS 'BEYOND THE COUCH' SERIES

Under the Skin: A Psychoanalytic Study of Body Modification Alessandra Lemma
Engaging with Climate Change: Psychoanalytic and Interdisciplinary Perspectives Edited by Sally Weintrobe

THE NEW LIBRARY OF PSYCHOANALYSIS

General Editor: Alessandra Lemma

The Violence of Emotions

Bion and post-Bionian psychoanalysis

Giuseppe Civitarese

Translated by
Ian Harvey

Routledge
Taylor & Francis Group
LONDON AND NEW YORK

First published 2013
by Routledge
27 Church Road, Hove, East Sussex BN3 2FA

Simultaneously published in the USA and Canada
by Routledge
711 Third Avenue, New York, NY 10017

Routledge is an imprint of the Taylor & Francis Group, an informa business

British Library Cataloguing in Publication Data
A catalogue record for this book is available from the British Library

Library of Congress Cataloging in Publication Data
Civitarese, Giuseppe, 1958-
[Violenza delle Emozioni. English]
The violence of emotions : Bion and post-Bionian psychoanalysis / Giuseppe Civitarese.
p. cm. -- (The new library of psychoanalysis)
Includes bibliographical references and index.
ISBN 978-0-415-69212-0 (hardback) -- ISBN 978-0-415-69213-7 (pbk.) 1. Medicine, Psychosomatic. 2. Emotions--Psychological aspects. 3. Psychoanalysis--Methodology. I. Title.
RC49.C47 2012
616.08--dc23
2012015188

ISBN: 978-0-415-69212-0 (hbk)
ISBN: 978-0-415-69213-7 (pbk)
ISBN: 978-0-203-08456-4 (ebk)

Typeset in Bembo
by Saxon Graphics Ltd, Derby

For Antonino Ferro, teacher and friend

Contents

Contents

Foreword

Andrea Sabbadini

Since psychoanalysis was introduced by Edoardo Weiss in Trieste in the 1920s, our discipline has only produced a handful of Italian analysts of international standing, among them Emilio Servadio, Cesare Musatti, Franco Fornari and Enrico Gaddini. In the last few years, however, several talented Italian colleagues have been emerging whose theories have come to the attention of a wider psychoanalytic community.

A new generation of analysts, including Giuseppe Civitarese, have helped to bring about a creative phase in the history of Italian psychoanalysis.[1] These colleagues often find their inspiration in the work of classic authors such as Ferenczi, Klein, Winnicott, Bion and Matte Blanco, whose ideas they then develop in their own original ways. Their active presence at international congresses, the publication of their papers in foreign journals and the translation of their books in other languages, especially English, have enabled them to gain recognition beyond the hitherto somewhat parochial confines of Italian psychoanalytic institutions.

Civitarese's latest book, *The Violence of Emotions*, originally appeared in 2011 in Italy, where it was deservedly praised; we now welcome its prompt publication in English. It is an organic sequel to a first volume of essays in which Civitarese had dwelt, *inter alia,* on the importance for his own thinking and practice of Willy and Madeleine Baranger's model of the bipersonal field.[2] *The Violence of Emotions* consists of eight psychoanalytic essays that touch on a variety of theoretical and clinical issues within the perspective of the expanding body of Bionian studies.[3] The book, however, is by no means only for the hardcore Bion faithful, nor for the post-Bionian analysts who have followed in his footsteps – and it is far from just a respectful homage to the Master.

Emotions, while not being intrinsically violent, may nevertheless make us feel overwhelmed by their intensity, their unexpectedness or their apparent inappropriateness, as they emerge from unconscious corners of our minds. They will then catch us unprepared to deal with them through what, from the outside, we would consider to be reasonable responses. This applies to all human beings in their daily interpersonal relationships, and more specifically to psychoanalysts and patients during sessions – a truth Civitarese does not hesitate to remind us about, and one which colours much of his clinical thinking. Indeed, it could be claimed that such 'emotionally violent' (or, better, 'irrational') processes constitute the essence itself of transference and counter-transference phenomena.

I am aware of two pitfalls that one could fall into when prefacing a book. The first is to reveal too much about its content (what film critics refer to as 'spoilers'), because one of the great pleasures of reading is the sense of anticipation; anything that gives away the element of surprise in the introductory pages will 'spoil' this enjoyable experience. The second danger consists in offering premature interpretations about the author's ideas. While of course such interpretations will represent nothing more than a subjective opinion, there is a risk that the appreciation of the book will be coloured rather than illuminated by them, and the reader will be left feeling short-changed.

These pitfalls notwithstanding, I still consider it my task to mention here at least some of the main themes of Civitarese's book. Particularly significant is what he calls the aesthetic and oneiric dimensions of psychoanalytic work, a view which he develops throughout the book. He considers the aesthetic experience as the most profound element in psychoanalysis, where conceptual reflection and clinical research can find a point of effective articulation. His understanding of aesthetic experiences, which he links to Bion's (and Ferro's) insistence on the oneiric quality of much mental activity (not just, that is, of the night dreams) is an extension of Meltzer's idea of an 'aesthetic conflict' originating in the baby's ambivalent attraction towards the maternal breast.

Keeping in mind the application to psychoanalysis of Keats's concept of 'negative capability' and Grotstein's description of our discipline as a 'mystical science' (something Civitarese agrees with only in the sense of its 'inexhaustible drive towards the unexplored and the ultimate meaning of things', p. 46), he develops Bion's views on the relationship between painting and 'the aesthetics of the real'. He argues that art has a similar function to psychoanalysis: to allow the surfacing of, and to put us in touch with, profound emotional experiences; to meet reality ('O', in Bionian language) while accepting that the knowledge ('K') of it could only offer us a distorted picture, based as it is on a state of 'normal hallucinosis' (he quotes Grotstein as saying that 'knowing reality involves dreaming it'). All of which has implications for our psychoanalytic work, as illustrated by Civitarese through a series of vignettes from his practice. The emphasis moves away from any attempt to reconstruct the past or even to account for current external events, towards the present aesthetic experience of the emotionally charged encounter between the internal worlds of analyst and patient, 'dreaming' the session together.

In the chapter on 'Caesura', Civitarese bravely links Bion's view that thoughts pre-date the activity of thinking to Descartes's theory of knowledge. Illustrated by some intriguing analytic material is the chapter on hypochondria: 'a malady not of the body but of relationships', the author claims, deriving from unresolved issues in the process of subjectivation, as 'a way of defending oneself from anxiety through a process of desubjectivization' (p. 69). Another important chapter is the one where Civitarese adopts the language of performing arts and literary representation (casting, improvization, acting, screenwriting, etc.) to describe the formation of the self and its relation to others, specifically in the analytic context of the transference. The author's familiarity with a vast cultural field, allowing him to provide relevant examples from the worlds of drama, film and literature, together with his clinical illustrations, make the reading of this chapter a stimulating experience.

In the last chapter Civitarese approaches the complex issue of mnestic traces, recollection of memories and *Nachträglichkeit* by elaborating on the differences between, on the one hand, Freud's view of the human being as a *tabula rasa* as reflected in his brilliant essay on the 'mystic writing-pad' (1924a) interpreted here according to Derrida's reading, and, on the other hand, Bion's (and Winnicott's) belief that 'the psychic surface on which the child inscribes the mental data of its experience at birth is the memory of the mother, that is to say, a page that is by no means immaculate but rather is already written' (p. 173) – thus supporting an interpersonal psychology.

Reading Civitarese's book, an activity sometimes demanding but always rewarding, I have been impressed by a number of its features. First of all, while rigorously adhering to a psychoanalytic perspective, if one rooted in Bion's often unconventional theories, the author's choice of topics shows an original independence from the traditional analytic canon. Related to such originality is the courage with which Civitarese develops his themes, allowing his own imagination to challenge preconceived ideas, to explore aspects of the human experience not often touched upon by other psychoanalysts, and never refraining from exposing his own therapeutic work in the service of illustrating his more abstract thoughts with vivid case material.

Another central feature of *The Violence of Emotions* is the solidity of Civitarese's scholarly approach – an approach rooted in his extensive understanding of a variety of psychoanalytic theories and in his familiarity with a wide spectrum of cultural concerns. This results in the introduction of stimulating and cogently argued parallels with ideas culled from other disciplines, such as philosophy and literature.

Last but not least, I value Civitarese's clarity of writing-style (a welcome departure from the gratuitous crypticism of some of his Italian colleagues), even when dealing with the most complex of issues.

At a time when many Cassandras rush to announce the death of psychoanalysis, *The Violence of Emotions* offers a powerful challenge to their gloomy predictions. The ideas running through our discipline, if not perhaps its professional practice, reveal that it is in a healthy state and that in our fast-paced time of easy but superficial communication and social networking, and of pervasive crises of identity, psychoanalysis is more needed than ever to provide reflections on the meanings of personal experiences, in contrast to the shortcuts to happiness recommended by other mental health practitioners.

The richness and intellectual rigour of Civitarese's book offers the best evidence that our impossible profession is still full of life – in its theoretical approach to the understanding of contemporary issues, in its engagement with creative interdisciplinary dialogues, and as a sophisticated method for the exploration of the deepest recesses of the human mind.

Acknowledgements

Chapter 1 is based on '"Caesura" as Bion's discourse on method', *International Journal of Psychoanalysis*, 89: 1123–1143, 2008. This chapter was translated by Philip Slotkin.

Chapter 2 is based on 'Bion e la ricerca dell'ambiguità', *L'educazione sentimentale*, 8: 121–132, 2006; *Revista de Psicanálise*, 14: 57–76, 2007.

Chapter 5 is based on 'Per un'estetica bioniana', *L'educazione sentimentale*, 11: 124–130, 2008; *Koinos: Gruppo e funzione analitica*, 29: 105–114, 2008. This chapter was translated by John Coggan.

Chapter 7 is based on 'Il disagio del setting interno dell'analista', *Gli Argonauti*, 30: 253–266, 2008.

Acknowledgements

Introduction

'Whose Bion?' was the title chosen by Edna O'Shaughnessy (2005) for her intervention in a debate organized some years ago by the *International Journal of Psychoanalysis* on the controversial readings that several authors have given to Bion's work. There followed other contributions by Ferro and Bianchedi, and the discussion continued in the form of some letters to the editor of the journal. One of these letters was from Grotstein (2006). He attributed Bion's dense style and his radical conception of dreaming (an activity of the mind that takes place both at night and during the day) to his habit of immersing himself in poetry and questions of aesthetics. My reading of Bion, which like any other is simply one possible reading, draws its inspiration from this insight of Grotstein's and from another of his ideas, namely, that aesthetic experience is the most profound element of psychoanalysis.

The thread that runs through all of this book, and that to my mind gives it unity, is indeed the exploration of the aesthetic theme, which I investigate from a dual perspective. On the one hand, I try to place Bion's conception of psychoanalysis along an axis of continuity with Freud and Melanie Klein, but as I develop my theoretical discourse I also seek to emphasize the moments of caesura; on the other hand, what I'm interested in is keeping Bion alive and taking useful conceptual tools from him for the daily work of analysis. The stimuli, models and ideas that he has left us are now no longer separable from the contribution of the scholars who have interpreted his thoughts in an original way and have expanded their theoretical and technical potential. Now, it seems to me that conceptual reflection and clinical research can find an effective pivot precisely in the theme of aesthetics (and dreaming).

The first problem that arises, then, is how to approach the 'secret' of Bion's creativity, and for this reason I have chosen to revisit a brief paper of Bion's from his last period, 'Caesura' (1977c), which is emblematic of his style – both difficult and fascinating, frustrating and brilliant. I read *Caesura* as the equivalent of Descartes' *Discourse on Method* (1637). By taking it to extremes and applying it to the very faculty of thought itself, the dictum of 'methodical' and 'hyperbolic doubt' became for Descartes the ultimate principle of philosophical and scientific research; in Bion's somewhat cryptic text it translates into the formula of 'transcending the caesura'. Bion focuses successively on the different opposing pairs of concepts that structure psychoanalytic discourse and demonstrates their paradoxical and non-separative logic. The binary system of meaning making is deconstructed through the systematic use of non-pathological – that is, not static but dynamic – reversal of perspective. A viewpoint that appears natural, self-evident and primary is plunged into crisis and proves to be founded on what the punctuation mark of the slash excludes. Yet rather than supplanting its predecessor, the new point of view adds to it. The conceptual opposition is not reversed, but merely destabilized in such a way as to keep up the creative tension that generates new thoughts. This shows the differential economy that regulates the operation. By this technique of wrong-footing the reader, Bion achieves what amounts to a Kuhnian revolution: the transition from Freud's semiotic or evidence-based paradigm to an aesthetic paradigm centred on emotional experience, a 'science of *at-one-ment*'. Finally, playing on the antithesis between censorship and caesura, I take a clinical vignette to illustrate some of the implications that this change has for psychoanalytic technique.

I then go on to look again at the subject of Bion's 'method' from another angle of vision. Meltzer (1978) discerns in Bion's style of writing a genuine search for ambiguity. His readers are certainly very familiar with this ambiguity, which they experience as a source of both delight and torment. Also the colleagues who attended his seminars had direct experience of it. But for Bion ambiguity has a defined value. It activates the psychoanalytic function of the mind. In his view, in fact, psychoanalysis can be seen as a special probe that explores the unknown of the psyche in an act of reconnaissance that continuously expands the field. Thus, Bion's darkness, the black light of dream projected on to things, is nothing other than the desire to be '*precisely* obscure' (Bion, 1975, p. 191), to achieve the ideal state of mind which he calls negative capability, and to free oneself as far as possible of preconceived ideas. To focus on knowledge you need to be able to tolerate the frustration that comes from not understanding, from paradox, from the aporias of reason, and what Freud called overdetermination, in other words, the plurality of possible meanings.

In Bion, *knowledge*, 'K', becomes a primary drive. It is equivalent to searching for food for the mind, the tension that constantly pushes the mind to personalize, or to dream, 'O'. What this evocative letter of the alphabet denotes – the real that is unknowable in itself – imposes itself on the ego through the thoughts waiting to be thought that are emotions; through the impact of the irrepressible biological imperatives of thirst, hunger and cold; and through the supreme need of the child to be soothed, comforted and held – the need that underlies every moral determination (Freud, 1895). And every knock, every encounter with 'O' with 'the other tiger',[1] is transformed into thought when the truth it expresses paradoxically takes on the guise of a lie. Because 'O', like sunlight, cannot be looked at without filters. A rhetoric of blindness and vision is what forms the weave of Bion's thought, and this perhaps explains Bion's fascination with the mystical writer (and poet) Saint John of the Cross.

In his books, Bion often refers to the hypochondriac experience, the subject of Chapter 3, and I think this is because this common form of 'somatic paranoia' takes on a paradigmatic meaning within his theory of mind. Here again, it is a question of how to regain – or acquire for the first time – visibility in the eyes of the objects of one's inner life. The starting point here is an illuminating observation in *Learning from Experience* (1962); here Bion sees the 'hypochondriac system' as an attempt to re-establish a connection with the reality of one's own emotions by replacing them with physical sensations and by obsessively investigating their meaning. The hypochondriac symptom shows how for the healthy psychological life it is essential to have not only the consensuality of the senses in perceiving the objects of physical reality, but also of the consensual emotional experience of consciousness – what Freud (1899) calls the sense organ for the perception of psychic qualities. This theme is reminiscent of Klein's notion of the importance of attaining the depressive position, that is, realising one's emotional ambivalence towards the object. It goes without saying that Bion addresses the concept of PS $\leftrightarrow$ D oscillation in an extremely original way, no longer from the diachronic perspective of how a process of maturation evolves, but from the synchronic point of view of a mode of functioning of the mind.

Hypochondria can be examined from an intrapsychic perspective, in line with classical metapsychology, or from an inter-psychic viewpoint. Both approaches are legitimate. In my view, however, the latter is a more accurate way of registering the field dynamics that can help the patient's psychic growth. If one is using the concept of waking dream thought, perhaps the most revolutionary of Bion's ideas, the story of hypochondriac suffering becomes one of the possible narrative genres that patient and analyst unconsciously choose to recount what is happening, moment by moment, in the analytic field. Finally, I go on to use the Freudian concept of the 'hypochondria of the dream' and the attendant idea of 'dream-work' because they show that hypochondriac symptoms can also stimulate symbolization.

In order to investigate this area of Bion's research from another point of view – in other words, looking into how the mind can acquire a 'binocular' vision of reality – and taking my cue from the idea of 'personifying' the split parts of the personality described in the article 'The imaginary twin' (which later became the first chapter of *Second Thoughts* (1967)), I go on to develop further Ferro's concept of casting (2007). The question is: what does the choice of a certain figure from the manifest text, or of a certain reverie, represent for the analytic dialogue and the process that underlies it? Once this choice is made, this character plays the part of a split-off aspect of the patient, that is, the role of a part of himself that performs, without an audience, in the theatre of his unconscious but which in the light of the concept of the field can also represent something that belongs to the analyst, or to both. There are clinical situations in which this decision is made in a felicitous and unexpected way, and others again where it proves difficult, and where, so to speak, the scene of the analysis appears empty. The concept of casting also offers an occasion for drawing attention to the aesthetic experience of analysis.

Bion's psychoanalytic theory can be described as 'aesthetic' for two reasons: both because it puts emotion, *aisthesis*, back at the centre of thought, and because it brings thinking back to its oneiric ground, to the operations Freud saw as composing the explicit text of the dream which are also involved in dreaming for the purpose of artistic creation. It is no accident that the first name for the α function was dream-work-α. I was originally stimulated to address this question by reading *Transformations* (1965), one of Bion's most demanding books; one of the peculiarities of this book is its repeated use of the metaphor of art, especially painting. My proposition is that one can read a theory of aesthetic experience between the lines of *Transformations* and that, conversely, it can illuminate the analytic experience. This chapter can be seen as putting forward a theoretical premise for the following chapter which deals with aesthetic conflict and the α function but does so by drawing on clinical practice.

Among the works that investigate the meaning of the aesthetic emotion there are very few that address the issue from the perspective of clinical practice. What's more, most of these articles make no distinction between the feeling of beauty evoked by nature and the apprehension of art. Here I would like to help fill both these gaps. I discuss a detailed clinical vignette in the light of Meltzer's concept of aesthetic conflict, Kristeva's concept of abjection and Bion's α function. Meltzer's insight, in fact, expresses its full heuristic potential only if supplemented by the Kristevian theory of aesthetic experience, and if seen in terms of the original idea of Bion's that lies behind it: 'In the beginning was the aesthetic object and the aesthetic object was the breast and the breast was the world' (Meltzer, 1986, p. 204).

The pathology of the aesthetic conflict (or in other words, the inability to experience beauty in an authentic fashion and the flight into the aestheticization and fetishization of art) seems to originate from a certain negative quality of the mother's reverie. What I emphasize about this negative reverie, which I describe by introducing the Barthesian notion of the *fading* of the object, is its primitively sensory character. Hence, conversely, I deduce what seem to me to be the essential elements of the aesthetic object: sensoriality, rhythm and fictionality. Finally, I define the aesthetic experience as an opportunity to restore body to the mind or, to put it another way, to promote a basic psycho-somatic reintegration, first and foremost to meet the need to structure a space where the ego can develop, 'this side of the pleasure principle' and prior to sublimation.

In Bion's theory, the attention paid to the way in which the mind apprehends the real 'aesthetically', and thus also to the psychoanalytic function of the mind, is constant. This results from the importance he gives to the concepts of container/contained, projective identification/reverie and negative capability/selected fact. How the analyst's mind functions, how it proves itself capable of reverie, of taking on and transforming the emotions transmitted by the patient – these questions become a central variable in therapy. Not only that: in a radically intersubjective dimension what are significant are the images that occur to both of the actors performing on the theatrical stage of analysis. The caesura between patient and analyst becomes dialectical: how do we know, Bion asks, what belongs to one and what belongs to the other? It is as if the concept of setting became internalized, and in fact we can speak of the institution of the internal setting. Compared to the idea that Freud probably had of it, the idea of internal setting, which is the subject of Chapter 7, is a richer and more versatile concept because it takes a 360° and no longer just a 180°. That is to say, it also takes in the analyst's mind. At the same time it radicalizes the oneiric paradigm in the session: there is at least one vertex from which all the facts of physical and factual reality can be referred back to the dream of the analysis. Consequently, the analyst feels more responsible when he decides, based on each individual situation, what to consider relevant to the transference and what to exclude from it.

The last chapter looks at the metaphor of the text in Freud and Bion. The idea is to bring out affinities and differences between the two authors within the general framework of the shift in contemporary psychoanalysis from a one-person to a two-person psychology. Admirably suited to this purpose is Freud's paper, as short as it is fascinating, on the mystic writing pad (1924a), about which Derrida wrote a memorable work (1967). By comparing the meaning of Freud's metaphor and Bion's Grid, I seek to show how in Bion the 'suitable lights' of the transference, which Freud used to read the impressions apparently cleared from the wax tablet of the writing pad (of memory), essentially become the reverie. While the concept of transference is characterized in a one-directional way, the notion of reverie, the phenomenic pole of an invisible α function of the mind, in fact introduces a 'strong' social theory of the subject. Related to the metaphor of the text is, then, that of translation and especially of how to translate the unsayable and the unrepresentable 'whiteness' of the trauma, and what has been experienced but has not been able to enter memory and that therefore does not belong to the sphere of repression. Things have become more complex. Even with those patients suffering from the most fragile form of narcissism that we now see in clinical practice, we must take account of a pre-linguistic unconscious; of memories stored in the body in the form of sedimented impressions of the original object relations. We have to get in touch with the primitive rhythms that underlie the 'aesthetics of being' (Bollas, 1987), to repair the background against which the ego can form, to define the margins within which it is possible to experience the world. This is why once again the aesthetic experience and the sense of truth that we usually attribute to it in some way ultimately inspire the work of analysis and enable it to escape the grip of excessively rigid conceptual oppositions. When the categories we use to interpret reality become too clear-cut, the field of experience begins to wither; art, on the other hand, is founded precisely on ambiguity, a plurality of points of view, a certain obscurity and a sense of surprise.

Finally, what is true for Bion, as perhaps for no other, is critical theory's assumption that the reader of a text is also its author. This is reflected in his style, which is at the same time both dazzling and undefined. It is not so much a question, one might say, of what Bion has really said, but of how we can creatively use the extraordinary legacy he has left us. For my part I would be satisfied if this book has succeeded in giving a sense of the incredible wealth of ideas that his thoughts contain and which can both stimulate our thinking about psychoanalytic theory and serve as a basis for living clinical practice. In this spirit I hope I have managed to convey the excitement I feel every time I go back to read Bion. My impression is that this feeling has much to do with the paradox that permeates his writings. They are often abstract and nigh on 'incomprehensible'; apparently, however, it is this not wanting to be understood that expresses Bion's most secret intention. His aim is to be truly understood in the most intimate meaning of his work – which, as in the consulting room, means running the risk of thinking for oneself and venturing beyond the already known.

1

'CAESURA' AS BION'S DISCOURSE ON METHOD

Bion inspires in his reader a sense of surprise and almost reverential fear by virtue of the creativity, courage and originality of his thought. I have always wondered what his secret is. On the infelicity of answers, he himself was fond of quoting Blanchot (1969, p. 13) – 'The answer is the question's misfortune, its adversity' – by which I mean only that the secret is destined to remain such. Nor would there be any point in following the evocative but insidious path of character and biography – partly because one interesting aspect of genius is the non-ineffable part made up of hard work. I have therefore attempted to proceed along a different track, in the hope, with any luck, of happening upon some fortunate discoveries. The clues I found led me to Descartes and his *Discourse on Method* (1637). I then reread 'Caesura' (Bion, 1977c) in the light of this classical text. The choice proved appropriate and, even if it does not reveal Bion's secret, it at least affords a glimpse of his toolbox.

On the same track

Bion's psychoanalytic research is based, in the purest Cartesian spirit, on the need to cast light on areas of darkness. It is not for nothing that the subtitle of *Attention and Interpretation* is 'A Scientific Approach to Insight in Psycho-Analysis and Groups' (Bion, 1970), while the subtitle of the Italian version of *Second Thoughts* (Bion, 1967) translates as 'The Analysis of Schizophrenics and the Psychoanalytic Method'. Again, it is only after a long journey that Bion arrives at ambiguity, aporia and paradox, and ultimately at a rhetoric of blindness and sight (Civitarese, 2007). Bion's interest in Descartes and his motivation is confirmed by an authoritative witness, André Green:

> During my conversations with Bion, I was struck by his great interest in Descartes. He thought that Descartes' aim to arrive at 'clear and distinct ideas' could also be applied to psychoanalysis. At least, this was a task that should be achieved in theory. Descartes' project was to arrive, as far as the mind was concerned, to the same degree of certainty that one experiences with mathematical demonstrations. Bion and Lacan, though starting from very different premises, were both on the same track, pursuing the same ultimate goal. But, as I said earlier, this ideal in the beginning of Bion's work led in the end to a disillusionment.
>
> (Green, 1998, p. 651)

So it is beyond question that Descartes was well known to Bion. The issue is in fact the extent of the philosopher's influence on him. It is my hypothesis that this was much more pervasive than is at first sight evident. Bion does not often mention him by name, as he does in the case of Kant, Plato and other classical and contemporary authors. However, when he does refer to Descartes, he certainly does not invariably cast him in the role of a mere extra. Indeed, on at least one occasion, Descartes appears centre-stage, considering that Bion actually disputes his *cogito*, the single founding postulate of the modern Western conception of the subject.

However, over and above the idea of providing a version of the *cogito* of his own, Bion borrows something even more precious from Descartes – namely, systematic doubt, which he adopts as his key principle on both the theoretical level of the psychoanalytic method and the clinical level of the analyst's self-discipline. Method, for both, is the central problem, and nothing less than a leitmotiv. In this connection, one intuits a profound consonance of sensibility, instruments and objectives between the two. So it is not difficult to imagine them linked by the bond of a continuous dialogue, albeit pursued mostly between the lines. The text in which Bion presents his rendering of radical doubt is 'Caesura'. 'Transcending' the caesuras that redraw the boundaries of settled thought is the only truly general, conscious and *strategic* criterion – which is therefore in the same way 'hyperbolic' (that is, at 360°) – that inspires Bion's thought.

That is the sense of the peremptory-sounding invitation to investigate the caesura which closes this brief text. As in Descartes, doubt does not lead to an absolute, sterile relativism; it is not an end in itself, but serves for the attainment of truth. As for Descartes with regard to the scientific and philosophical world of his time, the result for psychoanalysis is tantamount to a change of paradigm, which can be summed up in the following formula: from contents to relations; from the past to the processes of mental growth; and from traces to differences and to the functioning of the apparatus for thinking thoughts.

That, then, is why it is not a sterile exercise to reread 'Caesura' and the *Discourse on Method* with a view to identifying assonances between them, some of them only lexical, over and above the obvious differences. When we see him united with Descartes by a whole agenda of problems and by the espousal of a radically sceptical critique, a difficult author like Bion becomes more familiar to us. It is worth recalling the passage in Bion (1967) where he writes that, while the relationship between psychoanalysis and philosophy is not a happy one owing to the lack of mutual recognition, analysts feel that philosophy is more necessary to their work than it is to that of the philosophers themselves.

As an indication of the degree of kinship between the two thinkers, I shall attempt, however incompletely, to enumerate the points which they share: the rhetoric of light and the implicit analogy between knowing and seeing with the eyes, on the one hand, and between ideas and visual images, on the other; Descartes's appeal to 'good sense', reminiscent as it is of the concept of 'common sense', which Bion uses with the peculiar meaning of 'common to more than one sense' (Bion, 1963, p. 10); the importance of reflecting on the norms that govern scientific inquiry; the emphasis on the search for truth, but also on truth understood not as absolute knowledge but as subjective certainty; the frequent reminder of the unreliability of the senses and the errors of reason; the exaltation of the freedom of judgement and the rejection of preconceived opinions, of the authority principle, and of scholastic wisdom; the rule of systematic doubt and of the suspension of judgement (or of prejudices); the recourse to mathematics, albeit, for Bion, only in the sense of an analogy, and to symbols carefully contrived to render the nature of the problems addressed clearer and more transparent (it was, precisely, Descartes, who introduced the use of the final letters of the alphabet to denote mathematical unknowns); the practice, which Descartes calls 'analysis', of breaking down complex theoretical objects into simple elements that can be immediately apprehended (the parallel in Bion can be seen as the spirit of the Grid and its system of Cartesian coordinates); the theme of the possibility of dominating the passions by way of appropriate 'training'; a doctrine of invariants, which is represented in Descartes by the conception of matter as mere extension, and of infinite transformations; the concept of functions; the theoretical use of 'fables' (Descartes) or 'scientific fictions' (Bion, 1977b, p. 514); the idea that knowledge can grow by degrees, that the mind needs to be accustomed 'to the love and nourishment [*se repaître*] of truth, and to a distaste for all such reasonings as were unsound' (Descartes, 1637, Chapter 2), so that it can become 'gradually habituated to clearer and more distinct conception of its objects' (ibid.), and that the individual succeeds by experience – another highly significant term for both – in improving his or her self-awareness.

This is a key point. The Cartesian theory of perceptual experience serves as a model for Bion's theory of thought: Bion assigns the same function in the knowledge of self and of one's internal world to the 'internal sense-data', or the psychic qualities represented by the emotions, as Descartes does to sense impressions in relation to objects situated in time and space, in external reality – that is, the function of producing the same type of consensual vision. This, and nothing else, means getting in touch with one's own emotions: seeing the component parts of the landscape of one's own internal reality. Perceiving the object as a whole fuels the subject's mental growth (Bion, 1967). It is indeed the emotions that aesthetically organize the first elements of experience. Moreover, it is true that Descartes disembodies representation; however, he recovers its sensible basis by transferring it to the 'intrinsic evidence of the idea in so far as it is immanent in the subject' (Borutti, 2006, p. xviii, translated). Again, Marion (2001, pp. 109, 122) shows that, in spite of and contrary to all the dualisms of canonical interpretations, for Descartes there is ultimately an equation of feeling with thinking: 'Le *cogito* s'accomplit en chair ou ne s'accomplit pas … L'*ego* se reçoit donc de sa prise de chair et jamais de la réflexion qui l'égalerait à soi' ['The *cogito* is accomplished in flesh or it is not accomplished […]. The *ego* therefore comes into being by virtue of its assumption of flesh and never of the reflection that would equate it with itself] (1637). Bion likewise includes in thought the sensations, or rather the as yet indistinct sensory–emotional afferences bound up with corporeity – that is, the 'unthought thoughts' represented by β-elements (Fornaro, 1990). Once these crude emotions and impressions can be endowed with thought, they no longer need to be evacuated and they increase the subject's sense of reality, which is indispensable to the mind in the same way as food is to the body. A thought which lacks the emotional component that alone can give it vitality is a divided thought, which lives solely in the concrete world; it is, rather, a state of hallucinosis. Thought is emotion moulded into shape, but emotion is the guarantee of proximity to reality, the material that absorbs its stamp, what binds it to the real (in the twofold sense of a limit and opportunity), because it is more undifferentiated, closer to the corporeal, to the somato-psychic. From this point of view, the dualism of affects and cognition is plunged once and for all into crisis.

A more extensive comparative analysis of the two authors' texts, conducted with philological precision, which might also produce quite a few surprises, is beyond the scope of this chapter, whose sole aim is to suggest a new reading of 'Caesura'. However, I should like at least to draw attention to some other passages in the *Discourse* that are particularly reminiscent of Bion's theory. For instance, when Descartes (1637, Chapter 5) wonders

> what changes must take place in the brain to produce waking, sleep and dreams; how light, sounds, odors, tastes, heat, and all the other qualities of external objects impress it with different ideas by means of the senses; how hunger, thirst, and the other internal affections can likewise impress upon it divers ideas; what must be understood by the common sense (*sensus communis*) in which these ideas are received, by the memory which retains them, by the fantasy which can change them in various ways,

we are very close to Bion: sense impressions, transformations, passions, common sense, differences between waking and dreaming, the work of memory and so forth. The impression is indeed gained that, with changes of vocabulary and style, Bion is merely reformulating in his own language, and attempting to solve, the same problems that excited Descartes. Similarly, Descartes having pragmatically noted that 'it is sometimes necessary to adopt, as if above doubt, opinions which we discern to be highly uncertain' (ibid., Chapter 4), Bion echoes him by maintaining that it is necessary to tolerate insecurity and that 'the insecurity should be noticed but disregarded till it becomes relevant' (1967, p. 129).

Lies and Descartes's error

The part of the *Discourse* (Chapter 4) in which Descartes introduces the famous phrase 'I think, therefore I am' deserves to be treated at greater length, because Bion comments on it explicitly. Descartes offers a proof *ad absurdum*. Even if the waking state were only an illusion, a dream, and all our thoughts were false, we should nevertheless at least have the certainty of existing:

> [F]inally, when I considered that the very same thoughts (presentations) which we experience when awake may also be experienced when asleep, while there is at that time not one of them true, I supposed that all the objects (presentations) that had ever entered my mind when awake, had in them no more truth than the illusions of my dreams. But immediately upon this I observed that, whilst I thus wished to think that all was false, it was absolutely necessary that I, who thus thought, should be somewhat.
>
> (Descartes, 1637, Chapter 4)

This statement is so radical as to be scandalous. There is no reliable clue to distinguish waking from sleep. At any rate, Descartes extracts an indubitable truth from a twofold rhetorical fiction – namely, pretending to dream. Thought presupposes existence.

Bion positively reproaches Descartes for not having ultimately remained faithful to the principle of methodical doubt, and for having thus fallen into error, and he ventures to correct the *cogito*: 'Descartes's tacit assumption that thoughts presuppose a thinker is valid only for a lie' (Bion, 1970, p. 103). Bion's contention is not 'I think, therefore I am', but, if anything, 'I mentate, therefore I am'. A relationship of logical necessity exists only between the lie and the thinker, but not between (true) thought and the thinker. Oddly enough, Bion's critique is based on a – Platonic or neo-Platonic – doctrine of innate ideas, which both authors substantially share. Indeed, Sandler (2005) correctly recognizes that it was precisely Descartes who first formulated the idea of a thought without a thinker, albeit solely with the aim of drawing attention to its incongruity.

The Cartesian *cogito* is thus conceived anew and remains valid only for lies. In this regard, López-Corvo (2002) points out that the ancient inhabitants of Latium had already made the connection between the mind [*mens/mentis*] and lying [*mentior*]. However absurd this might appear in logical terms, the thesis is valuable as a paradox – as a 'logo-immune'[1] truth (Magrelli, 2006) – and for its heuristic value. Separating ideas from the apparatus for thinking thoughts, Bion gives prominence to the 'digestive' metaphor of the psyche; he establishes a concrete model of the internal world in the style of Melanie Klein; and, lastly, he emphasizes the social and ideological nature of thought: the development of the mind does not depend only on the management of frustration, as for Freud, *but needs another mind* (Neri *et al.*, 1987). The interplay of projective identification ↔ reverie – that is, the actual availability of this other mind for accepting the child's, or the patient's, emotions, for reliving them and for returning them after transformation (i.e. endowed with thought) – is the delicate mechanism of the container–contained function. Moreover, it must indeed be admitted that, from a certain point of view, there really are thoughts awaiting a sufficiently mature mind for them to be thinkable, thoughts pressing for the development of an apparatus to think them; thoughts that cannot not be thought – for example, the transience of things and the ineluctability of separation – except by relegating oneself to failed, false forms of existence. They are 'true' for Bion because, unlike lies, they are transformations of the 'unthought thoughts' represented by β-elements, or protosensations–emotions emanating from O – from what for Lacan constitutes the real and for the mystics the Divine.

The key idea is that emotions do not lie, because *they express a relationship of sense, a state of belonging to, and a coordination with, a world intuited as true but not directly knowable*, but in order to be used they must be re-cognized, shaped into ideas – that is, subjected to a function of synthesis or imaginative schematization. Emotion represents nothing unless it is pervaded by an idea. Making use, as Bion does, of the immediacy of emotions as proto-thoughts, their opaque, confused background, *is a way of transferring the criterion of truth to the interior of knowledge itself.* Yet it is a fact that, for Bion, the subject is at the same time paradoxically defined on the basis of the illusion of freeing itself from the limits imposed by reality by means of lies, delusions and hallucination – as if the subject could not be born other than in the unbridgeable gap of an impossible perfect fusion with the real.

Here again, however, Descartes's theory is found to be much more refined than might be suggested by the seemingly only too clear-cut caesura that separates Bion's conceptions from his. To claim, as Bion (1974a, p. 22) does, that 'Descartes, while suggesting philosophical doubt, failed completely to doubt philosophical doubt' may appear ungenerous. Whereas, for Descartes, all knowledge has its prerequisite in self-evident ideas, in intuition, it is nevertheless true that, in him, the shadow of doubt is so pervasive as to fall upon any other possible object, over and above the proof of the pure existence of the thinker. To preserve the correspondence between the ideas of the mind and external bodies, he is left with no alternative but to invoke God. Only God can keep one from error. Not being true in itself, knowledge is joined to truth only in His infinite goodness. For Descartes, as for Bion, knowledge (*K*) and truth (*O*) belong to different domains. Nor is it the case that for Descartes, in the final analysis – given that he after all applies the standard of rationality – the mind can be the ultimate measure of knowledge. As Nobus and Quinn (2005, p. 44) point out, in Descartes's philosophy, 'God is the guarantee of truth, but apart from their faith in God individuals have no guarantee that this is a truthful representation of God'. Hence 'God' is reduced to 'faith'.

Now it is not difficult to discern in Descartes's God an unexpected consonance with the Bionian concepts of O, of which God would be only one of the names, and of an 'act of faith'. This is because, for Bion, faith is a scientific attitude – the correlate in knowledge of a rational, disciplined and pragmatic passion that nevertheless makes use of negative logic; and, ultimately, the 'possibility of doubt' (Merleau-Ponty, 1964, p. 103) about what has been acquired: 'I do not waste time believing facts or anything I *know*. I save my credulity for what I do *not* know' (Bion, 1977e, p. 445). Yet, just as Bion uses a term borrowed from mystical thought to express a scientific concept, thus plunging any rigid dichotomy between the two systems of thought into crisis, so Descartes's God does not necessarily correspond to what it literally denotes: many commentators, including Bion himself, have not overlooked the instrumental and opportunistic character of Descartes's theological argument, and hence also the radical nature of his scepticism: 'Why does Descartes find himself defending a theological position? The explanation he gives is quite simple: he does not like what happened to Galileo, and he doesn't want to get into the same difficulty' (Bion, 2005, p. 45). By means of this dry comment, he thus re-evokes the nocturnal, gloomy, nihilistic Descartes, lost in the void of the world and terrified by the blind force of the dogmatists – the audacious, crazy figure sketched out by Derrida (1972). Cartesian doubt, like Bion's, is so vertiginous that it not only examines the contents but also informs the very faculty of thought. Indeed, he makes this inquiry into the intellect a necessary prerequisite, and stops only at the subjectivity of the *cogito*, since any 'metaphysical' certainty in relation to the object of knowledge is lost in the lack of distinction between waking and dreaming.

To sum up, the error with which Bion reproaches Descartes is, if anything, only the lie to which he resorts in order to conceal his radical scepticism. Descartes too could basically maintain that existence presupposes the lie – the distance between words and things. For in order to overcome this aporia and to be able to resort to a notion of truth, both place their trust in faith – theological in one case and secular in the other – in an infrasensible or ultrasensible reality. In order to survive, the subject cannot allow itself to depart too far from the real, from O, from God, from the One. At the same time, the subject 'ex-sists' only by coming *out of itself*; it is born of the fiction that it stems from the impossible absolute adherence to the real. Should this ever become possible, the subject would be annihilated as such, as actually happens in the *unio mystica*. One can perhaps discern in this 'desire for the indivisible mode' (Matte Blanco, 1988, p. 218), and for the abolition of all tension the only possible sense that we today can still assign to the notion of the death drive and its servant, the Nirvana principle.

Investigating the caesura

Bion addresses the subject of the caesura in a few short works: 'Emotional turbulence' (1977a), 'On a quotation from Freud' (1977b), 'Evidence' (1976) and 'Caesura' (1977c). These are his last non-posthumous publications, followed only by *Seven Servants*, the Paris Seminar, *Making the Best of a Bad Job*, and *The Tavistock Seminars*. In 'Caesura', a text so close to the 'caesura of death' to which he alludes in 'Evidence', and which therefore also assumes the significance of a spiritual testament, Bion focuses his attention *a posteriori*, when the major part of his work is already done, on the sole general principle that inspired his entire theoretical activity. This principle, which is analogous to Descartes's systematic doubt, can be summed up in the theoretical 'gesture' of transcending caesuras wherever they arise. In this way, Bion criticizes established ideas and current beliefs and opinions, opens up new fields of research and, at clinical level, forges for the analyst an instrument that will help him to suspend judgement, to achieve a mental state of receptivity and attention, and – as Descartes too demands –'gradually to weaken the strength of memories' (Massarenti, 2006, p. 151, translated).

'Caesura' is prefaced by an unusually large number of quotations – ten in all! Among these, the two taken from Freud stand out. The first, from 'Inhibitions, symptoms and anxiety' (Freud, 1926, p. 138) not only provides the title but also sets the tone of this contribution: 'There is much more continuity between intra-uterine life and earliest infancy than the impressive caesura of birth allows us to believe'.[2] The second, on the other hand, is taken from the letter to Lou Andreas-Salomé in which Freud tells her of his method of writing: 'I know that in writing I have to blind myself artificially in order to focus all the light on one dark spot, renouncing cohesion, harmony, edifying effects and everything which you call the symbolic element' (E. L. Freud, 1961, p. 312).[3] The discrepancy between these two sentences, which are followed by others from Martin Buber and Saint John of the Cross whose function seems to be more that of amplification, clarification and comment, is puzzling. However, if the two Freud quotations indicate the space in which the discourse that Bion develops in the text extends, what is his route from one to the other? Having started from the caesura of birth, how does he find his way to the concept of the ray of darkness, or 'negative capability'– what Saint John of the Cross would call *desnudez de espíritu* [nakedness of the spirit]? And lastly, what is this text really about?

'Caesura' is structured in such a way as immediately to establish an interplay between inside and outside. The quotations serve as a frame; the centre of the picture is occupied by the discussion of the epistemological problem, to which the theme of birth, mounted as it were *en abyme*, offers a model solution. From the very first lines Bion almost obsessively asserts that the issue of truth and falsehood in knowledge is crucial. However, he reminds us that this is precisely the field of analysis. Bion wonders whether a foetus does not – even if only in the form of physical pressure on the optic or auditory pits – feel the stimuli of the environment in which it is immersed, and whether traces of this blind, or 'embryological', intuition might not persist into postnatal and adult life. He comments that, in the analyst's consulting room, one sometimes encounters intense, formless emotions, perhaps bound up with fear or with inexpressible ideas which can usefully be thought of as if they were 'sub-thalamic, or sympathetic, or para-sympathetic' (Bion, 1977c, p. 43). The search for truth cannot dispense with these primitive forms of knowledge, 'empty' of concepts but awaiting the possibility of being formulated and communicated:

> From the point of view of the analyst the fact that the analysand is a grown man or woman can be so obtrusive, the evidence of the eyes so obtrusive, that it blinds him to feelings which are not so clearly presented to the optic apparatus.
>
> (Bion, 1977c, p. 43)

At times, the fact of managing to see a patient who may be experiencing sensations equivalent to those of intrauterine life as a foetus in the 'amniotic cavity' of the consulting room might, on the other hand, be indicative of the capacity to blind oneself to the evidence of the conversation between adults which is, after all, taking place. The truth has to do with emotions too, and not only with abstract ideas, but emotions are bound up precisely with those primitive, psychosomatic or somato-psychic, levels of the mind, and can therefore spring only from a twofold, bidirectional – actually simultaneous – movement from empty, blind or 'embryological' intuition to conceptualization and vice versa.

However, immediately this key analogy has been introduced, the discourse turns to methodology: *the caesura of birth is the model of the birth of every new thought.* Just as the caesura of birth makes one insensitive to the persistence of more primitive forms of knowledge and levels of the mind, so *every new idea establishes a new caesura, a barrier, an obstacle to other ideas, which are thrust back into a cone of shadow, if not positively 'killed'*: 'A foetal idea can kill itself or be killed, and that is not a metaphor *only*' (Bion, 1977d, pp. 417f.).

Transcending the caesura, or deconstructing the slash ('/'→'\')

However, to what caesuras is Bion referring? One need only read the text, which enumerates a whole series of them: between foetal and postnatal life; between body and psyche ('I have often had "echoes" of messages from my gills to my conscious mind' – Bion, 1977e, p. 449); between intuition (being at one with *O*) and concept (*K*); between outside and inside the analyst's consulting room ('What the patient does away from the session cannot be known to the analyst' – Bion, 1977c, p. 46), and hence between direct and indirect evidence; between past and present ('We exist in the *present*; we can do nothing about the past. It is, therefore, seriously misleading to think as if we dealt with the past' – ibid., p. 47); between the language of the analyst and that of the patient; between words worn out by daily use but absolutely suited to the formulation of an interpretation, on the one hand, and specialist jargon, on the other; between pathological and non-pathological splits; between nosographic classifications and non-objectivistic visions of the patient; between incorrect and correct interpretations; between mature and primitive levels of the mind; between the psychotic and the non-psychotic part of the personality; between night dreams and waking dreams; between emotions and thought; between subject and object; between knowing and not knowing ('"Understanding" is inappropriate' – Bion, 1974b, p. 203); between thought and the negativity of the no-thing; between literary and scientific discourse; and, finally, between transference and countertransference.

But if that is the way things are, Bion wonders, *how* is it possible to transcend the caesura? How can one '[break] through the barriers' (Bion, 1970, p. 114)? And lastly, what might be the 'means of communication' (ibid., p. 4), the 'Language of Achievement' (ibid., p. 2)? His answer is that we need to resort to non-pathological splits. This precept can be understood as an invitation to use a variety of viewpoints; that is, the caesura implicit in all discrimination must not inhibit thought or become reified or static. Only when this condition is satisfied does the shifting play of caesuras become equivalent to the respiration of the mind: 'the diaphragm is the important thing; the caesura is the important thing; that is the source of the thinking' (Bion, 1977b, p. 511). Transcending the caesura, or 'disturbing the binary system' (Magrelli, 2006) – or, as Grotstein (1981a) puts it, disturbing 'the universe'– which regulates the production of sense becomes the general model of a dynamic thought, of a thought that tolerates insecurity and ambiguity, or, in other words, the presence of a plurality of meanings, the paradox of more than one truth and the aporias of reason. The barrier can be broken through by the interplay of different points of view, the deconstruction permitted by free associations and the dissemination of sense, and by negative capability and *transitive* thought (thought which succeeds in overcoming the barriers).

It is only at this point that the reader is offered the possibility of grasping the sense of the parergonal[4] relationship between the numerous introductory quotations, each of which constitutes an ellipsis or preconception or embryonic thought with regard to the text. This is that one should put oneself in the position of adopting a number of different vertices which converge on a point to produce a consensual experience, each quotation as it were being a split that can be maintained but nevertheless also be recomposed – recomposed 'transitively'. In other words, the text is constructed in such a way as to generate, in the reader, the experience described in it. Again, language, pressed into performative use, seeks to denote something external to it, which cannot be clearly named but can only be suggested. If any doubts remained as to the nature of 'Caesura', as to the fact that its subject is method, and only secondarily birth, these must surely be dissipated once and for all by the closing sentences:

> There is much more continuity between autonomically appropriate quanta and the waves of conscious thought and feeling than the impressive caesura of transference and counter-transference would have us believe. So ...? Investigate the caesura [Bion admonishes] not the analyst; not the analysand; not the unconscious; not the conscious; not sanity; not insanity. But the caesura, the link, the synapse, the (counter-trans)ference, the transitive-intransitive mood – the movement ('trans'), which is retrograde ('counter'), of thought, or reversible perspective.
>
> (Bion, 1977c, p. 56)

The sudden change of tone here is clear-cut and introduces the text's coda in a manner tantamount to a *coup de théâtre*: there is also a caesura between the transference and the countertransference. Bion seems to be implying that the dynamic condensed in this pair of concepts does not suffice to explain the facts of analysis. One reason is that a 'fact' needs to be understood as what the analysand says he is experiencing, and that the 'important thing about the patient's state of mind is that it exists *at the time* he or she is seeing the analyst' (Bion, 1977d, p. 645). The current concept of transference, on the other hand, based as it is on more than one caesura, gives no indication of the extent to which every event in the relationship does not belong to one or other of the two actors on the stage, but is merely, albeit to different degrees, a point of condensation of the forces pervading the field. In this way, Bion is referring to a symbiotic–fusional level of the setting, which is first and foremost characteristic of intrauterine life, but which nevertheless continues to exist as a psychic dimension of transindividual functioning and participation in a formless and undifferentiated *basal* background of experience. This is the area which we describe, with different nuances of meaning, as the intersubjective matrix, the transitional space, the protomental area, the bipersonal field or the group mentality.

± RP

But how is one to make thought breathe, and to use non-pathological splits – that is undefended, negotiable boundaries? Sandler (2005) emphasizes the paradoxical nature of the concept of caesura as an event that simultaneously unites and separates, defining it as the mode of functioning of the contact barrier, of transformations and of invariants; he adds that the caesura becomes a split when it is not tolerated: it is the intolerance of frustration that establishes the cut, the breach, the pause, and which renders a viewpoint absolute and conceals continuity. A part of the figure disappears, and *one sees either the duck or the hare.* It is for this reason that Bion, in 'Caesura', makes himself the theoretician of continuity – because the dis-union is already obvious by itself. After all, in order to structure experience, we customarily resort to asymmetric logic (Matte Blanco, 1975) or separative logic (Bottiroli, 2006). Sandler (2005) is therefore right to point out that, notwithstanding its twofold, paradoxical nature as latent continuity and manifest discontinuity, the concept is used and rendered commonplace, in the sense of interruption. Bion's starting point, on the other hand, is, precisely, continuity.

What is evident in his method is that he systematically dynamizes a situation of static splitting that has arisen in consequence of a kind of reversal of perspective already established in the description of a certain phenomenon. In other words, Bion *re-reverses the perspective, but without eliminating the ambiguity resulting from the consciousness that more than one viewpoint exists, that these viewpoints cannot be reduced to one another, and that what we call reality is what our states of normal hallucinosis cause us to see.* It thus becomes clear that the concepts of negative capability, binocular vision, the vertex and dynamic splitting are all corollaries of transcending the caesura, and that the container–contained oscillations, which presuppose those between PI and reverie, as well as PS ↔ D and NC ↔ SF, are all, already, models of *reversibility*.

As described by Bion, reversible perspective (RP) is a defence against mental pain so intense that it would threaten the subject's psychic integration. As such, it may relate to several aspects of one and the same phenomenon, and acts in such a way as to render a dynamic situation static, with recourse if necessary to hallucination and delusion. 'The work of the analyst is to restore dynamic to a static situation and so make development possible' (Bion, 1963, p. 60). We could thus adopt the same approach as Bion by using a new sign, ± RP, to denote the twofold functionality of reversible perspective, preceding it by a plus sign (+) or a minus sign (−) according to whether it serves the purpose of dynamic or of static discrimination. An example of reversible perspective that makes for the development of thought (+ RP) – what Descartes might have called 'an overturning of my opinions' (Massarenti, 2006, p. 152, translated) – can be found in *Elements of Psycho-Analysis*, where Bion deconstructs the very antithesis between α and β:

> The dispersed β-elements, in so far as they seek the ♀, may be regarded as an abortive prototype of a container, a container loosely structured [...] the dispersal of β-elements has analogies with the preconception that is to be mated with a realization to produce a conception.
>
> (Bion, 1963, p. 40)

A temporary state of ambiguity (paradoxicality) thus corresponds to the development of the capacity of a container (♀) in which containeds (♂) are suspended. In what is said by the patient, and indeed also by the analyst, characters and plots can be seen as unconscious narrative derivatives of waking dream thought – of the continuous transformation of β-elements or protoemotions into visual images (pictograms or β-elements) which the mind is called upon to perform (Ferro, 2005). At the same time, however, a 'cloud of β-elements' represents not only the protoemotional and protosensory data awaiting filtration by the α-function, but also a protocontainer, or unthought thoughts. Upon every crystallization of sense, the β-elements reopen the process of assignment of meaning, thereby leading once again towards a certain tolerable ambiguity. The β-elements ultimately carry with them the drives, the transference, and redraw the field's lines of force on each occasion. Symbolization can be seen only as being in a state of continuous tension with its own undoing, like a continuous oscillation of the mind between the two poles of the pairs certainty/doubt and being moved/being confused. The decisive factor becomes the tolerance of frustration, which is a function of the time whereby the absence of the object is measured: 'Therefore "excessive" inability to tolerate frustration is likely to obstruct development of pre-conception' (Bion, 1970, p. 16). Consequently, there is at first no difference between β-elements and thoughts in the nascent state. Emotional turbulence, pain and states of psychological crisis are also inherent in mental growth. Furthermore, every 'true' interpretation is mediated by the analyst's experience of persecution, fear and depression.

This, then, is the nature of the method used by Bion as a theoretician of psychoanalysis: illuminating a central opposition and then deconstructing it to plunge it into a state of tension – and so he puts it to work. Each of these oppositions, or caesuras, may prove to be false unless their dual function of separating and uniting is apprehended, as in the case of the contact barrier. Nothing is taken for granted or established once and for all so that it becomes untouchable. No dogma or 'bigotry of certitude' (Bion, 1975, p. 34), of the type 'Here is something I don't understand – I'll kill it' (Bion, 1974a, p. 28), is immune to this approach. Freud's premonitory statement about the caesura of birth ultimately takes on the character of a paradigm.

In terms of technique, transcending each of the caesuras enumerated above is reflected in a precise indication. These indications are, in order: what matters is direct evidence in the present, in the analyst's consulting room, and not only the past; it is impossible to know what happens outside, in external reality; one should not confine oneself to what can be understood on the basis of logic, 'causal thought', 'plausible explanations' and 'rational interpretations', but should leave room for conjectures and daydreaming; one should not surrender to one's inability to apprehend the total situation; the analyst must know how to make use of the diseases of the field, wrong interpretations and mistaken decisions; he must know how to apprehend the subterranean continuity between the β and a levels of the mind, between what he can only intuit and what assumes a more abstract and sophisticated guise; the analyst must pay attention to the gap between his own language and that of the patient, which often diverge dramatically because of their differing viewpoints; he must relativize the caesura between knowing and not knowing, and see darkness not as the absence of light but as one of its functions, like the *agnosía* of the mystics, learned ignorance, or Eckhartian *Abgeschiedenheit* (detachment); and, last but not least, the analyst must realize that the transference itself is a caesura, in so far as, in the current version of a false connection, it combines within itself the caesuras of the past, of external reality, of the analyst's knowledge (or rather 'supposed' knowledge), and the split between subject and object – that is, between what belongs to the patient and what belongs to the analyst; and he must ask himself, as Bion does: 'Where does my personality end and someone else's start? Where does the analyst come to an end? And where does the patient start?' (Bion, 1974b, p. 177). Clearly, then, attention to how the analyst's mind functions, in its inmost recesses, becomes the central feature of this model.

Taken together, these methodological indications lead, as in Descartes, to an approach in which, in the vocabulary of Saussurian linguistics, the paradigmatic takes precedence over the syntagmatic.[5] For Ricoeur (1987), Descartes's theory, too, is one 'of the instant and of the caesura'. A consciousness in the self-reflective act in the here and now is also inherent in the Cartesian approach: Cottingham (1986, p. 36) points out that a correct English translation of the *cogito* should make use of the 'so-called continuous present' ('I am thinking') rather than the simple present, and emphasizes attention to im-mediate experience: 'so long as the mediator focuses on the proposition in question, then there is nothing that could be done to undermine its self-evident truth' (ibid., p. 69). In the same way, what matters in Bion's theory are emotion, at-one-ment, and hence the here and now.

Transcending the caesura and reversing perspective may be a process that initially leads to new ideas being 'felt' as if they possessed some of the qualities of bizarre objects – the objects that are created when the contact barrier is dispersed. When new thoughts are allowed to arise, this may call for an unaccustomed permeability of conscious to unconscious thought, which is then the mental state that is actively pursued by evenly suspended attention or negative capability. For this reason, many original ideas may at first appear strange or mad, and may give rise to a sensation of excessive ambiguity or even of confusion, to such an extent that their protagonists can uphold them only if they have 'faith' in the existence of a reality (O) which they are deemed to reflect. The contact barrier is seen to be unstable, and its state of permeability to be dynamic. Just as projective identification and the PS ↔ D oscillation have become physiological mechanisms of thought, so the mechanism of reversible perspective can be seen as not always pathological – at least when the subject, while switching between different viewpoints or reversing the figure, does not apply an absolute or once-for-all denial to the alternative perspective, but instead tolerates the ambiguity and frustration of not being able to see *both* the figure *and* the ground together. *The slash* (i.e. the punctuation mark) as it were *slopes the other way*. Throughout his oeuvre, Bion seems never to have proceeded in any other way. In a passage in *Learning from Experience* in which he describes how the selected fact may represent the factor, the caesura, that confers sense and coherence on formerly meaningless elements, he hints at this non-pathological dimension of RP, in noting that this event 'is accompanied by an emotion such as is experienced in regarding the object in reversible perspective' (Bion, 1962, p. 87).

Caesura or censorship?

After the summer holidays, I see Ada again. She has telephoned me the day before, at about the time when we would normally have had the first session of the week, apologizing for not having remembered when I had told her we would resume. She tells me that she came by mistake to my consulting room and rang – four times (she has four sessions a week) – but of course did not find me in. 'I couldn't remember when I was supposed to start again,' she explains. 'Yesterday I went all round the houses ... do you know what? Every so often I dreamt of you! I took you away with me ... We spent a month in a camper van. We covered a good six thousand kilometres, from Milan to Berlin. It was a positive experience, except for a few moments. One evening R. felt ill and suddenly passed out. Those sixty seconds were very nasty! I screamed: 'Help me!!' Then he regained consciousness by himself … But he won't let anyone examine him. We had an argument. He rolls too many joints. Then, when he came to, I felt like collapsing myself. I thought it might be photosensitive epilepsy … Ummmm! I also thought it might be a withdrawal symptom. But he won't have an EEG, he won't hear of it! A few evenings later, we talked about it again, and he also flew into a rage. I said something like: 'Can't you do without them?' I felt like a mother with a child having an epileptic fit!'

A: You caught a fright!

P: I was really shocked; I had to lie down. I was terrified … And then there was the frustration of not being listened to! And as if that was not enough, my mobile was locked, and I couldn't remember the PIN!

A: Did you unlock it when you phoned me to ask for the appointment?

P: No. The day before … You know, my friend S. – the fascinating blonde – called her analyst, and they talked for half an hour … The whole thing was along the lines of 'I was at the seaside', and how she was all right and not all right, and 'Then you'll tell me' … *He* actually called *her* to remind her that they were to see each other that day! [Laughing.] Fantastic service! I said to myself: 'I dare not. I'll go along and ring on the entryphone.' The fourth time …

A: So, basically, the service here is lousy!

P: Just a bit! No, I'm joking. But it really struck home. Actually calling her at home! But when we were in the Marche region, we felt fine. I also made some new friends … It was a very peaceful holiday. ABSOLUTELY ON THE SAME WAVELENGTH. I also managed to face up to the row and overcome it. Apart from that, I really felt good. Then, every so often, I think of Prince Charming …

A: One who phones you at home!

P: Yes. I didn't tell you, when I had the row with R. … I so much needed some emotional topping-up that I dreamed of everything under the sun … I abolished the setting … All sorts of things that basically never happened … NO! I can't do it … We've got time. In the dream I said: 'Why don't I know anything about you? Whereas you know everything about me.' You replied: 'No way, I can make an exception … All this neutrality …' And then …

A: And then …?

P: CENSORSHIP!! … On the very night when I was angry with R.!

A: You got yourself a bit of 'emotional topping-up'? ... You must have felt evicted from your home ... And having to stay in the camper van, the withdrawal symptoms, the frightened state, the rage, and the collapse. Perhaps it all has to do with us. Then the mobile that starts working again two days ago ... And an analyst who ... phones of his own accord ...

P: [Laughing.] Yes, it seems to me that you ... respect the setting from A to Z!

This text can be read in two (and, of course, many more) ways according to whether – on the basis of the single highly evocative word uttered by the patient – one applies Freud's concept of psychic censorship or Bion's of (transcending) the caesura. The general framework of the material brought by the patient is the pain of separation and the intrinsic violence of the limits imposed by the setting. The experience of loneliness suggests an earthquake (sheltering in the camper van), feeling ill, the *joints* of dependence, *collapse, photosensitive epilepsy, withdrawal symptoms*, frustration and the interruption of communication due to distance. In the first case (the evidential–archaeological paradigm), these events as narrated, which can also be read as 'transference neurosis', would be seen mostly as external and reduced, from the point of view of psychic censorship, to the patient's intrapsychic conflicts. The emphasis would be placed on sexuality-related contents. Ada stages a relationship of intimacy, characterized by the expression of passion between a female friend and rival and her friend's solicitous analyst; this would here be seen as a manifestation of jealousy and envy. Attention would be directed to the hints of erotization of the transference contained in the dream, which, censored as it is, alludes to a scene in which the analyst appears, as a resistance to the analytic process, an attempt to 'undo' the setting, and so on. The therapeutic action would lie in the interpretive translation of the defences and id impulses. I shall not dwell on this any longer, because it is the classical approach *par excellence.*

Let us now adopt a vertex based on Bion's invitation to transcend caesuras or to *reverse the perspective* presented by the classical Freudian binary opposition that have now become 'obvious', as stated in the previous section (external/internal; past/present; dreaming/waking; patient/analyst; logic/'mysticism'; light/darkness; etc.), but preserving a relationship of mutual tension – i.e. a non-disjunctive relationship

– between the two terms. This would concentrate on the interruptions in communication in the here and now (the aesthetic, or field, paradigm), developing along the Bionian lines of the absolute paradoxical simultaneity enshrined in the notion of 'without memory or desire'. Being unwilling to wait, feeling frustrated, noticing one's need for the other: these are feelings arising out of the *present* context of experience, on which waking dream thought confers an image-based form. The meeting that did not happen on the previous day and the repeated ringing of the bell are in effect shots from a film of the beginning of *this* session. All the verbs are conjugated in the present tense. It is in the present that Ada phones, fails to remember, rings the entry phone, fails to find me in, dreams of me, travels, feels ill, asks for help, gets worried, feels discouraged, struggles and is afraid. It is in the present that she recovers after I speak to her. She turns into a seductive blonde, while I become someone who phones – i.e. who succeeds in getting in touch again. Now she feels good; the climate is friendly. Contact becomes intimate again. The comment about the lousy service might sound like a reproach, as the caesura between outside and inside the analysis prevents me from seeing Ada herself in the friend whom she is telling me about and myself (or rather another representation of myself, or a synthetic function of the intersubjective field that comes into being at that instant) in the other analyst, who is so solicitous and seemingly uninhibited by the requirement to respect the setting. But she seems to take it well, because at this point we are 'absolutely on the same wavelength'. The row is followed by a reconciliation. Sometimes, fortunately, the tone is more important than the content. Furthermore, in the (censored) dream, she perhaps gives me the kiss that transforms me from a persecutor-because-absent into Prince Charming. The relationship becomes not only intimate but positively hot (Ada's invocation), but in a bashful tone – all that can be seen here of the right of censorship is a manner of speaking, a veil that constitutes an invitation to concentrate one's look. Indeed, it is obviously somewhat *too* hot, because, even if my intention is to help her to experience with less guilt the embarrassment of the presumed seductive scene of the dream, I do so by immediately adding a transference-type interpretation of the account of her holiday, straight out of a textbook. Perhaps, with hindsight, my aim is to create a distance between us, partly because I in effect feel that I have permission to do so by virtue of the dream's direct reference to the analyst; however, the response comes right on time: 'You always take your *A to Z* with you when you go out.'

The dialogue could in fact be visualized as resembling M. Night Shyamalan's film *The Sixth Sense*, and, in particular, the scene between the psychologist and the child who refuses to speak but who moves a few steps forward or backward depending on how he feels what is said to him: everything is reflected in an alternation of + closeness/−closeness, whereby the emotional distance undergoes constant regulation. Seen in this perspective, which is shared by Descartes and Bion, everything takes place as it were in the form of a live broadcast. The resumption of contact (being *absolutely on the same wavelength*) allows the rage of separation to be overcome – that is to say, it expands the container for violent and potentially destructive emotions, as the epileptic fit turns out to signify, being nothing less than the discharge of β-elements into the body. The psychoanalytic process appears to resume in a climate of rediscovered attunement, and Ada is able clearly to express her need for *emotional topping-up*. This type of awareness or emotional consensuality and contact with one's own needs is what Bion calls *food for the mind – that is, elements that allow the mental space to develop and become elastic.*

The vignette demonstrates Ada's fragility when she is confronted with the separations of life, holidays and weekend breaks, with the brief intervals between sessions, and with the microfractures of communication; *however, these in particular are manifest and can be apprehended by analyst and patient alike.* The epilepsy, the blonde, the other analyst and all the other characters of the session are there, outside, in external reality, but they are also *here* in the field – in the *camper* van[6] – and the main line of the history (the syntagmatic–diachronic–linear aspect) can be linked to that of the present (the paradigmatic–synchronic–coexisting–systemic aspect) only by virtue of a *permeable* caesura. What is specific to a model inspired by the overcoming of caesuras – i.e. a field model – is not only simultaneity (because there is always a duration to be considered, and hence a 'historical' dimension, if only of a few seconds), but also attention to the form of the content, to the system and structure of communication, considered, like language, as the dynamic realm of links and differences. Attention to the *transformational structure* of the analytic field permits a new vision of the text and a new form of analysis, focusing more on functional aspects and on the container than on the contained, but the two levels are interdependent: *it is the interaction with the syntagmatic aspect, by virtue of its selective function, that establishes itself as a limit to interpretive drift* (Civitarese, 2005, 2006a, 2008a, 2008b). I therefore believe that the guarantee of an effective junction between the two planes, of a type of thought that overcomes the antithesis between the history and the present, lies precisely in the mental state of receptivity permitted by negative capability, a preliminary art of self-negation and of sacrificing what one knows. Only in this way is it possible to allow oneself to be absorbed by the truth of the session – as intuition stemming from the feeling of the transference instant (Horovitz, 2007) – and only then does one have enough faith in the entirely passive possibility of being able to be surprised.

Reconciliation

'It is curious that this term "caesura" was misprinted in the original paper by Freud as "censure",[7] so that it was even then, accidentally of course, unconsciously described as a censor, an inhibition' (Bion, 1977a, p. 12). This sentence is astonishing for its (felicitous) ambiguity. On the one hand, it is difficult not to believe that Bion is playing the game of imputing a conceptual oversight to Freud (the 'accident' of having theorized about the censorship rather than the caesura) instead of assuming a material error on the part of the typesetter – that is, that Bion was pretending that Freud was responsible for the slip. On the other hand, he is inventing for himself a Bionian Freud – one who understands that the caesura of the birth of every new thought sets up a barrier, 'a resistance, a prohibition'. By virtue of the entirely fortuitous substitution of one or two letters, the censorship becomes a particular case of caesura, a function of the permeability gradients of the contact barrier. At any rate, this singular anecdote can be used as a vertex for conceptualizing the discrepancy between Freud's notion of what the subject-matter of analysis represents and Bion's – that is, in sum, between Freud's memory-as-store and Bion's waking dream memory; between a science of the archives, erasures and rejects of memory and a science of at-one-ment.

Both Freud and Bion set themselves the problem of how to arrive at a more integrated kind of mental functioning. To this end, the essential aspect for Freud is recovery of the text deleted by the censorship of repression or of the superego, which, in order to win over the subject for civilization, must stem the incontinence of the sexual drive, even at the cost of a degree of discontent. Bion, on the other hand, is more concerned to favour psychic growth, and hence only secondarily to overcome the fault lines between the various parts of the mind. This is achieved by aiming for the finest possible affective attunement, by attempting to proceed at the patient's pace, *with the same rhythm.* This constitutes a shift from a psychoanalysis of contents to a psychoanalysis of the container – that is, of the apparatus for thinking thoughts. Self-evidently, Bion's approach repeats the decisive step taken by Descartes, and subsequently by Kant – namely, the transcendental approach of inquiring into the intellect before considering the objects of knowledge. The problem of how to reconstruct the text of memory, with all its lacunae, becomes, in Bion, that of how to live together with the patient in O, in unison, and to increase the patient's capacity for symbolization. After all, the factor that allows the container to expand and splits to be overcome is not knowledge in itself but emotion, or rather shared emotion, at-one-ment, the *feeling of being in unison*, even if the two can go very well together. The historical dimension is not in the least evaded, because transcending the caesura does not signify overturning a binary opposition but instead tolerating the existence of paradox, assuming the (impossible) task of taking account of two truths at one and the same time.

At-one-ment, which also means 'reconciliation', is the only way in which an embryonic thought can be born: it is the moment when projective identification is received and can be transformed. *Basically, there is no other channel of communication*: after all, what could such a channel be when, for example, language has not yet developed? But then, even where the subject is capable of symbolization, do not the emotions, which are indispensable to life, continue to be mediated by projective identification? So 'unison' – but the English word is not confined to a single sensory modality – means 'message received', 'I know what you are thinking' or 'I feel what you are feeling'; it is an agreement, a consent, a communion – it is the communicability of the feeling. It is not a vague 'being completely at one' once and for all, but the way in which the subject constantly seeks to reconcile himself with the real, of which the other is a part. In this, understanding appears essentially as a type of aesthetic intelligence. Developing thought means acquiring, in the interaction with another mind, the capacity to feel the form of experience through the play of similarities and differences.

Whereas Freud's vision of psychic life is eminently conflictual and unipersonal, Bion's is developmental and bipersonal; he believes that, in general, not enough importance is assigned in psychoanalytic theory to the problem of psychic growth. Sexuality is no longer the primal locus of conflict, and the way it is experienced varies according to the degree of security of the self and of development of thought. The sexuality of minds precedes the specific sexuality of the sexual drive, and in the *intimate room* in which analysis takes place, it is more a narration of relational + closeness/− closeness (Ferro, 2002a, 2005). From this point of view, censorship is a particular case of the caesura, while sexuality, although retaining its meaning, is nevertheless subordinated to the confirmation of identity, to filling the primal lacuna of being – that is, the primal trauma of birth – to the continuous reconstruction of the self. In a passage of *A Memoir of the Future* that is as extraordinary as it is irreverent, Bion resorts once again to the image, used in 'Caesura', of waves (transmissible elements) and quanta (proto-thoughts, 'in effect mental concentrates with a very low proportion of shareable emotional and verbal meaning' (Neri *et al.*, 1987, p. 38, translated), and very clearly lays down a number of concepts. These are: the technical primacy of simultaneity (of the paradigmatic) in the session over the historical and referential dimension; the need for the two planes nevertheless to be linked in order for the experience of analysis to be significant, and for the fictional truths of the virtual reality of the setting to colour the history and confer upon it the emotional substance without which it would be a mere chronicle; and the subordination of drive-related to relational factors, expressed paradoxically in sexual language. Here is the passage concerned:

'The phenomena which I regard as conjoined and mental are more full of meaning if I conceive of them as contemporaneous.

Bion: You do not regard them as historically distributed?

Myself: I do, but not exclusively. In fact, I would find it helpful to borrow from a schizophrenic patient a capacity for a transference relationship which was alternatively penetrating and planar; deep and confused, or superficial and of great 'spread', like a monomolecular film. At the same time these states, though apparently mutually exclusive, are reconciled and coexistent – like wave motion and quanta, objects in a pattern conforming to a Poisson distribution displayed on two planes – one temporal, one spatial – at right angles to each other. Seen from the temporal plane, the other 'transference' spreads monomolecular-wise: seen from the vertex of the spatial plane, the 'transference' is penetrating.

Bion: I don't think I understand. You mean that from an historical vertex events are distributed sequentially one after another in what we call time, *but that it is possible to regard them, by ignoring the temporal vertex, as distributed in space, not time?*

Myself: Yes, but then two views are obtained, one which is very narrow and extremely penetrating, the other very broad and spread out without depth or penetration.

Alice: So what? Is this any different from what I and any girl friends have always known? Our boy friends are all the same – either forever pawing us about though it's clear it doesn't mean a thing, or 'poking' us, having what they call sex, which doesn't mean a thing either.'

(Bion, 1975, pp. 193f., my italics)

By her foul-mouthed, caustic style, Alice reminds the analysts that time and space, the referential and the relational, amorous effusions and sexual intercourse ought not to be split, and that the same applies to the syntagmatic, that is, the linear chain of events (the history), and the paradigmatic, that is, the structure (the present context) and its network of differential relationships. There is not only a temporal, planar, superficial and extensive transference, but also one that is spatial, deep and penetrating, the two being linked in one and the same graph of Cartesian coordinates on two planes at right angles to each other. A static caesura between these two planes would be a form of schizophrenia, and indeed Bion establishes a logic of the supplement, based on a conjunctive rather than separative rationality between inside and outside. The main problem, however, is to make visible the other part of the figure, the landscape of the internal world, the extension of the mental space, which we are prevented from seeing by the normal hallucinosis of daily life – which is the paradoxical guarantee of subjectivity, for the subject as it were is born of the lie. When this condition is satisfied, the caesura takes on the full meaning assigned to it by Bion, which could hardly find better expression than in the following line from Hölderlin: 'Versöhnung ist mitten im Streit und alles Getrennte findet sich wieder' ['Reconciliation is there, even in the midst of strife, and all things that are parted find one another again'] (Hölderlin, 1965 [1797–1799], p. 170).

2

UNDER THE COVER OF DARKNESS

Bion: Is there anything new in this? You must often have heard, as I have, people say they don't know what you are talking about and that you are being deliberately obscure.

Myself: They are flattering me. I am suggesting an aim, an ambition, which, if I could achieve it, would enable me to be deliberately and *precisely* obscure: in which I could use certain words which activate precisely and instantaneously, in the mind of the listener a thought or train of thought that came between him and the thoughts and ideas already accessible and available to him.

Rosemary: Oh, my God!

(Wilfred R. Bion, *A Memoir of the Future. Book 1 – The Dream*)

In his book on the clinical significance of Bion's work, the last of the trilogy entitled *The Kleinian Development*, on more than one occasion Meltzer (1978) uses the expression 'search for ambiguity' to characterize Bion's style. And indeed Bion's conceptual path takes him from an absolute demand for rigour and precision, and from an attendant project similar to Descartes' aim to formulate only 'clear and distinct ideas' (Green, 1998, p. 651), to a 'mystical' perspective, the use of disciplined intuition, and the art of blinding. A rhetoric of blindness and vision (the intention to be '*precisely* obscure') represents the point of arrival of a theory that calls for tolerance towards the aporias of reason, that is to say, undecidable logical contradictions; towards the indeterminacy resulting from the presence of several possible meanings; and towards paradox, or in other words, propositions at odds with common sense but which upon closer examination contain elements of truth.

Blindness and vision

'It is characteristic of Bion's playfulness,' observes Meltzer (1978, p. 273), 'that he should use ambiguity to allow the reader both to misconstrue his meaning and to remain puzzled and uncertain for some time before clarification arrives.' He adds that for Bion the search for ambiguity takes the form of a 'playful "patience" in the interest of allowing others to have experiences [. . .] [Ambiguity and idiosyncrasy are] essential tools of Bion's methods of both investigation and exposition' (ibid., p. 274). The search for ambiguity also lies behind many of the stimulating ideas that Bion drew over the years from the field of mathematics, and one of the factors, along with his idiosyncratic use of many words, that define the poetic quality of his language, which is at once 'evocative and incomprehensible' (ibid., p. 295).

Meltzer does not hide his view that at times he finds Bion's prose exasperating, obscure, irritating, abstruse, oppressive, even absurd. He even suggests that Bion idealizes what one might consider the negative version of ambiguity, or in other words, confusion. But he alternates these negative adjectives with others of a very different nature: astonishing, brilliant, original, dazzling. 'Dazzling', in particular, is a term rich in meaning, reflecting as it probably does his ambivalence towards Bion, but also his perception of an essential aspect of Bion's thought: this is the point where, by inadvertently suggesting the idea of error, mistake and obfuscation, Meltzer endorses Bion's rhetoric of blindness and vision.

The fact is that Bion discovered the path of creative work and encouraged others to follow this same course. Meltzer shows that he has understood this very well. Likewise it is true that, if it makes sense to point to ambiguity as one of the components of creative work – one need only think of the classic study by Empson (1930) – Bion also seems for this reason to envy poets and philosophers their syntax and the richness of associations of the words they use. In 'Evidence' (1976), for example, he recalls Plato's remark about the enormous advantage that despite the apparent precision, despite the fact that Socrates and Phaedrus apparently speak in a very accurate language, they are in fact using extremely ambiguous terms.

Elsewhere, Bion (1962, p. 5) acknowledges that he too has chosen certain words precisely for their ambiguity quotient, and he declares equally directly that he wishes to keep this ambiguity and is concerned not to forgo nuances of meaning: 'I wish the ambiguity to remain: I want the reader to be reminded of mathematics, philosophy and common usage because a characteristic of the human mind I am discussing may develop in such a way that it is seen at a later stage to be classifiable under these headings – and others.'

Part of this is his desire to use 'empty' terms or terms void of a codified meaning – such as the 'α function' – using them like variables or unknowns in mathematics whose value can be gradually made more precise through usage. Many of his formulations, moreover, have the same 'mythical' status as elements belonging to the C-category on the Grid, in other words, they are 'science fictions'. The same can also be said of the 'moral' or philosophical dialogues in *A Memoir of the Future* (1975).

As we have said, Bion begins with a self-imposed aspiration for Cartesian light, but precisely his desire for rigour causes him disillusionment and leads him to the mystical model, even if only to draw inspiration from it. In this respect his intellectual journey is not unlike that of Wittgenstein (1953), who moved from the stringent logical positivism of his early writings to the 'anti-realist' concept of the language game in his *Philosophical Investigations*. Eventually, what remained of an impossible mathematical version of psychoanalysis was mathematics seen only as a dream of precision and a repertoire of analogies for the phylo- and ontogenetic development of thought.

Here it becomes clear why the figure of the blind man with a stick is the central allegory of Bion's way of understanding psychoanalysis, as it had been for Descartes and his philosophical system.[1] To some extent this also applies to Freud, who in his letter to Lou Andreas-Salomé dated 25 May 1916, described his method of writing, explaining that he felt the need to project a ray of darkness onto the material he was investigating.[2] Psychoanalysis as the probe that expands the field it investigates is nothing other than the prosthesis of a blind man: 'Psychoanalysis tells you nothing: it is an instrument, like the blind man's stick, that extends the power to gather information' (Bion, 1992, p. 356). The thing-in-itself (noumenon, ultimate reality, the unconscious, the gods, 'O') is unknowable, invisible, but can be intuited (seen) through the eyes of interiority.[3] As in the Platonic myth of the cave, itself a highly theatrical setting, the world shows itself only through the pale reflections of phenomena. The form of things changes depending on the angle of light and is itself the result of the process of the irreducible virtualization of reality performed by the senses.

Consistent with this basic approach, most of Bion's concepts could be ordered according to the pairs light/darkness or blindness/insight. One need only think of terms such as reversible perspective, vertex, binocular vision; the truth as *phós*, and the obscurity of negative capability, unsaturation and pre-conception; the invisibility of absolute or transcendental reality. The Bionian lexicon itself may be seen as the gropings of a sceptic: conjecture, hypothesis, speculative imagination, uncertainty, guesswork, doubt, erring/wandering, and so on.

Memory and desire, too, erect a screen against the sunlight of knowledge. What remain are acts of faith; Bion does not mean these in the religious sense, however, but as scientific propositions, that is, as the feeling that characterizes the mental state of openness towards the idea of the existence of an ultimate truth or reality which it is possible to approach. But, as Derrida with his usual *agudeza* points out (1990, p. 30), even faith 'in the moment proper to it, is blind. It sacrifices sight, even if it does so with an eye to seeing at last'. All blind men 'must *advance*, advance or commit themselves, that is, expose themselves, run through space as if running a risk. They are apprehensive about space, they apprehend it with their groping, wandering hands; they draw in this space in a way that is at once cautious and bold; they calculate, they count on the invisible' (ibid., p. 5). This is also what analysts do, as they strive to be *precise* in darkness, gropingly exploring the space around them.

In Bion, then, the ascendancy of seeing over saying is absolute. The primacy of the visual is ultimately ensured by the centrality of the concept of the α function and by the related concept of waking dream thought. The 'mysterious' α function produces α-elements, *visual* images that become part of the construction of dream thoughts and enter into memory's repository of experience in the form of 'clouds of uncertainty', or β-elements. With the concept of the α function Bion reverses the Freudian approach and rewrites the theory of dreams. The emphasis is less on meaning and more on the process of signification. Now the dream creates and distinguishes the conscious from the unconscious.[4] In this way Bion also takes to extremes the Kleinian model of the inner world as a theatre where meaning is generated which then permeates the objects of the external world. The external world, after Klein, is a world between inverted commas. It is seen '*as*, that is as a reflection of internal relations from the point of view of meaning and significance' (Meltzer, 1978, p. 312). By emphasizing this aspect of Kleinian theory, Bion arguably makes his greatest contribution to a theory of ambiguity and creativity. The subject assimilates the world through a mental process regulated by the same mechanisms as those of the dream – a waking dream – as in the theatre.[5]

The theatricalization of reality

'To what extent,' Bion asks himself (1992, pp. 137–138), 'are the mechanisms of dream-work evident elsewhere? [...] is it not possible that the mechanisms that Freud described as peculiar to dream-work are in reality found to be operating over a wide area of the psyche and in a great number of different functional fields?'. Thus, if all language is ultimately metaphorical, as post-structuralist critical theory would argue, surely the operations that structure it will be the same as those of the dream, and not (only) those that are strictly logical and rational, purified of all passion, such as might be suggested by the identification of thought with the conscious and the ingenuous practical realism we all possess? While the question is, of course, rhetorical, it should not be forgotten that Bion himself valorises the social nature of *common sense* as the factor that allows a consensuality of sensory and emotional impressions, and that he focuses on the role of the individual in the group and of the group in the individual.

In Bion the dream is the model of a functioning mind which precisely for this reason is able to create the unconscious and keep it separate from the conscious by means of a permeable barrier – the 'contact-barrier' (once again, an oxymoron). Integrated, or 'binocular', vision, namely the simultaneous use of the conscious and the unconscious, enables the subject to enjoy positive contact with external and internal reality. So, when the individual is awake he can continue to function by remaining asleep to a range of stimuli that, although constantly assimilated, cannot invade his mind but are contained and remain for the most part unconscious.

When this is not possible, it is as if the subject were in the same situation as a newborn child whose rudimentary consciousness 'is not associated with an unconscious. All impressions of the self are of equal value; all are conscious' (Bion, 1967, p. 116). Consciousness in these conditions, just like the hyper-memory of *Funes*, the character in Borges' famous story, would not be able to perform its functions. It is for this reason that at birth the newborn child has an absolute need of someone who filters sensory impressions for him and takes on the violence of primitive emotions. This means that he needs both a receptor for his projective identifications and maternal reverie if he is to be helped to internalize an α function – the definition that sums up this process. The mother 'dreams' the child, that is, she acts as if they were one and contains its projective identifications (as always, imperfectly; the realization is for this reason necessarily negative), which are the result of the previous splitting and evacuation of emotions that cannot be treated in any other way, and she *negotiates* a possible meaning for them. The mother's dream is the first place in which the (PS and D) positions are negotiated.[6]

On the other hand, perfect adherence to reality, where things mean only themselves and nothing else, where everything is clear, hyper-luminous like a screen memory, factual, non-ambiguous – a vision which is too natural, solely external or literal – is nothing other than an 'effect of reality', a β-world, the perverted dream of *The Matrix*. Bion would talk of transformation in hallucinosis, produced by the operations of splitting and projective identification *in excess* of the reversible perspective, which gives the false impression of possessing absolute truth; not hallucinations of objects but the perception of false relations. This is the mark of psychotic thought (which can in fact be found in part in any personality), which presents itself as 'rational thought characterized by a peculiar lack of "resonance" [...] one dimensional, [which] has no overtones or undertones of meaning [...] It and has no capacity to evoke a train of thought' (Bion, 1970, pp. 15–16). *It's like saying that psychotic thinking, inhibited thought, is characterized by the fact that it betrays no ambiguity!* From this viewpoint, Bion's conception is inherently aporetic, in that it sees rationality in its rigid form as a dead end street – and not just individual logical *impasses*.

In short, the difference lies between the permeability of the contact barrier, which is a dynamic caesura whose 'social' or inter-psychic origin has already been mentioned, and the rigid impenetrability of the β screen, a static type of caesura that is produced not by the α function but by its reverse. The fact is that the dream becomes the very paradigm of the functioning of a mind that generates meaning and learns from reality. Given the obvious difference in degree of focused attention, for Bion the ability to dream – that is, to symbolize – and the ability to think are the very same thing. Now, what is more ambiguous than the dream? Think of the sense of suspended time and the rarefied atmosphere we find in surrealist painting; think, for example, of paintings by Delvaux, Breton and Dalí, which deploy ambiguity in their attempt to grasp the essential nature of the dream. Now for the first time the Greek tragedians' idea of life as a dream has begun to receive serious scientific consideration and a kind of validation. With its shifting imagery and its sophisticated rhetoric, the dream, which Freud modelled on the theatre set, captures the world in its poetic guise, in other words, in the cognitively most complex way possible, that is, from several points of view simultaneously and in an emotionally more meaningful manner.

If Egginton's compelling hypothesis (2003) is true – namely the idea that the modern, Cartesian concept of the self-reflexive subject was linked to the emergence between the sixteenth and seventeenth centuries of a new sensibility that resulted from the new forms of space in the theatre – the same can also be said of Freud's inversion of the *cogito*. The medium of the theatre provided him with the model that enabled him to develop his idea of the dream within a scientific framework. Not only that, but theatre is the medium best suited to serve as a metaphor for the analytic setting. For, as in the theatre, knowledge is attained through experience in a dimension which is sensory (illusion, presence, performance, action, *práxis*, confined and limited space), mythical (*mythos*, fictionality of plot), and passionate (*páthos*, emotions). The difference between the narration of facts and dialogue or action in the here-and-now is the same as that which, according to Aristotle, makes tragedy superior to epic (Weber, 2004). In Bion the same gap separates T → O from T → K.

But the new *theatricality*, which Finotti (2004) has called 'the rhetoric of diffraction', is such that it not only constructs but at the same time also *deconstructs* the conceptual oppositions that define it, namely outside/inside, stage/auditorium, actors/audience, reality/illusion, and so on. Accordingly, if the dream is the template of the theatrical set, now that Bion has made it *the* model of the mind, one can say that *reality itself becomes theatre* – and thus *becomes more ambiguous*.

Negative capability

The concept that encapsulates the characteristics I have been attributing to Bion's thinking is that of 'negative capability' for it is paradoxical in its very formulation,[7] it creates ambiguity or in other words provokes new thoughts, and, as it is based on an engagement with the limits of pure rationality, it is aporetic. Often the concept of negative capability, a state of mind 'like being almost thoughtless' (Bion, 1997, p. 32), is examined as a concept in itself. The result is that, despite the evocative references to the passage in Keats's letter to his brother in which the poet coined the expression,[8] it becomes difficult to capture its essence. It is better to consider it as one of the nodes in the network that includes the notions of reverie, selected fact, insights, transformations in O, preconception-realization, reversal of perspective etc. What distinguishes Bion's thought, owing to the peculiar use he makes of analogy[9] and the construction of models, is the fact that the individual elements, taken in isolation, are either felt to be inadequate to express our knowledge of a certain phenomenon or lend themselves to sterile, stereotypical use, which is completely at odds with the dynamic and problematic essence that marks them out. Taken together, however, in their interrelations, these same elements prove extremely convincing.

For example, negative capability, the state of mind that best describes the lack of memory and desire, the *impossible* task of stripping oneself of the *a priori* assumptions that guide observation and knowledge, is not just a question of remaining in the paranoid-schizoid (PS) position (but beware: the interplay of positions is unconscious), because this suspension only makes sense as the prelude to a movement towards the depressive position (D). What is important is that there should be an ordering principle that intervenes to allow us to move from patience to safety, even though every transformation which goes in the direction of integration never halts the search for meaning but presents new obstacles to understanding.

Negative capability is tied to the emotional competence acquired through tolerating doubt (another synonym for 'aporia'). It has to do with knowing how to allow the gradual development of a container in which the contents (♂) that reflect a prevailing state of PS – a 'cloud of uncertainty' of β-elements – are able to disperse and remain in this state for a certain period of time before some surprise event comes along to organize them into something coherent. Now, this container is no abstract entity. Its fine tissues are made up of emotions. The capacity to tolerate doubt, uncertainty and paradox provides this vital connective tissue with the qualities of flexibility needed to accommodate ♂ elements, and thus to make K possible, or rather O → K: not purely rational knowledge, but that which comes from being able to learn from experience, ultimately from the introjection of the interplay between projective identification and maternal reverie and the consequent ability to make use of the consensuality of emotions.

The concept of negative capability is often misunderstood because of the gap that separates the two terms of the activity/passivity dichotomy. It is the *active* search for memory and the *active* exercise of desire that Bion proposes to inhibit (actively – another paradox!), and not their emergence from a background of passivity. In this case memory is configured as a reverie; not so much as knowledge (K) but as an 'evolution' of the analyst (T → O), in the same way as Zen practice teaches that what matters is not the quality of the solution to the koan proposed by the master but the experience of the search. For the analyst, giving up memory and desire means that each session is a new session. Negative capability is another name for the *epochè* which Freud brilliantly adopted to circumvent the impassibility of aporia, the predominance of the conscious, and logical, rational thinking. It is way of radicalizing and restoring effectiveness to his concept of evenly suspended attention.

The concept of negative capability also coincides with a principle of hospitality and compassion for the suffering of others, rather than expressing a rule which, however useful, may in concrete terms encourage persistent arrogance and pride. On a clinical level it is the translation into the form of a technical guideline of the methodical doubt that Bion, à la Descartes, maintained that it must be part of every analyst's set of tools.[10] The same principle is expressed at a theoretical level by the invitation to investigate and to 'transcend the caesura' (Bion, 1977a). From a meta-theoretical viewpoint, however, systematic doubt is at the origin of the steady, largely underground flow of epistemic reflections to be found throughout Bion's books – and, for that matter, also in Freud. These notes led him to criticize the opposition between ideology and science (also to be found in psychoanalysis), and to express himself increasingly in 'science fictions', that is, overtly narrative forms. In this respect, Bion is in line with Derrida's deconstruction of the dichotomy between narrative-literary and scientific-philosophical discourse. Green (1992, p. 587) has focused on this aspect with great precision:

> Bion's conception of the relations between psychoanalysis and science, at a time these matters are acutely topical, is interesting in that it constitutes a total *reversal* of the usual approach to these relations. Instead of wishing for a psychoanalysis carried along in the wake of science, seeking validation procedures agreeable to scientists, Bion, on the contrary, maintains for example that what a community deems to be 'scientific' dictates what fantasies are to be externalized in the prevalent cosmology and which are to achieve some other outlet. [...] The deductive scientific system is that defined by its place in the hierarchy of thought processes; it is at one and the same time the topmost level of a particular system and the basis whereby lower-level systems (in terms of generalization) can be used.

The key word in this passage is *reversal* because it echoes the concept of 'reversible perspective'. (Pathological) reversible perspective expresses the specific loss of ambiguity, intolerance towards paradox. The case Green alludes to, however, is an example of the *non-pathological* reversal of perspective because the paradoxical nature of simultaneous points of view embodied in the couple of science/psychoanalysis is maintained. In agreement with Green, Sandler (2005) too notes that perhaps if we want to clarify the way in which Bion comes to conceive of the analytic attitude it would be better to refer to his later works, especially *A Memoir of the Future*, where a quasi-theatrical or poetic prose takes the place of mathematical formulas and concepts drawn from philosophy. The subtitle is also significant: *A fable for our time*, which appeared in *Cogitations*, dated July 1971.

Right from the beginning, for Bion the use of a language that requires taking a new look via abstract symbols borrowed from geometry and via the 'void' of concepts such as the α function, as well as philosophical terms already laden with meaning, was a way of repeating Freud's act of decentralizing the conscious subject of the psychology and philosophy of his time – a project that was anti-Cartesian in content but highly Cartesian in spirit and method. Both things are true. Ever since his early work, Bion had a precise awareness of the limits of the scientific formalization of psychoanalysis, but only over the years did that knowledge turn into real disillusionment. Hence one can see continuity where Meltzer (1978), towards the end of *Transformations* (Bion, 1965), identified a sharp break in the shift from the mathematical to the mystical vertex. The break *would* be clean only if one could speak in the proper sense of mysticism and not, here again, of sophisticated *bricolage*, in other words, the construction of conceptual models using materials taken from other forms of knowledge that share the same object of investigation.

Analogies set up transferences of properties and relationships between different realities, some better known than others. This is why they are heuristic and hermeneutic or interpretative tools. They serve to construct models and theories. Analogical language, which includes similes, metaphors, allegories, parables, comparisons, myths, etc. stands, in fact, between equivocity and univocity. Ambiguity occupies this intermediate area, which is the area of creativity. Bion's terms have an analogical meaning, in other words, they are positioned between the impossible, aporetic uniqueness of phenomena that cannot be understood because they are not knowable any other way, or because they are too complex, and the confusing and totally unproductive ambiguity which is closer to psychotic thought (with or without quotation marks).

The opposite of the search for ambiguity – the meaning of which I have tried to explain by taking on board Meltzer's near-provocation – is the search for *concreteness*, for material as opposed to psychic reality, quantity as opposed to quality, the inanimate instead of the animate. In this way individuals can get rid of the emotions and turmoil that affect the mind by giving up the perceptual consensuality they provide. Confusion and concreteness correspond to the unconscious and the conscious when these two domains of the mind fail to function simultaneously, as they should, albeit with constant fluctuations. When, however, conscious and unconscious function in synchrony, steering clear of both the prison of uniqueness and the risks of misunderstanding, the subject is able to grasp the ambiguities of reality, to appreciate the paradoxes of existence and to tolerate the impasses of reason.

A mystical science?

In his book on dreams, Resnik (1987) points out that in Greek the word *theoréin*, the word from which we get the term *theory*, also means 'to contemplate'. This verb recurs obsessively (mostly as 'dark contemplation') in the *Dark Night of the Soul* by Saint John of the Cross (1618), a work that describes the path of enlightenment that leads to divine communion with God. *Dark Night* is an extraordinary work because it can be interpreted in different ways: from its declared theological standpoint, from a psychological or from an erotic perspective (it can be read as if it had been written by de Sade, and again, as in Poe's *Purloined Letter*; basically there is no better way to hide something than to put it on display for all to see). A comparison with Bion's terminology and concepts proves illuminating. For example, the explicit sexual metaphor in Saint John of the Cross is reminiscent of Bion's similar metaphor of the container and the contained (♀ ♂); 'becoming O' translates the mystical expression of the *pati divina* ('suffering God'); the union of love with God is equivalent to atonement/unison; the transformations of the soul as it approaches things divine recalls Bion's theory of transformations; the parallel drawn between the journey and both a struggle and a 'tempestuous and horrible night' (ibid., p. 71) invokes Bion's idea of 'without memory and desire'. The author of *Dark Night* insists on this point throughout the book: one should free oneself from 'ignoble exercises of sense and meditation' (ibid., p. 36 but seek a state of passive receptivity, of emptiness and 'poverty of spirit' (ibid., p. 25); voiding oneself of intelligence, will and memory, so as to be struck by the 'ray of darkness' (ibid., p. 64) of the divine light, which can only be a black light.

For Saint John of the Cross, in its search for the divine spouse (the truth) the soul must escape at night while the house is dark, that is, when the servants are asleep and can do nothing to stop it:

> It is needful for the enamoured soul, in order to attain to its desired end, to do likewise, going forth at night, when all the domestics in its house are sleeping and at rest – that is, when the low operations, passions and desires of the soul (who are the people of the household) are, because it is night, sleeping and at rest. When these are awake, they invariably hinder the soul from seeking its good, since they are opposed to its going forth in freedom.
>
> (Ibid., p. 95)

Only then can one travel the paths of knowledge that are precluded to mere intelligence:

> The reason, again, why the soul not only travels securely, when it travels thus *in the darkness*, but also achieves even greater gain and progress, is that usually, when the soul is receiving fresh advantage and profit, this comes by a way that it least understands – indeed, it quite commonly believes that it is losing ground. For, as it has never experienced that new feeling which drives it forth and dazzles it and makes it depart recklessly from its former way of life, it thinks itself to be losing ground rather than gaining and progressing, since it sees that it is losing with respect to that which it knew and enjoyed, and is going by a way which it knows not and wherein it finds no enjoyment.
>
> (Ibid., p. 100)

Doubt as a form of dark knowledge is necessary if one is to reach something new and not limit oneself to the things one already knows. Finally, Bion is not even a stranger to the triad of faith, hope and charity, which appears somewhat surprisingly in the final chapters of the *Dark Night* as the real key to interpretation:

> Hope voids and withdraws the memory from all creature possessions; for, as Saint Paul says, hope is for that which is not possessed; and thus it withdraws the memory from that which it is capable of possessing, and sets it on that for which it hopes. And for this cause hope in God alone prepares the memory purely for union with God. Charity, in the same way, voids and annihilates the affections and desires of the will for whatever is not God, and sets them upon Him alone.
>
> (Ibid., p. 116)

Grotstein (2007) wrote that the type of science which Bion considers appropriate to psychoanalysis is a 'mystical science'.[11] By this he means a nonlinear science that knows how to think about complexity, infinity and indeterminacy; a science that arises from an aesthetic vertex, a term he uses to imply the dream as imagination, fiction and creativity. But in my view the mystical element that should be maintained more than any other is the inexhaustible drive towards the unexplored and the ultimate meaning of things and, in all other respects, that mysticism is to be translated through dialectics and the systematic exercise of doubt. For Bion's 'mysticism' was nothing other than the systematic transcending of caesuras, in other words, the restoration of dialectical tension to the two terms of binary oppositions that organize meaning in psychoanalytic theory. In this way, they are released back into a field in which each of the two is de-identified and becomes indistinguishable from the other except as its reflection: ultimately, what is this if not the logic of the dream?

Beyond Bion, silence in words

The Bionian search for ambiguity has been picked up by the theory of the analytic field, where it enhanced the contributions of the Barangers to form an original synthesis (Ferro, 1992, 1999, 2002b, 2005, 2006; Ferro *et al.*, 2007; Civitarese, 2008b; Fabbrici, 2008; Ferro and Basile, 2009).[12] The ambiguity of unsaturated or veiled speech that characterizes this model comes from an awareness of the limits of knowledge and from the attention paid to the effects that interpretation has on the patient. This means that the analyst's mental procedures, which are specific to psychoanalytic understanding, are carried out in a different scene, in an internal setting, which enables him to monitor the status of the emotional field and to adjust his interpretative presence accordingly.

Psychoanalysis has asked itself many questions about the silence of the patient, but it is only since Bion's concept of 'negative capability' and transformations into K and into O, and since their subsequent theoretical extensions into concepts of weak or unsaturated interpretation (Bezoari and Ferro, 1989) that we can speak of silence as something that not only indicates the presence or absence of words, but can be *in* the words themselves. The point, then, is not the quantitative aspect of the analyst's discourse but above all its quality. The way the analyst uses his language – which is always also a performative, namely speech that *produces* what it purports only to describe – becomes an important parameter with regard to the manifest text of the interpretation.

Bion maintains that the analytic dialogue should resemble an ordinary conversation, but he also says that the art of conversation in psychoanalysis requires an 'extension into the realm of non-conversation' (Bion, 1975, p. 190), where even pauses, breaks and gaps are important. This is why silence is also an important factor in the consulting room and is closely linked to other technical parameters of the therapy, such as free association and evenly suspended attention.

And, I would add, especially silence *in* the words, that is, a way of participating in the analytic relationship which privileges the use of so-called weak or unsaturated interpretations. This results in a clinical practice based on abstinence, omission, reserve, indeterminacy, and made up of respect, sensitivity and tact – all of which can ultimately be linked to the exercise of 'negative capability'.

Thus, dialogue, though produced by a generative grammar that can be equated with the specific interpretative procedures of analytic work, takes place on a superficial level, but is only at one remove from a second or third level which, as with the various layers of writing on a palimpsest, may be less visible but should nonetheless not be overlooked. The emotional truth towards which the interpretation moves can at times be largely implied. It is approached indirectly. Because it is not the absolute truth, but a reflection of truth, an *armistice*, as suggested by the probable common derivation of the words *truth* and *truce* from the same root *trewe* (faith, loyal, faithful) (Weber, 2004).

This way of working puts great faith in the power of speech; in the possibilities inherent in the device of analysis to restore weight, consistency and density to the word; to bring words back to a kind of auroral state, at their best not far from the magic of poetry; and in its ability to coin its own metaphors and forge its own dialects. The analytic discourse, however, is not only valuable, it is also perishable. It can decline into jargon, falsehood and violence – and certainly not the 'necessary' violence Aulagnier (1975) has introduced into our thinking.

Ideally, the analyst seeks to free himself from doctrine. He aims to be natural and spontaneous, but at the same time disciplined. He cultivates within himself an awareness of the relative, provisional, conjectural nature of his knowledge. He sees all knowledge as something that is always under review and can always be amended. He is impervious to certainty, arrogance and assertiveness. He scrutinizes the living presence and changes of emotions in details of speech that might appear banal or insignificant. He uses a language which is transparent, colloquial, simple. He does not dress his words in sumptuous clothes.

He rejects the definitive closure of meaning, and with his unsaturated, open interpretation calls upon the other to engage in imaginative work. The dialogue can then develop along unforeseen lines. A hospitable atmosphere is created, just right for the perception of nuances. The gaze becomes more acute. The 'playing of the unconscious' (Bollas, 1999, p. 164) is seen as a source of pleasure. It can sometimes be useful to resort to an evocative, elliptical use of language which is allusive (from the Latin *ad* + *ludere*), which makes suggestions but does not resolve all questions of meaning. It is a way of leaving room for the other, for the unsaid, even for reticence. It is an *eloquent silence*, not opaque or closed in on itself; a silence that creates a concave receptive space, which is opposed to noise and not to the word. It is open to the unexpected, the unknown, the unconscious (*unbewußt*). In this way the patient experiences the analyst as someone who tolerates uncertainty, contradictions, complexity; who puts up with not understanding everything right away and who knows how to look out over the abyss of pain and the insignificance of the human condition; but equally as someone who not only has his own humanity but also a method by which, in the face of all of this, he hopes to acquire – and hopes to help the patient to acquire – growth of thought.

The analytic attitude outlined here may seem minimalist, but it is by no means oracular or gnomic, nor does it have anything aestheticizing. The field model deconstructs the rigid caesura between transference and countertransference and between analysand and analyst; and it makes even more meaningful Bion's concept of thought without a thinker. Truth as food for the mind is a constant goal; if anything, it is seen, as Sandler (2011) writes, as 'a very fragile species' and the search for it is carried out with a more acute sensitivity, which is less likely to be found in those who claim to possess knowledge 'about' the other. It is, on the contrary, a technical approach marked by a strong ethical tone. The analyst takes full responsibility towards the patient. He knows that in the theatre of analysis, as Bion never tires of repeating, pain, fear and danger are always present. He thinks that ultimately the truth of the basic loneliness of the human condition should come to the surface. Ideally, when the analysis is over, the patient should, as he takes his leave, also take with him the secret, as Montale teaches, of the illusory nature of reality.[13] Or he should have seen the demon described in the lines by Coleridge that Bion (1970, p. 46) refers to in *Attention and Interpretation*, the sense of the transience of things or, as Searles has it, the acceptance of the inevitability of suffering and death.[14] This is, after all, the same lucid pessimism that Freud possessed, or rather the tenderness of a well-tempered scepticism void of any idealization of the negative.

3

THE BURNING BODY

The perception of psychic qualities and hypochondria

> Are we going to dismiss X by saying 'Oh, he's terribly hypochondriacal' – finish; we thank God we don't have to bother any further? Or should we *listen* to what he says? Should we expose ourselves to what this individual is trying to communicate?
>
> (Wilfred R. Bion, *The Tavistock Seminars*)

The ego, as Freud says 'is first and foremost a bodily ego' (1922, p. 26), and in a note added in 1927 to the English translation of *The Ego and the Id*, he explains that it 'is ultimately derived from bodily sensations, chiefly from those springing from the surface of the body. It may thus be regarded as a mental projection of the surface of the body, besides, as we have seen above, representing the superficies of the mental apparatus'. This idea, which inextricably links mind and body, is now firmly established. Less obvious, however, is the idea that the body itself is in its turn something that is 'produced' from birth on. Sensations and perceptions are not pure or natural, but somehow also learned, that is to say, shaped by the mother's discourse. The first homeland of the ego is a pre-symbolic language made up of rhythms, tones of voice, sounds, words, silences, gestures, expressions, smells and colours. The construction of identity starts in the play of assonance and dissonance, absence and non-absence. A fluid bundle of sensory experiences marked from the very beginning by caesuras, gaps and spacing provides 'the principal *media for the creation of psychological meaning* and the rudiments of the experience of self [... a] non-self-reflective sense of "going on being"' (Ogden, 1989, pp. 52–54). The first experiences of contact or, in the literal sense, the first impressions, which correspond fully to the autistic forms described by Tustin (1986), later become associated with ideas of security, protection, relaxation, and as a rule ensure *the silence of the body* (Pragier, 1995).

The process whereby a person becomes a subject and comes to structure a feeling of self-cohesion thus implies submission to a certain symbolic order, in other words, the incorporation of codes, rules and regulations.[1] The identity defined by the sexed body has a performative dimension,[2] it is the result of attributions of meaning that give shape to reality in the very act of naming it, and it springs from the ritualized, embodied repetition of actions. At one extreme it is the 'hallucinatory effect of naturalized gestures' (Butler, 1999, p. xv). Thus, the body has always been a significant body, a text being written and rewritten within an intersubjective matrix, within a 'web of relationships woven on a loom of flesh'[3] (Magrelli, 2006, p. 9). The semiotic functioning of this text reflects its vitality. Once internalized, the frame of 'productive, regulatory and contestatory relations' (Butler, 1997, p. 99) continues to produce its effects in a constant iteration or unconscious 'execution' of memory traces laid down by experience. The ego's activity of self-production is not, however, a closed system, but is always contaminated by external reality. In its reiteration, the meaning of the text articulated by the body changes, because with each re-writing it finds a modified local context and is constantly generating new readings.

I use the concept of performative identity, a correlative of the theory of gender performativity (Butler, 1990), because it culturizes perceptions and sensations more incisively than the psychoanalytic theories that in fact provide its inspiration;[4] and because it supports a 'strong' theory of the body as an entity that always and everywhere speaks a language, as the term itself attests, which equates meaning with one of its organs. Sensory experience dominates not only at birth, but also later, when during development it accompanies the more specialized forms of thought, and is preserved as 'the *barely perceptible* background of sensory groundedness of all subsequent subjective states' (Ogden, 1989, p. 50). Basically, the body is generated partly, but inescapably, by its own lived material nature, and by the way in which it is already marked by, and inseparable from, discursive strategies. Sensations are not pure emanations of the body – it is not as if a language could ever reflect what it denominates as its referent, reality itself, the thing itself, of which it is incidentally a part – nor are they opposed to the body; but they have to do with it and they dovetail and fuse drive and culture into one.

De-subjectification

In hypochondria this background changes. The path of subjectification is traced backwards in a repeated attempt at sensorial self-containment. The reintegration of the self proceeds like the decryption of a text that has become inexplicably obscure and in which the body once again comes to the fore. The right to citizenship acquired through the original and necessary subservience to the symbolic order is lost. The conscious ego lives as if it were in exile and feels as though it were inhabiting a body it is impossible to decode, which is experienced as threatening, no longer transparent or natural. The sensations that constitute the vocabulary and syntax of the discourse of hypochondria translate a feeling of disorientation, whose essential paradigm is Freud's concept of the *unheimlich*. The world suddenly becomes alien, but it is a world which is above all the other as an object of passionate attachment. The exile of the body from the ego and of the ego from the body is unconsciously experienced as something preordained. The other as an ideal object upon whom one's psychic survival depends is absent and becomes the fantasmatic space in which the subject becomes more and more distressed, as it moves in a maze, in a foreign land where it does not speak the language. This regression is the internalized reflection of the crisis of the intersubjective matrix that generates and maintains the process of identity construction. The loss of familiarity with one's own body translates the subject's unconscious feeling of being evicted from a house which is 'a substitute for the mother's womb, the first lodging' of being (Freud, 1930, p. 91). This is what happens when the subject's need to be recognized meets in the other a defective α function or chronically deficient reverie.

The state of exile restores a precarious para-excitatory system by lowering the level of psychic tension, similar to what happens to refugees fleeing from a devastating political conflict. Although steeped in nostalgia, it still allows a certain ego functioning. It does not exclude one entirely from the sphere of social relations, since there is still a 'text' written on the body, however opaque it may be. At the same time, the status of being an exile expresses the urgent need for a narcissistic re-equilibrium in relational exchanges. When this request is not understood or accepted, the malaise that affects more and more differentiated levels of meaning-making can turn into paranoia, melancholia or somatization, and can thus lead the subject to withdraw to strongholds where defences are even more primitive and limiting. This is why hypochondria is seen as a sort of *crossroads* between several disevolutionary paths and cannot be reduced to a psychopathological entity of its own. If it has any specific characteristics, on the one hand it is a regressive move towards the sensory pole of production of experience; and, on the other hand, in treatment, it prompts the analyst's reverie to a particular sensitivity towards this level of interaction.

Hypochondria as a narrative genre

In hypochondria the gaze scans a body/landscape that has become an ambiguous area encroached upon by intolerable anxiety. If he focuses on this level during the session, however, the analyst objectifies the patient and sees his condition as a fact, as reality, or he gives an interpretation which is based solely on a one-person psychology. He does not grasp the communicative meaning of the symptom and its value as an alarm signal warning about what is happening in the here-and-now (Robutti, 1992). From an intersubjective point of view, on the other hand, the discourse of hypochondria is the dyke the patient erects to hold back the lava of emotions he is unable to contain in the immediate context of experience. The fact is that the 'body' is also a 'character' of the field, a fiction, or rather a second-degree fiction, *and not only the real body* (Ferro, 2006). It is the story of the events of the analysis as they happen, and in this case it can be a disorder afflicting the analytic field. Explaining to the patient that he is suffering from an imaginary disease is not very useful, because on another level, perhaps the most important level for the treatment, paradoxically, it is a 'real' and even necessary disease – but a disease of the relationship, not of the body. From the transference point of view, the doctors the patient calls upon to make a diagnosis stand for the analyst himself who does not give credence to his version of events. In an involuntary parody of medical jargon, which moreover illuminates its performative function, as already brilliantly highlighted by Foucault (1963) in his now classic work on the birth of the clinic, the patient, who turns himself into a clinician, rebels and offers a glimpse of what emotions he is defending himself from. From this point of view, the discourse of hypochondria in the consulting room has to be put into context. The real body has to be put between quotation marks. As in the construction of identity there is no prediscursive, essential, natural body, just as in the fiction of the setting there is no body outside the text of analysis.

Respecting the surface level of the patient's discourse, while trying at the same time to read its transference meaning between the lines may be the most effective way to facilitate the transformations that at some point may render the symptoms superfluous. It is necessary, then, to play along with the game of the body so as to suggest, as soon as the patient acquires a minimum of trust, a more ambiguous perspective on reality. In this way one can help the patient tell his story in new ways and open it up again to unexpected possibilities for development (Ferro, 2006).

The classic meta-psychological vertex, then, can be considered secondary (because it is less intimate, warm and involving; but the formation and transformation of the subject is not possible without a bond of passion!), and in the session is itself a place in the field. *Indeed, by referring to the genealogy of the ego and the temporality of an individual's history, a radical social theory of the subject, such as that proposed by Bion, stands in a relationship of reciprocal implication with respect to a clinical approach of the bi-personal or field type*. If the body is always a text, in other words, an inscribed surface (though not purely passive, because otherwise it could not form an *agency*) of a socio-cultural order, and if the process of subjectification involves a subjugation that entails a certain symbolic dimension, it is clear that any anomaly in the sensations that produce it socially, and which from an objectivistic point of view would tend to be seen as an effect of the (dys)functioning of a natural body, can only also express a crisis within the *present* intersubjective identity matrix. That's why the concept of subjectification as a performative construction of the ego can be the theoretical key which articulates both an external and an internal vision of psychopathology, both the intra- and the interpsychic.

From the lava of emotion to the dream of the volcano

I shall now present some clinical material from the first two years of an analysis. I have deliberately adopted a narrative form that although it avoids confusion leaves some initial margin for ambiguity in distinguishing the voices – the key question is: 'Who is speaking?'[5] The idea is to encourage a decentred kind of listening, to bring out the game of identification between analyst and patient, and to emphasize that the text of the analysis is constructed by two people, but also, paradoxically, that it is a text written by an author and therefore 'fictitious'. The word 'fictitious' also applies, however, to the hypochondriac discourse if it is understood in terms of transference as a possible narrative genre with which to recount what happens in the virtual field of analysis.

The Human Torch

I went to play volleyball, which is something I used to be terrified of when I was a girl. *Every Saturday was a real trauma,* having to play matches against *strangers*. There was a time when I would have said no. But now … I feel changed. When I am with other people I am relaxed, different from usual, even extroverted. It was nice to tell my elder sister what I'm learning here, really satisfying … especially when I think of the relationship we have always had. A breach has opened, a space; to put it in legal terms, 'a precedent'. We talked about our parents' lack of affection for us and how we both tried to fill the *gaps*.

It seems that this is another game one can now play … without too much fear of strangers [one can leave the other without feeling bad] …

I felt appreciated for what I really am … When I got a little upset because of my state of health, my mum told me about some episodes from my childhood. When I was small I used to fall ill easily, *my immune defences were low*, so I was never taken outdoors. I remember the feeling of being a bit of a recluse at home, unable to do the things that others were doing … I had been given a Human Torch as a present, one of the Fantastic Four. One evening I began saying: 'Voio Omo-To'ciaa!' ('Wanna Uman Torrch'). I just started talking. My mum did not understand me and I got more and more angry. Then she would despair. When I was a child, and she had to go somewhere, she always did so in secret. I don't remember this. When she told me about it, the feeling of anguish I felt then came back ... This very probably had an influence on my *fear of loved ones going away*. That's why I become obsessive! She told me something else. I was always hungry and *she*[6] didn't realize. She told me that I was always hungry as a child. I don't know, but when you're little, affection can also be interpreted in terms of food.

This story of the Human Torch has aroused my curiosity ...

It's what I told you ... when I got something new I had to take it to bed with me ... I clearly remember the feeling of helplessness and my mother not understanding.

... And what did the Human Torch do?

One of the Fantastic Four was a woman, then there was another character, who was strong and whose flesh was made of stone (just between the two of us, that was my friend S.), then, the intellectual of the group, who was able to stretch his body, and this was my other friend A.; and me, the smallest, I was the Human Torch, the one who could generate flames. *His body caught fire and he could fly and became a superhero*. I was very fond of this character.

The woman?

She wasn't assigned to anybody. *There were no women among us*. Women were also somewhat looked down upon.

I try to reformulate the situation to myself. We have become a little alien to each other after the weekend ... The gap of separation ... It doesn't take much to make her feel bad ... The mother who goes away in secret ... The female member of the Fantastic Four (the sessions?) is missing, and, as in the comic, has the power to become invisible ... She was back to being a little girl, lacking the words (*in-fans)* to ask for food/affection after the two weeks of starvation over the Christmas holidays ... the Human Torch ... the fire that burns, consumes, suffocates with smoke (passions?) ... but perhaps also light and heat.

After her first rather long period away from analysis, Carla is once again also worried about her health.

I've got that pain in my back again.

I ask her when she first had it.

Even as a child I had this weakness in my back ... I got it soon after I was able to stand up. The first time I experienced it ... I had been seeing Piero for six months. I was under exam stress. It was probably bad posture that gave me pinched nerves (*compressione*). I had a feeling of tightness (*oppressione*) in my legs which I had interpreted as a tumour. I was really anxious. It got a little better when I started going to see a chiropractor. It was also hard for Piero, because I involved him in the whole thing. *That was the beginning of the discomfort I felt at being influenced by these disorders in my relationships with others* ... I went to see a doctor. I was undecided whether to go or not because I did not want to indulge my fears. He told me that my back muscles were contracted. He prescribed anti-inflammatory drugs. They had very little effect. Then I also got colitis ... This discomfort in the back ... makes me feel ill. When I went to see the doctor, he said: *'Maybe you've caught a chill.'* For a day my worries disappeared, but then they came back. I can't understand what's causing it, and I don't know how to react. I'm tired. By now I've tried every medicine available.

A chill ...?!

I had been going out with Sandro for some time and everything was going fine. But then, after New Year, I felt that he had cooled off. I started asking myself again what he thought of me, what he felt about me. I used to be able to rely on him. *Maybe it was just the fact that we hadn't seen each other for a while.*

So you need a touch of the Human Torch?

Yes, it's like desperately asking 'Wanna Uman Torrch!' and nobody understands me ... I want to know whether Sandro wants to see me, whether he wants to talk to me ... Yes, the Human Torch ... at this moment for me it would be demonstrations of affection that I don't know how to recognise, how to stimulate, how to provoke ...

During this period of the analysis the important thing is to help Carla to make some sense of the experiences that cause her so much distress and which she sometimes explains to herself as signs of some as yet undiagnosed neurological condition. And clearly she is the one who, interpreting the meaning of 'chill', finds a connection between illness and affection, between physical discomfort and relationships, with continual overlaps between past and present. My words are cautious, at times allusive, and my remarks are elliptical, though mostly quite simple. I welcome her contributions and try to respect her ability to address something that until now she had felt the need to turn away from. I try to do some groundwork, on the level of recognizing and naming emotions; it's like compiling a kind of primer of feelings. Sometimes, however, I interpret the transference more directly when I have the impression, which *a posteriori* does not always prove to be correct, that she does not experience this as persecutory, or that 'the terror of double meaning', as another patient of mine once called it, does not impede communication nor does it encase him in its 'heavy suit of armour.' However, despite these precautions, this fragment of dialogue reflects a clear demand for less pressure from me (it is repeated twice: the Italian word for pressure (*pressione*) appears in both *com/pressione* and *op/pressione*), that I should be more (chiro-) practical, in other words, less abstract. Otherwise the contractures, the inhibitions, the silences will make their appearance. To put it briefly, Carla is asking for more demonstrations of 'affection.' And this is the latent meaning behind my question-comment which responds to her identification with the Marvel Comics superhero.

The Human Torch, one of the Fantastic Four, is the character Johnny Storm (!) becomes after his spaceship is bombarded with cosmic rays during an interstellar voyage. One of the consequent mutagenic effects is that he gains the power to generate fiery plasma. Impetuous and immature, he discovers that he can transform his body into flames at will. In such a state he can fly and project flames with various degrees of intensity, even reaching the temperature of a supernova.

The burning body seems to me to be a way of encapsulating violent emotions in a hypochondriac symptom.[7] It is an exposed body because it is covered with sores from burns; it is too permeable, it has no boundaries or barriers. It is a body from the *inferus* world, as suggested by the flames. It is the pride of exile Verlaine talks about in the poem we shall examine below. It's the blaze of narcissistic rage, the fire of passion, destructive, regenerative and cruel, but also the warmth and the light that illuminates and indicates the need for treatment. It is the body that screams how painful and dangerous contact has become; and for this reason it appeals for bandages, relief from pain, hospitality, sterile rooms. It is the body burning with desire.

AIDS

Carla is a humanities student. She is twenty years old. After much hesitation she had asked to start an analysis the year before, just at the beginning of summer. While doing an internship abroad she had had unprotected sexual intercourse with a young man, and she was convinced that she had caught AIDS. Despite numerous tests, her feeling of anguish had never entirely disappeared. Some months before this episode her boyfriend, Piero, a fellow-student at the Faculty of Letters, had left her and she had suffered a lot as a result. She had kept up the keen interest in volcanoes Piero had transmitted to her, *so much so that she would regularly visit a dedicated website to enjoy the shots taken by a webcam pointed at the mouth of an active volcano.* We had agreed that her analysis should begin in September. During our first sessions that autumn she told me that she suffered from a colicky disorder for which her doctor had prescribed a spasmolytic that also contains a tranquilliser. She was a little suspicious because she knew that these drugs could be addictive, but she felt better immediately. I wondered whether this might not be the first result of our sessions and presaged well for her therapy. She then said that she was looking for a new boyfriend, adding however that she would be very cold with whoever it happened to be, as that was her nature.

I had been warned. It was cold, winter would last some time. I should have put her at ease, but I already knew that sometimes coldness could become *lava, glowing plasma* and *flashes of lightning*, and that it was not advisable to get too close. One could imagine a 'colitic' functioning of the mind, controlled, obsessive, but with fits of rebellion, outbursts of anger, or the 'incontinence' of physical disorders. I gained some first impressions: there had been the vacuum/vacation of the summer … the gloomy climate, the nostalgia for Piero … she had fallen back on her body, 'a contraction'. Some positive, pain-killing effects had appeared at once, but the expression of her fear of depending on someone was equally immediate. In short, Carla's words provided me with the coordinates within which our relationship would be able to move for the time being. She was asking me for tact, a bit of darkness; for now, she wanted me to observe things quite rapidly, without looking or understanding too much. She was worried that 'unprotected' contacts might lead to terrible and uncontrollable things, LAVA-AIDS.

In the meantime I get to know more about her story. She is a great hoarder of objects. Sales slips, museum tickets, receipts have accumulated in special containers, 'so you can revisit the past with precision.' For a time she even kept the advertising flyers she found in her mailbox. She says she feels second-rate. She doesn't like herself. At home she never felt she was given much support in her self-esteem. The atmosphere was severe. At home they only watched Hollywood classics on TV. The films her friends watched were frowned upon. *No Fantozzi or Italian comedies or anything like that.*

A Place in the Sun

This explains why, when at some point she begins to become fond of a new TV soap opera, I feel that something is changing between us.

> There is a soap opera on every night at eight thirty, *Un posto al sole (A Place in the Sun).* It's awful, but I watch it because it always makes me laugh. It's obvious ... that the actors are not very good. The situations are predictable. I feel really ashamed before my flatmates. I watch it although I tell myself that I couldn't care less about it. But I still watch it. And the others think I'm an idiot. I know that's the impression I'm giving. But I like it. I've grown fond of it.

I ask her what she likes most about it. I do not feel that there is space to allude to what are probably her mixed feelings about the analysis.

> If I have to be objective, then nothing at all! Perhaps the story line, the feelings, the love affairs ... The attraction is to see how things work out. Every evening we now have this ritual of having dinner watching this soap opera that everyone hates. However, because the television is mine, I force everyone to watch it. The angrier the others get, the more I enjoy it!

Do you remember the scene in Nanni Moretti's Caro Diario? *– I ask. The scene with the intellectual who's fed up with the abstractions of philosophy and fascinated by the passions of* Beautiful, *who sees a group of American tourists on top of the volcano of Stromboli, and loudly asks them to tell him what had happened in the most recent episodes that had already gone out on American TV?*

I want it to be clear to her that I've perhaps understood something of the sense of constriction she must have felt and which has now become part of her character.

> Of course, I think back to the ban on seeing certain films. I don't like people who think in compartments, those who are talented in their field, but when it comes to more down-to-earth things, whatever ... football, say, go into a panic and show all their prejudices. For example, saying that something is stupid a priori, like my mother, who says things like, 'People who go to discos are idiots.' My friends judge everything in such a superficial way, like when they say, 'Analysis is useless ... '

A new young man comes on the scene, Giulio. And they watch *A Place in the Sun* together.

> There was immediately a feeling[8] between us ... a point of contact ... Two weeks ago the gastroenterologist ... gave me some pills for my colitis, some dietary supplements. I still haven't started taking them. Maybe that means something.

Yes, but what? It is true that she comes across as less tense, although I realize that certain 'films' still cannot be watched. The analysis as a place in the sun, or as the South, I think, but above all as a room where you can also watch soap operas together: that is, life with all its messiness, imperfection, simplicity and immediacy. It seems to me important that she is intrigued by the story-lines. That's what it's all about: 'How does the story end?' Immediately, however, reference is made to the need for supplements, a possible allusion to the indigestible emotions that arise from excessively intimate contacts and not being able for the time being to do without the defensive splittings which the ego uses to preserves itself. Carla intimates to me in many different ways the difficulty she has in letting herself go and the mixture of envy and admiration she feels for her next-door neighbour, A., 'who could even have a conversation with a rock, a likeable guy'. In some way, she says, she wants to be like him.

The association with the Nanni Moretti film is one of my reveries, but in retrospect it shows how gradually it becomes possible to approach the volcano of emotions together.

Lava

The months pass, and our bond grows closer. The day before, another patient had arrived very early and Carla showed that she was annoyed.

> Changing the subject ... Yesterday I was very angry. There is one thing that drives me crazy. I felt a enormous sense of rage when I heard that a friend of mine's girlfriend was coming and what's more they're supposed to sleep in my bed and I have to find somewhere else to sleep. I am very possessive. There's a reason why I have the single room. The other guy said he would give her the room willingly, and that he thought my attitude was childish ... that's not true! ... he doesn't understand me. I dislike the girl. But it's the fact in itself. When he said that I was behaving like a little girl, I felt this incredible desire to attack him ...
>
> The giant comes out...
>
> Yes, because he said I was behaving like a child. I wanted to talk about the many times that *he* behaved like a child. The fact is, when it comes to my room and my things, there is absolutely no room for rational argument. Yes, maybe I am rigid. But that's the way it is ... *I'm possessive about my room*!

On this point, the fact she's so jealous ... there is almost no room for debate, no compromise ... what comes to mind ... it's almost as if she felt compelled to behave differently depending each time on the situation: either like a dwarf or a giant; either she suffers and take a step back or she gets angry.

> The point about the giant or the dwarf is true. If I had to come to Pavia [but she's talking to me in Pavia!], *I would explode*. I'd do a Hulk, if I had to sleep in the other room. I would refuse to wait and see ... in this house ... So instead, by staying in S * or P *, I'm being the dwarf, I'm running away. In Pavia I would explode. MY ROOM! ... It's part of me. *I project on to that room so many of my dreams*. It's so full of meaning! It's not just a physical space. The idea of giving it up is unbearable. It's an act of violence! And I know that my repressed anger will come out. At the first sign of tension it will come out ... Then, perhaps we'll have one of our usual arguments, but it will come out.
>
> The lava!

There is no need to say much about these lines of dialogue, but it is worth pointing out the high level of awareness that Carla is sometimes capable of achieving. Our by now well-established relationship enables her to bring out the 'angry giant' that is inside her and that is usually forced into an overly rigid container and therefore constantly runs the risk of shattering. That the analysis, then, has become for her the 'room of passion', to repeat an expression of hers that is all the more sincere because it refers to something else, seems to me obvious.

A few days later, the situation is repeated, but with reversed roles. This time she turns up for the session in the morning instead of at midday! When we talk about it later, the discussion ends up focusing on the fact that her mother often forgets things that matter to her. She complains that her mother doesn't cook anything, or if she does, then badly, and on Sundays they never eat before half past two … if at all! Often in S * she has to sort something out herself if she wants to eat. She already has to do that in Pavia.

Well, of course it is annoying when one is hungry and there is nothing ready on the table, and, especially on Sundays! – I comment.

Yes, and I talked to my mum about it when I was little. I used to eat baby food from a feeding bottle with such eagerness that I ended up vomiting. Then she took a dummy which she adjusted to limit the flow of milk. But then I was famished! I sucked desperately and I had to struggle with the dummy to get something out of it. And it was only later that my mother realized what was going on. I have a complicated relationship with food, what with these attacks of colitis … I felt I was treated badly by my mum. Not that she should spend all day in the kitchen! My neighbour's mother gives him meatballs and omelettes to bring back with him, but the most my mother can do is to go to the supermarket and buy some mozzarella.

It's not nice when you think you are not receiving enough … Today you decided to eat early! 'Now I'm coming and I'm going to eat some meatballs!'

Yes, maybe I hoped something more would come out of yesterday's anxiety, a flash of insight. But then, not even on a day when I wasn't supposed to come …!

The mother cooks – I say – but not at half past two … at ten past twelve!

She laughs.

> And as soon as I left I thought that I must tell my mum! For a long time she said I was anorexic and I often got angry. She of all people! ... turning round and telling me these things when she was the one responsible for my problems with food!
>
> Is that her way of saying it's not her fault?
>
> Yes, it highlights this relationship between me and food, but *without shouldering any responsibility*. Every time I have physical problems, the first thing she says is: 'Are you eating properly?'! *A good way to make me even angrier and to bring on my disorders*!

Here Carla explains very clearly the dynamics of her disorders, of her anger, of her supposed anorexia (refusal to eat or vomiting the food of analysis). This is what happens when, like her mum, I choose the wrong words/dummy for her and perhaps see a problem in terms of an objective pathology of hers which might in fact relate to the field. That old scene, with a mother who could not quite shelter her from over-intense stimuli, is played out again in the parapraxis and in the timetable game. Her mother's reaction to her sense of malaise ('Are you eating properly?') is the paradigm of the parodistic, persecutory relationship that becomes established between hypochondriac and doctors. Occasionally I fell into the same trap myself, exasperated by her refusal to grasp the obvious emotional nature of her recurring physical disorders, and even more so by the denigrating tone with which she accused me of not being able to understand her, and worried about the invasive diagnostic procedures she was about to undergo. But then, reflecting on my countertransference, I understood that I had entered into an interaction that perhaps represented the only genuine opportunity for me to perceive the meaning and measure of her exasperation.

Floods

It is almost mid-November. After almost a year and a half of analysis Carla is now sitting her university exams according to plan, but still a certain uneasiness comes to the fore: a draught … a contracture in her shoulder and arm … blood pressure minimum value slightly too high … a touch of tachycardia.

The Ticino river in Pavia has flooded its banks. Carla talks about this with me at length and it becomes an image that allows us to address the issue of her mental dikes and how severely they are put to the test. She tells me that sometimes as a child she warmed up the thermometer on the radiator to make the temperature go up (which is like transforming herself into the Human Torch), so as to get off school. But the real problems have arisen since the disappointment of breaking up with Piero.

Sometimes she would go to two doctors during the same period, keeping each ignorant about the other and continuing to distrust both. At the moment she has something wrong with her ear, it seems to be blocked up. A doctor has told her that the problem with her ear comes from an inflammation of the jaw, because she chews her food badly or because she grits her teeth at night. I suggest she reflect on the expressions 'gnashing of teeth', 'masticare amaro' (lit. chewing bitter; nursing resentment) and then 'showing one's teeth'. Then she also has pains in her neck. During this period, she says, 'Giulio is cold,' Piero even 'frosty'. The peak of the crisis coincides with her recounting a conversation with her mother.

> A week ago my mother told me that my dad used to call my sister *The Only One*, as a way of saying that he did not want any more children. Looking back, in fact, I've always felt a little 'out of place'. Maybe subconsciously this was passed on to me ... THE IDEA THAT I WASN'T SUPPOSED TO BE! Sometimes I thought about running away from home, absconding ... even though I was crying because of something completely different. I imagined I was saying, I'll stop bothering you, I'll get out of your way.

In this way the analysis makes it possible to re-instate essential aspects of her story which, to paraphrase Bollas, we could say are known but not thought. I am surprised and moved. Here Carla has a unique insight into herself because she discovers the origin of the paranoid core hidden inside her hypochondriac suffering, the feeling of BEING IN EXILE.

The dream of the volcano

Upon returning from the Easter holidays, after nearly two years of analysis, she tells me that Piero, who happened to be in town, had stayed at her place and that they had ended up in bed together.

> I needed to experience once again this kind of physical contact and I did it with the person I feel most relaxed with. It wasn't like in England, where I was wracked with fear.

However, now that she has resumed her sex life, which in terms of the text of the analysis can be seen as the ability to tolerate a higher level of intimacy, the seismic activity starts up again:

She dreams of going to see an active volcano in the company of a volcanologist. You feel the tremor of an earthquake.

We've got to get out of here because there's going to be an eruption soon! she shouts.

I've been studying it for two years, I don't think it's going to erupt! replies the volcanologist.

And I've been watching it for four years on the website! she says.

The volcano erupts but they manage to escape. The lava catches up with them. But it is rubbery, and less dangerous than expected. They walk over it.

They were both right, we comment, the analyst/volcanologist and the amateur volcanologist.

There are still some eruptions, but they are no longer so destructive. We are dealing now with emotions one can begin to walk on, which no longer burn the earth under one's feet. A rubbery, soft lava … a bit like *Morositas* gumdrops[9] is her association.

After these two years of analysis it cannot be said that Carla, to use a metaphor suggested by another patient of mine, has resolved her feeling of exile and that she is dreaming in the language of the new country which is no longer alien to her, but *she has begun to dream again*. The obsessive image of the webcam trained on the mouth of the volcano has become a scene in the film by Nanni Moretti that was my reverie (and/or weak interpretation) and finally the dream of the volcano.

If she still suspects that the bond between us is no more than cool and professional or convenient, as in the case of the former boyfriend who was passing through and needed a place to stay for a while, Carla recognizes that over time, Piero ('Piero', if seen as a character in the analytic field) has become more affectionate.

I say that she is beginning to be able to bear 'hotter' emotional levels in her relationships, that a passionate Piero may return to the scene, but free of the fear of AIDS. And I think that the analysis might allow her to draw ever closer to this *Piero-Morosito* level, so to speak; perhaps closer to a mother not experienced as constantly on the verge of disappearing, in the double meaning of secretly running away from home, or rather, emotionally speaking, into depression.

Towards a theory of hypochondria

Et mon coeur, mon coeur trop sensible
Dit à mon âme : Est-il possible,
Est-il possible, – le fût-il –
Ce fier exil, ce triste exil?

(Paul Verlaine, *Ô triste, triste était mon âme*)

From an intrapsychic point of view,[10] outside the session (which of course is another possible way of being 'in' the session, that is, taking an off-centre perspective, not from the main vertex of the transference, and to achieve a sort of bifocal, near-far vision of the field, but also – and possibly without knowing it! – *not* being in the relationship), if I reflect on the type of text that I wrote together with the patient, on its content, I can get an idea of its poetics. I would even hypothesize a transference repetition of the significant scripts of her inner world and her childhood history. Within the hypochondriac discourse the body appears to me to be the living text, printed in letters that are hard to decipher (β?), of a disorder in the relationship – in Italian the word *relazione* has the dual meaning of account and connection – with the object. I imagine the black ink of these characters as the product of a real or phantasy object loss and the resulting narcissistic wearing effect. I note that the loss, in being denied, is not tolerable. And in fact the patient finds the text unreadable and insists on the physical nature of her disorders. But unconsciously she comes back and recites it again and by doing so continues to produce herself as a subject.

Identity is a matter of doing more than being; it is action.[11] All that changes are the plots. The basic prototype of the play that is staged in/on the hypochondriac's body is to be found in Kafka's short story *In the Penal Colony*, where the inscription of guilt is on the skin.

Abnormal sensations, like ideograms printed on the body,[12] dramatize the past and/or present history of a relationship with the persecutory object that mainly affects the sensory level of the production of experience. Passing through the transduction operated by the 'psychic slips of paper' of Freud's mystic writing pad,[13] they become part of the store of memory traces from whose dynamic and differential functioning, like any other writing apparatus or semiotic system, meaning emerges clearly – and with it a first draft of the ego.

At any rate, what is visible is a self-reflexive closure, the self-absorption of consciousness, the subject turning in on itself. He acts as if he had lost the natural experience of the body; of a body that sends disquieting signals and from which the ego feels separate as from that which founds it more than anything else. An exiled self is subversive, condemned by the law of its native country.[14] Its own subversion reveals the existence of an essential order. What is thrown into crisis is the internalized 'violence' of the origin which is an essential condition of subjectification. The problem of hypochondria is not comprehensible unless it is seen within the context of the subject as a social entity and the ego as a product of a discourse of power. Power, however, is not only suffered but also assumed by the subject, and within certain limits can also be modified. It is true that the sense of guilt is coextensive with the ego, but it is also true that a certain narcissistic equilibrium must have altered if it has called this ego before a court that has become so ruthless as to banish him into exile, once he has been defeated, and to feed his need for punishment.

The various forms of the production of experience that contribute to the construction of the subject – the autistic-contiguous, paranoid-schizoid and depressive positions (Ogden, 1989) – all depend on an optimal balance between objecthood and narcissism. If a crisis occurs in this equilibrium, a paranoid core is created that can be expressed as a hypochondriac state on various levels: a) abnormal sensations that keep up the fear/conviction of being ill, a form of sensoriality as self containment or projection of the lost object onto the sensorial and thus persecutory ego (*somatic paranoia*),[15] b) idealizing transference onto caregivers and attendant ambivalence, which in analysis can be rationalized as a negative therapeutic reaction (*external paranoia*),[16] c) introjection and identification with the lost object and with a cruel and destructive critical agency (*internal paranoia*).[17]

One can observe the regressive impact of all the ways of creating meaning and thus of ego-building. And at all these levels the same persecutory core[18] appears, which is reflected on the phenomenological level by the triad of *sadness, idealizing persecutory transference to doctors and conviction that one has a sick body.* These aspects are hinted at in the poem by Verlaine used as an epigraph to this section: loss (*loin de cette femme*), anger/paranoia (*ce fier exil*), sadness (*triste était mon âme*), and the sick body (*mon coeur trop sensible*). The symptoms translate the past *and* present quality of the intersubjective matrix that produces identity. If the analytic field contracts the patient's illness (to a tolerable extent), it is also true that, if it is *of* the patient it refers to a history of the subject. But from the vertex of the treatment its recurrence means that it should also be regarded as a disease of the field.

From a more general point of view, hypochondria can be: a) a physiological stage in the reorganization of self, as occurs in adolescence, b) the initial stage of a more structured mental illness (somatization, paranoia, melancholia), in which case its acts as a 'crossroads' or, c) it can harden into a very specific configuration of a pathology when a given imbalance between the various dialectically interrelated modes of production of experience eventually crystallize.

The molecular psychopathological mechanism never varies: hypochondria is the result of intolerable frustrations at a hyper-influx of β-elements, defects in the α function, lack of reverie by the object. *The subject, then, combats an experience of loss by organizing a paranoid core.* The choice of the disease remains mysterious, although it is reasonable to think that it is not a real choice and that it is determined by the internal and external context, and by the structure of the personality (Ferro, 2006). In general, the degree of individual tolerability is the critical factor that marks the dividing line between the work of mourning which constructs the subject and the irresistible seduction of the black sun of melancholia.

Hypochondria is both a way of defending oneself from anxiety through a process of desubjectivization, in other words, a way of denying a loss that would otherwise be devastating by retreating to a less differentiated but also less exposed level of functioning, and a distress signal (Stolorow, 1977, 1979). In staging the relationship between the past and present object, hypochondria organizes a possible meaning and seeks to restore a better narcissistic balance. Evident in this second function is the Freudian concept of the 'hypochondria of dreams' (Freud, 1917b), that is to say, the hyperbolic over-intensity in dreams, which comes to take on a self-diagnostic significance, of physical sensations still silent during waking hours, and the 'work of hypochondria' (Aisenstein and Gibeault, 1991), or hypochondria seen as symbolizing activity.

Freud makes a significant comment on this point:

> A person's own body, and above all its surface, is a place from which both external and internal perceptions may spring. [...] *Pain, too, seems to play a part in the process, and the way in which we gain new knowledge of our organs during painful illnesses is perhaps a model of the way by which in general we arrive at the idea of our body.*
>
> (Freud, 1922, pp. 25–26, my italics)

Freud's observation is echoed by Bion: 'Hypochondriacal symptoms may therefore be signs of an attempt to establish contact with psychic quality by substituting physical sensation for the missing sense data of psychical quality' (1962, p. 53).

According to this extraordinary insight of Bion's, one achieves a sense of the coherence of one's inner world, as it is the case for the consensuality of the perceptions that structure the space-time coordinates of the outside world, through the perception of emotions. The 'hypochondriac system' is both a symptom of the failure of this activity and a sign that an attempt is being made to restore it.

Living in a language

As we have already said, in the session the hypochondriac discourse can be considered one narrative genre among others, chosen perhaps because it corresponds to certain sequences of α-elements (Ferro, 1999, p. 32). From this angle of vision the hypochondriac symptom does not require a specific mode of listening. In clinical work the essential thing is what the patient communicates about the body-environment of the setting and the establishment (or not) in the relationship of impasse or unconscious pair defences (what the Barangers (2008) refer to as 'bastions'). What is important is not so much decoding the content but giving back to the patient the ability to interpret reality. Analysis is not so much an interpretation of content but an interpretation of interpretation, a reflection on how interpretation is carried out.

On the other hand, interpreting to the hypochondriac patient the symbolic or transference meaning of *his* symptom threatens to cause the field to cave in, and often elicits strong protests. When that happens, the patient has good reason to protest. Not only because it shows that he does not yet have a psychic space for interpretation, but because, seeing his suffering pigeonholed into a certain nosographic category, he realizes that his perceptions are being disparaged and he does not feel understood. The doctor's gaze desubjectifies even further a symptom that presents itself as disconnected from his personal history (Brusset, 2002).

The hypochondriac body, then, is a metonymic body, doubly entangled in the objectification of medical and psychopathological symptomatology, reduced in both cases to the reified meaning of the part of him that is suffering. It is a paradox: even the relational explanation of the meaning of a hypochondriacal symptom – *as* hypochondriacal and not as an 'open' text, in other words, a lively account of emotions that permeate the field – triggers rejection, because it looks more like an interpretation deriving from a delusion of transparency of intuition (Meltzer, 1976), an understanding to which the patient has not really contributed in the relational game but that has formed in the analyst 'without the shadow of the other' (Ferruta, 2004). Such interventions mimic the patient's obstinate beliefs about his disorders, and ultimately represent a way of acting out a paranoia-inducing transference.

The body that the hypochondriac discourse speaks of is the field, the relationship, the analytic third, interpsychic space, the setting. And not because the dynamics of the transference do not re-present empathic failures and past traumas, or specific vulnerabilities. Far from it. But if what matters is re-opening the history of the patient to new paths of meaning, it is well to look especially at the elements that best promise to enhance the ability to think, temporarily putting the others aside, knowing that in any case they too will emerge transformed. And it is the patient himself who reports the level of tuning that he needs most at any given moment during the treatment. Often interpretations that are too saturated with meaning will not be tolerated, but are seen as attacks (Civitarese, 2007). What are easier to tolerate, however, are discrete, non-intrusive interventions in which the analyst does not play the part of the main actor but is a stage hand.

The hypochondriac patient relives in the transference the trauma of a 'fallen' consciousness'. If he is exiled in his body/Ego, what one can do is to give him hospitality, help him become re-inscribed in a symbolic order, in a shared language. *For this reason I find the image of the exile valuable, because it forces us to see that hypochondria is a problem between different 'cultures', between several subjects.*[19] In Verlaine's poem (quoted in the epigraph to this section) the loss of the beloved causes the heart – fascinatingly, the old Italian or Latin word 'cor' is contained in and identified with cor/po (body) – to feel exiled from the world. The indifference and the absence of the other become the fantasmatic space inhabited by the subject. When the work of mourning is stuck, it can happen that the boundaries of this world narrow to coincide with those of the body and its organ or apparatus. One has a heart, then, exiled in a body-world. But the body itself, which in French has a plural form (*corps*), as if the intuition of the dual matrix from which the ego emerges were inscribed on it (De Toffoli, 2001), is in its turn exiled from the other, excluded from interpersonal contact. Hypochondriacal worries are then a retreat to a primitive level of subjectification, a defensive narrowing of the living horizon, a request for the other to re-tune *to that level.* If the needs that these complaints express are ignored, the fall from grace from the feeling of being the subject can be even more disastrous.

Within an inter-subjective model interpretation is intended as a gift of meaning and an offer of hospitality. Precisely because he bases himself on a rationality that he considers rhetorically weak, the analyst assumes more responsibility towards the patient. He informs his work with a principle of tolerance and a feeling of solidarity, compassion and sympathy for the suffering of the other that springs from respect for difference. Authentic hospitality, however, means first taking responsibility for one's own numerous selves, the constitutive alterity of the ego, of everything that is human. The exile needs to regain a place to live, an abode (in its various meanings: sojourn, pause, room, delay, slowness, time). This is what happens when one is in a foreign country and at some point realizes that one is beginning to have dreams in the language of that country, as another patient of mine told me one day, much to my surprise. He too was afflicted with a dysmorphophobic form of hypochondria and he told me this to explain something that he felt within himself as a positive change. In his case this change coincided with the dramatic reopening of a space for listening and dialogue with his parents. When things start to go well, this sets in motion the work of mourning. The patient becomes aware of the new situation, his new identity, and accepts it even though it means giving up something else and coming to terms with the loss. Finally, what he develops is a new feeling of belonging to a new country/maternal object. The Ego comes back to inhabit its own body, a body that has also always been the mysterious and inscrutable body of the other.

4

THE CAT'S EYES

Internal focalization and casting in the psychoanalytic dialogue

> The emotions fulfil for the psyche a function similar to that of the senses in relation to objects in space and time: that is to say, the counterpart of the commonsense view in private knowledge is the common emotional view; a sense of truth is experienced if the view of an object which is hated can be conjoined to a view of the same object when it is loved, and the conjunction confirms that the object experienced by different emotions is the same object. A correlation is established.
>
> (Wilfred R. Bion,
> *Second Thoughts: Selected Papers on Psycho-Analysis*)

Six emotions in search of an actor

In 'Totem and taboo', Freud writes that the patient '*turns* his *emotional cathexes* into *persons*, he peoples the world with them' (1912–1913, p. 92, italics mine). This statement contains everything necessary to frame a theory of character in the text of the analysis and a theory of therapeutic action: what is involved is transforming characters back into emotional cathexes for which the patient is ready to take responsibility. The more mature and balanced the person is, the more he is in touch with reality – not just the material reality he perceives with the senses, but also internal reality. One can be in contact almost exclusively with material reality, or with fractions of psychic reality, or with both. One may be capable, for example, of sophisticated reasoning and rigorous logic but singularly lacking in emotional resonance. This could be a form of pseudo-integration, a defence born out of the early failure of sufficient experiences of the psyche in-dwelling in the body (to use Winnicott's term) (Bonaminio, 2009). However, when excessively large sections of reality are inaccessible, the subject becomes impoverished and does not live up to his true potential; he fails to become what he is.

In a paper entitled 'The imaginary twin' Bion talks about two patients (referred to as A and B) and points out their differing abilities to personify their split-off parts in dialogue. While A's liveliness suggests a setting of child psychoanalysis and play, B on the other hand prompts very few associations, is monotonous, and makes constant hypochondriac complaints. 'Is it possible,' Bion asks, 'that the capacity to personify splittings of the personality is in some way analogous to a capacity for symbol formation'? (1967, p. 20). Similarly, Bion thought that the ability to recover the split-off parts of the mind gave the individual a binocular vision of things, a vision of reality that was coherent, clear and possessed of a sense of depth.

In the same way as sense impressions ensure consensuality about the objects of the outside world, so the recognition of emotions ensures consensuality about the objects of the inner world. Put simply, psychic well-being means being able to live in registers of reality, in the world of symbols and imagination, and having a good enough contact with their emotional colouring. This is why it is so important to map emotions. Without emotions, perception would be a chaotic assortment of data. Thinking or symbolizing, being able to grasp the differences between words and things, realizing that the link that brings them together in language is arbitrary, necessarily involves the ability to assign an emotional value to experience, to put a plus or a minus sign before an object. But for a patient, as for a child, gaining this ability means living through an endless series of moments of harmony or unison with the other.

When the patient comes to therapy, his or her ability to form mental images or to symbolize is always inhibited to some extent. The degree of inhibition is, however, quite varied and can range from slight and temporary dysfunctions to severe and persistent defective states. Making him into a better actor-director-critic-spectator of his own stories means encouraging the maturation of his thinking skills and helping him to integrate his experience into a narrative that will gradually work better in his life. Just as at the theatre, the more effective the analytic 'show' is dramatically (aesthetically) speaking, the more the spectator is moved and changed. This is why Bion says the interpretation should take place in the dimensions of sense (it should be a directly observable experience), of myth (it should tell a particular story which is concrete and meaningful; and it must possesses the truth value of fiction that only art, myth and dream have), and of passion (it must be emotionally intense, and express a bond of love, hate or knowledge). In short, it must have both the cohesion and focus of the present that we find in the theatre, and the dreamlike dimension more typical of film.

For Bion, the analyst's attention should be directed at the paradigmatic axis, at the present. This idea echoes the traditional theme of the superiority of tragedy over epic, which is due to the compactness and effectiveness that characterizes action on stage: 'It is possible,' he wrote in *A Memoir of the Future*, 'that the only phenomenon which could be described as a "fact" is what the analysand says he feels' (1977b, p. 609). The important thing about the patient's state of mind 'is that it exists *at the time* he or she is seeing the analyst' (ibid., p. 645). We should therefore pay the utmost attention to the quality of the relationship in the here-and-now because virtually speaking this is the most transformative level. The paradigmatic axis, however, necessarily correlates with the syntagmatic axis – with history. In fact, it is precisely the attempt to grasp the maximum emotional truth in the present and in the analytic relationship that constitutes the *royal road* to constructing and reconstructing the infantile neurosis, in the same way as the emotions experienced in the theatre lend meaning and flavour to everyday life and to our memories of the past.

In order to achieve the necessary immersive and interactive quality of the relationship, like the dresser in the eponymous film by Peter Yates (1983), depending on the occasion the analyst finds himself playing for the 'lead' (the patient) the function of fan, critic, assistant, friend, director, spectator, prompter and casting director. In the following pages I would like to focus on this last aspect, namely, how to choose the actors who are right for the roles that are played out on the stage of the setting.

First, we should clarify what we mean by character, actor, casting, and internal focalization.

Character

A character in the theatre or in a film is an actor playing a role, or rather the paper character, what stands in the text written by the playwright or screenwriter. Basically, characters are conveyors of emotions, feelings, passions that may belong to the patient, to the analyst, or to both; ultimately, they are what propels the action (Hamon, 1977). Each character, in fact, is a subject that has a type of bond with an object whose vector – strength, direction, point of application – is expressed in affective states. 'Characters' can be seen as relationships, types of bond (in Bion's terminology: H stands for hate, L for love, and K for knowledge); or, following Propp's (1928) notion of the fairy tale, they can be seen as functions. Here by the term 'character' I mean an emotion, that is to say, a role or part of the unconscious text of the analytic dialogue in search of an actor and a narrative development. Possible models for the characters of the patient's unconscious life that appear in the analytic dialogue are Freud's personifications of dreams, Klein's internal objects externalized in dream or in children's games, or the split-off parts of the mind referred to by Bion.

Even on a simple reading the reader imagines faces and sets, that is, he chooses the actors to project the film of the text in his mind, and he can enjoy a fulfilling aesthetic experience. The analytic device, however, is in effect built like a stage set, and it is only when the actor appears before the public that the magic of theatre is produced: Othello or jealousy, Richard III or revenge, Ajax or pride etc. Until there is a flesh-and-blood actor who undertakes to 'play' these parts no performance can be put on, nor is it possible to live through the exciting, intense and engaging experience that is the theatre.

However, unlike a play that has already entered the repertoire, the production of the analytic text has to be completely invented. Initially we only have fragments of stories, plots that are difficult to understand, characters that are barely sketched out. We do not know if we are going to be dealing with Uncle Vanya, Phaedra or Ivan Karamazov. Maybe they are already there in the play script, but they only really make sense when they can come to life again on the stage of the analysis. Only as the analysis gradually progresses are the parts assigned and performed; the plot becomes clearer, the psychology of the characters more defined: and, of course, everything proceeds simultaneously.

Actor

By actor I mean a character who makes his appearance in the *manifest* text of the analysis and puts himself forward to convey an unconscious affective state. The actual number of emotional states is limited. Indeed, even if they can be combined in all kinds of ways, it would appear that there are only six basic emotions: surprise, disgust, sadness, fear, happiness, anger. This simplification can be useful to help us realize that after all we are working with primary elements. For this reason the action is more important than the actors, because it corresponds to the link, the unconscious emotion that connects them. The characters that offer themselves as actors and are willing to put their identity aside are relatively interchangeable, as long as they know how to act a certain part. There can be various narrative genres, but the links, the emotions, the relationships do not vary. *Therefore it is irrelevant whether the story that is being told is set in the past, present or future, whether it is realistic or imaginary, whether it relates directly to the analysis or not.*

There is, however, a problem. There are some patients who arrive with ready-made actors, some who have nothing against acting as extras and some who are willing to take on more challenging roles. Occasionally, however, we have actors who have no interest at all in acting, perhaps because they are too afraid of the audience. This is what happens with patients who cling to reality and who are not aware of the fictional nature of the setting, just as they are not sufficiently in touch with their inner life and their dreams. For these patients, the point is to gradually bring them closer to the oneiric and mythical dimension of analysis and to save them from drowning in a sea of exterior events and objectivity. And it is here that the choice of the right actors becomes a key moment in the whole analytic process.

Casting

In the world of entertainment, casting is the process of selecting actors before putting on a play or making a film or television drama. For example, you decide who gets the part of Winnie, who is Ljuba, and so on. The person whose job it is to choose actors from a cast list, where each character is briefly described in terms of their psychological and physical features, is known as the casting director. To decide on the actor for the part he or she holds auditions specifically for the part or involving interaction, i.e., with individual players or with a group of actors. It is worth remembering that the verb 'to cast' has various meanings: to give/receive shape, to mould, to produce 'impressions', and also to carve out a certain view of things. In the theatrical context, the meaning of cast as a noun derived from the idea of the form a thing takes after it has been thrown.

In analysis, however, we have a manifest and a latent script. The play, which is the patient's life, does not work well enough because the discrepancy between the two scripts is too great – significantly, in Italian one possible version of the script is called the 'soggetto/subject'. It is, therefore, a question of bringing them together and bringing out their secret correspondences. The analyst selects (or helps to select) a character in the plaintext of the analytic dialogue and assigns a role in the text that is woven on the latent level of the relationship; he does this first indirectly (weak or narrative interpretation) and later possibly in a more direct way (transference interpretation). When choosing an actor for a role-emotion, he is guided by the derivatives of the waking dream thought, the logic of transference, his associations and reveries, and the feedback that the patient gives as a spectator, when he signals whether the audition was successful or not.

The α function of the analyst's mind becomes the special locus of the treatment; but, one could at this point say, the α function of the system made up of the patient–analyst dyad – what Corrao has called the γ function (1981) – to which the two parties contribute to varying degrees. The characters are also an essential tool for monitoring the state of this function and for restoring it when it gives the impression of not doing a good job. By taking care of the casting, the analyst gives form to an emotional experience not yet transformed or thinkable. Symbolizing means moving from β to α, from protoemotions and raw feelings to images that can then be used to dream and to think.

These are the transformations that concern us most. Mentalization means realizing the distance that separates one's emotions and thoughts and those of others from material reality, in other words, leaving behind the 'psychic equivalence' between mental states and the physical world (Fonagy, 2001), entering the world of *as if* or the potential dimension of psychic reality, waking up from one's dreams and even from the dream of reality. First of all, then, it is necessary to achieve that feeling of coherence and truth in the perception of emotions that Bion mentions in the quotation used as the epigraph to this chapter.

To summarize, by casting in analysis I mean (together with Ferro, to whom we owe the first formulation of this concept, 2007) the act of identifying a figure in the analytic discourse as an actor and assigning him the task of conveying a certain emotion that plays a nodal function that has not been recognized in the patient's life story and in the therapeutic relationship. But, and this is the essential point, usually it is an emotion of which he is not (sufficiently) aware. For example, I take, let's say, the angry cat that a patient talks to me about and try to see if from now on it could be the actor playing the role of her split-off part which is frightened-angry because it has been humiliated and treated like something that, without her knowing it, conditions her life and is reflected in the transference; or I try to see it as a character in an unconscious scenario. Mostly, though, I use it to get an idea of how she/we is/are dreaming the emotional waves that are disturbing the field of analysis. It also serves, however, to avoid saturating meaning too soon and helps to open up the narrative game to unexpected and surprising developments.

Internal focalization

When working on casting, the analyst makes use of the technique of internal focalization. That is to say, he sees things from the perspective of the character. This device has also been called 'vision with' or restricted field (Blin, 1989). Typically, internal focalization in a narrative produces a polyphonic effect. Like the principles of poetics for writers, for the analyst the different types of focalization express the explicit and implicit theoretical principles that inform his style of work. A classical analyst would tend to zero focalization, which corresponds to neutral and omniscient narration, and in film to the static objective shot. A more sceptical analyst, who is used to casting a more disbelieving light on things, will tend rather to adopt multiple internal focalization which, as in Pirandello, only relates what a certain character knows or sees, and identifies several, at most undecidable, points of view. This style is more subjective and immediate, and thus one can see it as being more appropriate to narratives in analysis, where the important thing is to gradually guide the patient towards a complex vision of things, to help him/her to relativize his/her experiences and judgements, to see reality from multiple perspectives and to come to recognize its ambiguities. Each point of view, in fact, establishes a certain framework for the experience and, ultimately, helps to structure it.

Now, any character in the analytic field can be thought of as the product of the encounter between the patient's and the analyst's projective identifications, ultimately β bands of emotions waiting to become thinkable, and, as in a hologram, to produce a three-dimensional image. The image is three dimensional only if it actually gives form to emotions; otherwise it remains flat, banal, lacking in resonance. Analyst and patient do not contribute equally to this construction. Nevertheless, it is impossible to project into the void. The participation of both is essential. A character is never the exclusive creation of one or the other.

The interplay of points of view becomes important insofar as the fulcrum of the therapeutic action is seen not so much in the translation from unconscious to conscious[1] as in the emotional tuning that provides the ego with its setting. For this reason we must be ready to respond to the countless perspectives through which the patient reveals how he sees the interaction with the analyst in the here-and-now. In short, we need to understand how he sees or fails to see things, because what is important is putting ourselves on the same wavelength – 'vision with' the patient, not 'vision on' the patient. The main therapeutic factor becomes the development of the α function which is obtained through the 'playing of the unconscious', through the increase in the analysand's narrative – but ultimately also personal – competence which the analyst aims to foster by removing caesuras from the text, suggesting new story lines, expressing his curiosity, opening up perspectives upon other possible worlds, transgressing the narrative frames, identifying with the characters, suffering because of their vicissitudes, and so on. If transference does not just mean perceptual distortion but also the ability to see points of contact to hold on to and then to bind together different terms – not just the repetition of the infantile neurosis but also a basic cognitive principle of mental functioning – then the only way out of a pathological transference could be to make room for *more transferences*.

One could order all the characters of the analytic dialogue in a three-dimensional diagram along the gradients real/unreal, past/

present and outside/inside, while always remaining within a framework of reality. But it is only through the introduction of the fourth dimension of the conscious/unconscious pair, the distinctive feature of Freud's theory, that treatment becomes possible, although it may not necessarily be explained to the analysand. The more the patient espouses the points of view of the various characters who move around and fill up this diagram, the greater his ability to contain emotions, to see things from the perspective of others, but also from radically different and even opposite angles of vision. The shifts and metamorphoses of the characters in this mental space are equivalent to transformations, to changes in the vertex. They correspond to incremental movements in the development of the ability to think and to tolerate the paradoxes of psychic life and existence that are schematized in the Cartesian system of coordinates that is Bion's Grid. The goal of the analysis is to generate as many of these transformations as possible.

Escaped from a book

> It is wonderful to think that one may live and yet be ignorant of the fact that under one's very nose there may be a book in which one's whole life is described as in a picture. Never should I have guessed that, as soon as ever one begins to read such a book, it sets one on both to remember and to consider and to foretell events. [...] one may read such works, one reads such a book as YOURS as easily as though it had been written by oneself, and had taken possession of one's heart, and turned it inside out for inspection, and were describing it in detail as a matter of perfect simplicity.
>
> (Fyodor Dostoyevsky, *Poor Folk*)

It sometimes happens that a patient at the very first session, or at one of the first sessions, brings along the novel of his life, or rather he reveals that he has identified with some fictional character and that his story has, in effect, already been written. If some key twentieth-century novels were inspired by psychoanalysis (Svevo's *Confessions of Zeno*, Berto's *Il male oscuro (The Dark Illness)* and Roth's *Portnoy's Complaint* are the first that come to mind), here it is the analysis itself that starts from literature. For the analyst, the indication is valuable because the interpretation proposed by the patient contains a number of ideas that are already well developed. Bion often expressed his regret at not being able to communicate with the same accuracy as artists,[2] but in this case his dream of precision is fulfilled. A character from literature or film can fascinate the analyst and enable him to achieve a more intense emotional involvement insofar as the aesthetic experience provides a moment of encounter with the analysand.

If, as Tolstoy said in the opening sentence of *Anna Karenina*, happy families are all alike but every unhappy family is unhappy in its own way, in the book that contains his life we find something of the particular sensitivity and unhappiness of the person who refers to it. It is as if he/she were looking for a new author, someone to invent a new story or to shoot a film with a different ending.

These situations are thought provoking also because they bring to mind the self-conscious narratives that are typical of what we now call the postmodern landscape but which had already been explored by Baroque theatre; narratives, namely, where the game of self-reflection and the display of rhetorical devices are pushed to extremes. A case in point is a story by Woody Allen where the reader has an affair with Emma Bovary, the 'paper' heroine of Flaubert's novel, but there are many others.

It is as if the patient immediately showed that he was aware of the fact that the analysis takes place on a stage set, within a framework that makes him sensitive to psychic reality and all that is part of it. Presenting himself as a character in a book, and thus as the protagonist of a metalepsis,[3] is a way of pointing to the first shattering of the narrative framework, of the secret passages between the material world and the inner world, between reality and dream, which lead to mentalization. It's a lucky start: the patient already knows that he is inside an area where playfulness, dream and psychic reality reign.

Further, from another point of view, the literary self-portrait has the same meaning as the overture to the first dream the patient recounts. Like a dream from the early stage of analysis, it sets the seal on the entire treatment, and marks a point to which one always returns in order to make numerous and ever-varying interpretations. All the other stories that come later can be seen as developments or comments on that first essential narrative.

Closed unspoken forces

> Oh, empty wagon on the railway siding, / Here for you the coarse freight of knocks / And thuds. Laden now you weigh / On the stretched looms; / But with surging gasps / Collapses smoking and comes / Sniffing with horrible fascination / The machine to yoke you up / Away from your absorbed space / Towards the harsh rolling of steel / Towards the shuddering screeches of brakes, / Chained in the herd / By the unchanging law / Of the ever open chimney: / And as you are dragged you pass on / And rigid you hold back / The closed unspoken forces / On nearby wheels and rails / Beyond connection and oppressed, / Beneath the leaping heaven / In the labyrinth of days / At the crossroads of the seasons / Unleashing eternity against boredom, / Piercing the expanse towards love, / And does not die and wants to, and does not live and wants to, / While the earth asks it for its word / Is passionate in its unripe wanting / Pays for its faith with blood alone.
>
> (Clemente Rebora, *Poems* (1913–1957))

It is a touching moment when Laura, after a few weeks of therapy, in speaking of the slight sense of excitement she feels about meeting a friend at work who intrigues her quotes a line from Virgil: 'Agnosco veteris vestigia flammae' (which in Dante becomes: 'I recognise the signs of the ancient flame').[4] Is this the moment when the transference is kindled? I wonder what possible changes, movements, developments it might foreshadow. No longer and not only is she identifying with the 'empty wagon' and the 'closed unspoken forces' from the wonderful poem by Rebora that she recited at one of the first sessions. That was her way – gentle, sensitive, intense – to let me into her world of pain. A life interrupted, a painful emotional stasis. The expectation of inexorable abandonment, imminent, already announced. And, in the background, the obsession with time.

And the fact that it was the kindling of transference later became clear: not every day is a farewell for a short period of vacation as poignant as that which can be read between the lines of this Madrigal by Tasso. Apparently talking about something else, Laura recites it before the Easter holidays:

> Qual rugiada o qual pianto / Quai lacrime eran quelle / Che sparger vidi dal notturno manto / E dal candido volto delle stelle?

/ E perché seminò la bianca luna / Di cristalline stille un puro nembo / A l'erba fresca in grembo? / Perché ne l'aria bruna / S'udian quasi dolendo intorno / Gir l'aure insino al giorno? / Fur segni forse de la tua partita / Vita de la mia vita?[5]

Ajax, the fatally named

And pity, O king, thy son, who without thee
To foster his youth, must live the orphaned ward
Of loveless guardians. Think how great a sorrow
Dying thou wilt bequeath to him and me.

(Sophocles, *Ajax*[6])

When she talks about it, Sara is moved. She had been struck by the story of Ajax ever since she first heard it as a teenager at school, and Ajax 'the fatally named' (δυσώνυμος Αίας, that is, the bad, hateful, fatal name), as Sophocles calls him, had become her hero. Ajax commits suicide because when Achilles dies his weapons are given to the astute Ulysses and not to him. The strongest of the Achaeans, he is seized by a rage so uncontrollable as to drive him insane. Aloof, isolated, he hatches a plan for revenge. Wishing to visit terrible punishment upon the Atreides, Agamemnon and Menelaus, who he feels have betrayed him, one night he slaughters the animals that are part of his army's war booty. Ostracized from the community of men, he becomes wicked and loses what Bion calls 'common sense'.

After regaining clarity of mind and now ashamed of his wrong-doing, Ajax kills himself. His death provokes a dispute among his men, because the Greek leaders want to deny him burial. They too behave excessively and, just as he had done, defy the gods. It falls to Ulysses, the compassionate hero and wise man who knows he is a man among men ('For I see well, nought else are we but mere Phantoms, all we that live, mere fleeting shadows', he says; ibid., p. 8) and who for this reason has greater emotional maturity and is better able to identify with others, to overcome his hatred, to understand the tragic grandeur of Ajax, and to persuade them to render him the last honours.

A warrior who has made valour his *raison d'être*, 'for his downfall, a man of one sole virtue, proudly brandished' (Starobinski, 1974, p. 22), and who is unable to tolerate narcissistic collapse, thus becomes for Sara the reflection of her fragility as an orphan (her father, with whom she had a love-hate relationship, took his own life when she was in her early teens), and her urge to win, to be the first, to be recognized, to redeem her father and to be redeemed in his eyes. Guilt, anxiety and expiation blend in a transference involving this great figure from classical literature.

Due to her double identification – with Ajax and with his son Eurysaces – Sara's compulsion to succeed, heightened by oedipal rivalry, entails on the one hand an unconscious need for punishment, and on the other the risk of losing herself, the catastrophe of failure. There are no half measures. And there were no half measures when she developed a violent negative transference towards me in the course of the analysis, and I realized that I was beginning to suffer from a kind of cardiac anxiety (δυσ-ώνυμος → dysrhythmia) during our sessions. My physical symptoms became a kind of alarming sensory reverie. It was a way of feeling – in my body and in the organ that symbolizes affection – the primitive deficiencies of emotional attunement that Sara must have suffered at birth and which were later reactivated in her subsequent mourning. Thanks to repetition in a new context – this is the transference[7] – perhaps we were able to work through / translate into thought the more distant and the more recent injury that lie behind her great fragility and extraordinary urge to exist. And indeed, after the fury, by way of reparation she quoted the lines in which Tecmessa, Ajax's wife, absolves her husband for what he has done and acknowledges that there was something good in him. The figure of Ajax came back several times during our conversations – a way, to paraphrase Sophocles, of saying the unsayable.

The Day After Tomorrow

– I saw a really bad film last night, you know, one of those typically vacuous Hollywood films … all about disasters, environmental change, a new ice age …

– [After several minutes of silence] So … you didn't like it?!

– [Humorously] It's just that while I was watching it … there was a real earth tremor.

– So it wasn't just your Home Theatre!

– Oh, no! We have a really battered old TV; you can hardly hear anything. Anyway, we sat there for a bit, and then it was over.

– That's a very British way of behaving, self-control and all that.

– Yes, right. It makes me think of ... The other day I was just about to enter a bookshop, when suddenly an immigrant on a bicycle ran into me. Incredible! He could have mown me down! Anyway, I wasn't injured. So I turned round. Phlegmatic. I put a hand on his shoulder, I looked him in the eyes. I saw his panic, and I said: 'Calm down. No problem.'

– Ice cold.

– Yes, ice cold.

– Like in the film, between father and son. Don't you agree with me that it wasn't so much a question of climatic disasters or, rather, that the ice age was between the two of them?! As a matter of fact, the father goes on a tough journey to New York to save his son who has taken shelter in the Public Library. A father who is always on the move doing his research ...

– If that was a frosty relationship ... then what about the relationship between me and my father! To save himself, the boy in the film does what his dad, a paleo-climatologist, tells him to do ...

– The father is important to him, of course. That's why he gets angry when his father is never there.

– But then he almost dies of the cold when he tries to phone him from the library to ask for help.

– A desperate plea for help ... But, I wonder, might not your silence sometimes have the same meaning?!

– It was one of those situations that would have been just right for xenophobic feelings ... In the film, it now occurs to me, there's something quite remarkable: the Americans are forced to cross the Mexican border to save themselves; for once they are the immigrants ... the re-integration of the different!

– Or the immigrant.

– [in a mixture of admiration and mockery] ... SO EVEN YOU WATCH THESE TRASHY MOVIES ...! Anyway, we're all post-modern now, aren't we?!

– If you want ... we can be post-modern, too!

– And still, he manages to save him ... Of course, at the cost of taking out half America!

– They have to reposition themselves in the south, in Mexico, in the heat ... In any case, woe betide anyone who underestimates ecology and sustainable development!

Here, the heat border is where the patient meets the analyst, at the moment when he finds out that the *analyst watches the same films*, when he realizes that he is willing to see things from his vantage point. The danger area represented *by the immigrant*, by everything that divides them, is diminished; but equally, on the intrapsychic level, there is less that is split off, that is to say, less anger that would tend to sever the link. It reverses the perspective: now it's the Americans who need the Mexicans, or the father is no longer just the famous paleo-climatologist always travelling around the world, but also someone who loves him and who risks his life to save him. However, in order to produce – the term is appropriate – the 'catastrophic change', you first need frost, the disease of the field.

The porter

It was with a sense of wonder and excitement I could barely restrain that I listened to Paolo telling me, during the umpteenth rather grey session dominated by silence, that he had bought one of my favourite books: *The Unconsoled*, by Kazuo Ishiguro. The book had left me with the memory of its dream-like atmosphere and recognizable yet original Kafkaesque tone. I had enjoyed the precision and clarity of the author's writing and his way of building up surreal scenarios. Just to outline briefly the main storyline: in an attempt to raise its profile, a culturally impoverished town is putting on an important piano concert – a clear echo of Musil's Parallel Action. But the pianist is anxious at the desired prospect of at long last having his parents in the audience when he gives his great performance. He has been separated from them by an old wound that yet has to heal. But the concert does not come up to his expectations. Then there is the image of an extraordinary second-tier character, a porter, a dutiful professional who never sets down the heavy cases he has to carry for the hotel guests, even in the lift. Each has his secret grief, in short. Everyone, each in his own way, is unconsoled.

Then Paolo, a man without qualities (although, just like Ulrich, he was in fact full of many qualities, albeit unspoken or mortified), came across Svevo and discovered the incredible resemblance between Zeno Cosini's ill-fated attempts to quit smoking and his own. There then followed declarations of intent, plans, and constantly he would fix the date of his last cigarette. He suggested that I adopt an appropriately pedagogical tone and interpreted every failure as evidence of the obvious ineffectiveness of the therapy. Paolo did not stop smoking, but the affectionate irony with which he depicted himself, and pictured *me*, was undoubtedly an indication of a more freely functioning libido, a sign that his self-consciousness was less rigidly self-punishing, that he was relaxing his tendency towards sacrifice. Until then his neurotic solution had been on the one hand his aspiration, with all the exhausting work attendant on it, to perform his work brilliantly and memorably, as a *soloist*, and on the other an underworld of transgressive fantasies that became inevitably tinged with guilt and condemned him to apathy and depression in atonement.

The fact is that, in a happy moment for the analysis, the porter's bags became the vivid and emotionally intense image of the burden that can sometimes be the business of living – which is what it had come to be for him.

The Knight of the Lions

He was laughing and crying at the same time as he read me out a passage from the second volume of *Don Quixote*. Don Quixote appeared to have been cured. The curate and the barber were pleased to see that their friend had come to his senses. But they wanted to be sure. So the curate approached him and commenced by telling him that he had heard that the Turkish troops were gathering. Obviously they were determined to wage war against the Christians. Don Quixote, who until then had been conversing reasonably, came out with a remark that left no doubt about his madness. He said that certainly all problems would be resolved if only people decided to assemble together all the knights-errant, or even only half a dozen of them, or indeed only one. He went on to ask the rhetorical question whether it would be the first time that a knight-errant had defeated an army of some two hundred thousand men as if they were made of sugar paste. To which the curate's comment was that, well, of course, as long as they avoided touching on matters of chivalry...! And it was this mixture of compassion, scorn, pity and scepticism that reflected Mauro's state. He, too, in fact, despite much progress, still felt very vulnerable to his ghosts. And through his sobs he kept repeating to me: 'YES, OF COURSE, AS LONG AS THEY AVOID TOUCHING ON MATTERS OF CHIVALRY!'.

Later Mauro returned to the same subject in another episode in Cervantes' masterpiece. Don Quixote met a carter transporting two lions and asked him to open the cage; to him this was obviously a test of his courage and he would have to challenge and defeat the lions. The carter held out for some time but there was little he could do in the face of Don Quixote's stubbornness and threats. However, when the cage door was opened, something unexpected happened: one of the lions, 'more courteous than arrogant', lazily eyed the knight, yawned and turned the other way, showing him his rear parts. Don Quixote was offended, but the carter was able to convince him that in fact the lion was just bowing to his greatness and had recognized his superiority. That was enough to satisfy his pride, so much so that he decided from then on to rename himself – no longer the Knight of the Rueful Countenance but the Knight of the Lions.

The 'more courteous than arrogant' lion later became a character we both invested with emotion, a reminder of and a way of re-living a shared emotion. This allowed us to see the meaning of Mauro's often difficult life situations in terms of an old pain that lay behind the susceptibility of being 'skinless', the wound that often poisoned relations that might otherwise have nourished and sustained him more.

The King of Hell

Now for a very special case: here the patient himself is the author of his own novel, in this case a comic strip that showed signs of real talent on the part of A., who gave it to me for Christmas; what follows is the dialogue. Starring: Satan and a random devil.

– ... I am speechless! I knew you would do yourself proud! You're a legend! You deserve a reward! You can have whatever you want!

– Sure! I want to become the Master of Hell … NOW!

– WHAT !!!???

– I am also more powerful than you … Are you ready to fight? … I'll explain it again!

STUD!

FSSSH!

SWISSH!

– UH!?!

– You are too slow for me!

– You bug! You will pay dearly for your insolence!

– Is that it?

– You asked for it!

– Go on, hit me!

– Rest assured I will!

STUD

STUD

SWISSH!

– You are no longer what you once were! All this time spent doing nothing … it's turned you into a wimp!

SHAAH!

– Aaaaah !!!!!!

KA-BOOM!

– NO … I can't believe it …

– It's the harsh law of the jungle …

WOAHH!

– Ah! Ah! Ah! Ah!

– Hail, Your Majesty!

– NOW I AM THE KING OF HELL! … MMM …

In a dramatic fight sequence A. sums up his fall into a world where all values are negative. The transformation into Lucifer, a measure of his distance from his interior gods, is his way of alleviating tension and living through his conflicts. The King of Hell has become the ideal actor to express his excessive anger and his paradoxical pride at being a *drop-out.*

Alie-n-ation

A second strip cartoon (again I give the text) that A. has dedicated to me bears the title Alie-n-ation.

– ... Giò, it's just a movie. So just shut up about the aliens. OK?

– ... Look, if you want to continue being blind, just follow your stick ... As for me, I'm keeping my eyes open ...

– Now ... I'm going to kill him ...

– You still refuse to believe.

– Once and for all! There will never be any aliens on earth! Got it?!

– GULP!

– And what's wrong now?

– ... Look, could I just ask you a quick question? Then I'll stop talking about aliens ...

– ... What the f... is that?! EH?!

– Do you think they have come in peace ...?!?

– You ask them ...

WOAMH !!!!!!!!!!!

BLAM!

– CHRIST !!!!!!!!

– Aaaah !!!!!!

– ... I'm thinking they probably didn't come in peace ... Do you know ...?

– DON'T TELL ME ...

THE END ...?

This cartoon illustrates the necessary alienation that gives rise to the subject, the need to live in a place that is the language of the other. But it also shows what happens when trust is missing, and when there are insufficient shared points of view on things. A traumatic situation develops that can crop up again at any time in life and in therapy. The others then become aliens from another planet, and, as in a modern version of the thunderbolts of the gods, they burn the fragile, nascent forms of mental life. And here it would be: 'See what happens if you don't believe my "delusions", if you don't see things from my point of view, if you stick to what is sensible, real.' In other words, it becomes an alienating unconscious identification (in the negative sense of a primary identification with an object that brings with it intolerable elements of violence) with a protective maternal shield that 'fails in its revitalizing function and in its ability to modulate the experience of the child' (De Cesarei, 2001).

It is quite evident, especially in borderline patients, that the function that mirrors and integrates affective states has been lacking. This leads to deficiencies in the ability to symbolize and to differentiate between psychic and material reality, as well as to a readiness to use forms of violence against self and others (Fonagy, 2001). The killer contents of the mind, then, can be seen as the product of micro-traumatic experiences of non-recognition (essentially perceived as expressions of hate on the part of the object), alienated aspects of self that correspond to an equal number of holes in the fabric of identity and healthy narcissistic functioning. Thus, the ego is exposed to the devastating experience of shame – 'the sign of a self starved of love is shame' (ibid.), perhaps the most social, the most peculiarly human of emotions, because it can be felt only in relationship with another – and hence, in the attempt to protect itself, it is also exposed to violent and angry reactions.

Of course, the gift has a reparative as well as a communicative value, and in any event mobilizes the resources of creativity that A. fortunately possesses. Psychic pain is not a question of all or nothing. There may be some very diseased areas alongside others that are highly evolved. Giving a name and a meaning to these Hulkian areas of the mind – which is what happens in his cartoons and in the context of the psychotherapy that has stimulated them – is like trying to map a minefield and clear it of mines at the same time. Both the image of hell and of Satan and that of the aliens as avatars from the virtual world of the setting enter into this difficult process as valuable coordinates of a psychic geography that becomes increasingly well defined.

Regarding the obvious superiority of Stupendous-Man over Superman

– I saw a movie with Superman. It's always a learning curve. Clark Kent was talking to his girlfriend, and she asked him, amazed and incredulous, 'So you're ... Superman?!?'. WHAT A DIMWIT! They're identical! And then, he's someone who keeps all his memories frozen at the Arctic Pole. Stupendous-Man is much much better!

– At least he knows it's all a fake.

– That's right! SUPERMAN THINKS HE REALLY IS SUPERMAN! Instead, when Hobbes, the tiger, asks Stupendous-Man, that is, Calvin, when the world will disappear, he ...

Stupendous-Man against Superman has become the way we repeatedly used to inform each other, between the lines, about the risks of a megalomaniac turning in on oneself. Humour and playfulness were useful to 'unfreeze' the traumas and memories of a relational atmosphere where the object was often cold and inhospitable as only a place like the Arctic Pole can be, and to find a healthier narcissistic functioning: from the psychosis of Superman to the normal neurosis of Stupendous Man.

Of course, the word 'dimwit' expresses his belittling view of women from the position of superiority he has adopted in order to regain control after the fall. It's as if Superman could only be recognized by putting on a mask, a false self. In this way the genuine and humiliated identity of Clark Kent is able to keep others at a distance. However, as Mario explains, if Superman engages in conversation with a woman, a catastrophe will immediately follow: for example, a coach will fall, and straightaway everybody will forget his past heroics and start rebuking him. The woman's exclamation is ambiguous. It can be seen not only as her disbelief that Superman is Kent, but also as incredulity at Superman's psychosis. The cartoon also highlights the importance of gaining access to the 'fiction' of psychic reality – a reality different from material reality – so as to move on from delusion to play.

Calvin's mom

Ten minutes of silence at the beginning. R. starts criticizing psychoanalysis: The people who do analysis are perfectly well and they do it because they can afford it. The real sufferers would go mad ... TODAY YOU CAN FREE ASSOCIATE ON YOUR OWN! Ten more minutes of silence. I met A. who goes to the analyst, Dr. L. It is disturbing that all my friends either have been, are at present or will at some point be in analysis: and what are the results? The fact is, this man is in a terrible state. Because he is afraid of depending on the analyst. So I say, 'You smoke fourteen packs of cigarettes a day, you're an alcoholic, you parachute jump. You let yourself be hoodwinked all day by your girl-friend ... Nice way of being terrified of 'dependance on your analyst'!'. But if you think about it, everybody does the same thing, within certain limits.

SILENCE.

More criticisms.

SILENCE.

It's the last minute of the session. R. reflects on the fact that he has spent the entire hour speaking ill of psychoanalysis. And he's still got lots more to say! And in fact he immediately piles on more criticism. Perhaps, he continues, he should read books on psychoanalysis, but he's afraid he'll find out that it could all be a load of b....

SILENCE.

The session is about to end. R. chuckles to himself and says – this session makes me think of ... a cartoon with Calvin and Hobbes. Calvin gets out of bed, goes downstairs and runs around the house turning everything upside down and shouting: 'I'M AWAKE! I'M AWAKE! I'M NOT IN BED.' Then we see his mother picking him up and taking him back upstairs to bed, and he goes, 'SHE'S GOT TO WORK HARD FOR IT!!!'.

A little parable about how effective silence, and not just words, can be in containing a patient's anxiety, but also about the extraordinary resource that great actors like Linus can offer, or the youngest of the Fusco Brothers, Al, a lifetime spent in analysis with the half-asleep Dr. Kapuchnik, or the wonderful Calvin in Calvin & Hobbes.

On the other hand, however, Green (1983, pp. 290–291) points out that in the area of narcissistic disorders silence can sometimes plunge analysis into 'funereal boredom'. Consequently he suggests that the analyst should use the setting as a transitional space and act as an 'ever-living, interested and constantly awake object'. Only in this way can he prove his vitality to the patient: by his associative links, but without ever leaving his neutrality and without falling into intrusive interpretation.

Commedia dell'arte masks

There are also poor actors, either amateur or semi-professional; or professional actors who, fresh out of the Academy of Dramatic Arts, tend to impose their drama school style of acting; or, again, actors stuck within standardize roles, as in the *Commedia dell'arte*. At other times the characters are already part of the grammar of a moral tale: the Wife, the Father, the Lover, the Girlfriend, etc., or, similar in some respects to Giotto's allegories (Prudence, Fortitude, Temperance, Justice, Faith, Charity, Hope, Despair, Envy, Infidelity, Injustice, Anger, Inconstancy, Folly), they are taken to depict vices and virtues. These actors do not appear very willing to take on new roles, and the patient himself realizes their characters are stereotypes. The point becomes whether you can force them to leave behind the repetitive patterns they are usually called upon to act out. The same problem can arise with actors who are so successful and such consummate artists, like Al Pacino or Robert De Niro, that now all they can do is play themselves, and here again the important thing is to show humility and take a step back towards what we know little about or towards that which we do not already know everything about from the start.

The boyfriend

– My boyfriend goes hunting for wild boar every day!

The interpretation may be accurate, but if it outstrips the patient's ability to take it on board, it can prove unbearable. Thus understood, the boyfriend plays the role of the analyst who terrifies the patient with his target practice. Of course, most of the time this terror is so intense because it almost always has its origin in old, painful experiences of disparagement that have made the patient's identity all too porous and fragile.

The girlfriend

– My girlfriend is in therapy with Dr. A.

– Ah!

– [Laughs] 'The Ninja psychiatrist!'

The Ninja warriors are terrifying turtle-like warriors. For a split second I feel flattered by the implicit comparison with my colleague. Paolo's ironic comment reflects our (collusive) victory as a pair. But immediately I sense a bittersweet note, the moment the micro-fire of the internal analytic theatre is extinguished and the tough warrior returns to the battlefield of the here-and-now where it legitimately belongs.

The husband

– Marcello and I make love for a long time but he cannot come. Which is very frustrating. I feel that he does it out of duty, that it's not something pleasant for him. Do you think it's a serious matter? Will we ever manage to solve it?

– What do you think?

– I think it's serious, but we should be able to solve it.

– ... Ah!

Ostensibly, a question of desire. I think of the side effects of anti-serotonin on sexuality, but seeing them as a character in the analytic field, I hypothesise my/our temporary drop in tone/understanding or 'depression'. Suddenly I feel the sense of boredom that for some time now has permeated our sessions and which it now is perhaps time to reflect on.

The other

– I was in the car with Anna. She was driving. BADLY. She broke all the car's mirrors. I've no great desire to see her any more.

The 'mirrors' suggest Lacan and Kohut, but also dreams that reflect the session as a paradigm for the analysis. It is as if the patient were signalling to the analyst that he is not being attentive enough to see what is happening between them in terms of the dream of the session. And, as we know, every broken mirror …

The mother

> – She has this uncanny knack of phoning every time the film I'm watching is about to end. 'How are you? What are you doing? What's the weather like? Are you tired? Is everything okay?' She just can't seem to understand that I have my own life, that maybe I'm doing other things and I want to be left in peace. Then I answer hastily and say I don't want to talk to dad right now, I'll talk to him later. She[8] is upset and then when we meet, 'You're always angry!' she says. It must be because she is lonely. I feel sorry for her and I'm also sorry she doesn't understand.

What can I say? 'You can't interrupt a film – or an emotion!'

Actors taken from the streets

Actors can be professional, semi-professional, or makeshift. Some directors, such as Pasolini, but recently also Garrone, the director of *Gomorrah* (2008), prefer to use actors taken from the streets. Often they even do without a proper audition. They just make sure that the actor's appearance corresponds as closely as possible to the character. What matters most is that they are spontaneous. Sometimes they are even called upon to play themselves.

The angry cat

The tragicomic story of an epic struggle to get a cat driven wild by fear to come off a sideboard is the theme of a memorable session. Assorted blandishments and threats were all in vain. Various figures intervened, but to no avail. It is only when they had all decided to leave the cat time and space to recover from its terror that the unexpected guest left the room. How could I ever forget that furious cat and the significant lesson in technique it taught me? But let's listen to Sofia:

– As you know, I adore cats, but on Tuesday something amazing happened. There's a cat that hangs around the block of flats where we live. It must be a wild cat. It got into our flat and we couldn't get it out. It was terrified when we got out a broom. It began to dart here and there. From wall to wall. It was wounded. It was beginning to leave bloodstains on the wall. Everybody was screaming. The next-door neighbour was crying. Michele was getting more and more pissed off. The cat's fur was ruffled and it had two enormous eyes! … It was hissing like crazy! The fur on its tail was all puffed up, its ears flattened. It was perched on a sideboard, out of reach. Then I called the vet, who said she couldn't come but told me to be careful. At that point, it immediately jumped on a neighbour who had come to see what was going on, and scratched her. Rather than let anyone come close, it was ready to commit suicide. It was dangerous. Jumping on people's heads. Blood everywhere. The flat was wrecked. The neighbour was screaming and crying. So I called the fire brigade. Five firemen arrived. They thought I was an idiot, but even they weren't able to catch the cat! They got scratched too. So they put on their helmets. They were getting more and more annoyed, saying it was absurd calling out the fire brigade for a cat. BUT … THIS WAS MORE THAN A CAT! Then they left. The cat was still there and they refused to come back. I couldn't wait outside all night for it to come out. So I begged them, and one of the younger, nicer firemen came back inside. By now the cat had crept under the sofa. They tried to catch it using a blanket. But it looked like it had disappeared. … I can't tell you what state the house was in, what with the cat and the firemen who had moved everything around!

It looked as if it had gone and so the firemen left … We go to bed. Time passes. At some point I think I hear a meow! OH NOOO!! During the night you could hear meowing. It's still there. A wild animal, totally beyond taming. An almost eerie presence, the ghost of this cat wandering around the house. I know I'll be awake all night. It's there. You can't see it but it's still there. It scares me. Never seen such a thing … I THINK IT MUST BE JUST LIKE COMING FACE TO FACE WITH A TIGER! I washed and cleaned everything. But today I picked up a plate and I thought I could still see bloodstains. What if it is injured? What if it needs help? If only the firemen had gone upstairs and looked around properly! It's true that it gets between the balcony and the closet and avoids being caught. A band of idiots …

Now Michele says that this whole cat business has really stressed him out. He went out this morning and I wasted half the day looking for the cat. And he says: 'You have to be cold-blooded, you can't let emotion take over ...' And I wanted to give it a bang on the head with a broom to knock it[9] out. But I didn't feel like doing something that violent. But if he had seen the cat jumping! It walked on the ceiling! I understand why people in the Middle Ages thought cats were in league with the devil. The situation had got out of control ... Its meowing was plaintive, not angry ... While all this was going on, the neighbour took some Ativan! And I took a sleeping pill as well.

– 'I put myself in the cat's position,' you said.

– Yes, then I too thought that the only thing was to try and tame it. There's this thing about the claustrum, from the point of view of the cat. From my point of view, what worries me is that it moves, that it is beyond control ... It's there, but you can't see it. It can't be pinned down. It's a bit like with spiders. Although, with spiders ... No, my fear of spiders paralyzes me. Three weeks ago, I came home, and there was a big black spider on the stairs. I stood there unable to breathe, motionless. I felt as if it were on top of me. I had the sensation it was moving over my body. As a child I couldn't handle spiders, I'd get stuck; now I can pull myself together and react. I went inside and got the spray. I sprayed half a bottle all over this cat ... – oops! – spider!

I feel that comment here would be superfluous; however, there are at least two points I would like to underline where the ambiguity of the account proves productive. The first comes when it is not clear who Sofia wants to knock it/him out with a broom: the cat or the person giving her sensible advice. The second is the slip about the cat and the spider, when for a moment she confuses a creature that evokes a strong sense of persecution, and is usually interpreted as a mother figure, with a domestic cat seen here primarily as an embodiment of her wild fear. But the cat also stands for Michele's terror and for the presence of the analyst which at times she experiences as disturbing. The slip, finally, demonstrates the typical misunderstandings of transference: cats that seem to be tigers or spiders, the familiar that becomes uncanny.

The lamp

Even the objects in the consulting room can become actors playing unexpected characters. There's an IKEA lamp on a small table near the couch that has on occasions been unable to withstand the weight of what Maria was telling me at that moment! This had the immediate effect of defusing the situation and emphasizing the comic side of things. From time to time we would then wonder how this affectionately ironic and sceptical lamp might have reacted to certain other challenging propositions. Sometimes that was enough to activate gently a radically different, 'unofficial' perspective on some of the things we were talking about.

Spiders

– I cannot say this to my husband, but the real reason I want to move house is because I can't stand all the spiders coming into the house during the summer, they're so black and disgusting. He doesn't know, BUT I'VE GOT ARACHNOPHOBIA!

Here again the question arises: what do the spiders represent for Laura? And could wanting to move house be a way of giving notice of wanting to terminate the analysis?

The cat on the roof

Giorgio tells me that when he happens to stay away from home for a while on business, on his return for a few days the cat stays on the roof and every time he has to go and coax it back down again. It does this to get its own back. It would be perfectly capable of getting down unaided. And so his neighbours find themselves observing with great compassion the spectacle of a serious professional man, a respected manager in his company, standing there meowing in an attempt to persuade the cat – whom he is enormously fond of – to come back inside.

What should one think of this delightful story that the patient tells me on return from the holiday season? Perhaps that the analyst should also learn how to meow?!

The mobile phone

On several occasion during sessions Anna and I have been witnessing some amazing special effects and watching unexpected plot developments unfold when, suddenly, her cell phone would go off from inside her handbag, but each time with a different ring tone – depending on whether it was a simple ring, an SMS, an MMS or a normal call. In these unforeseen alignments between the noises as punctuation marks in her discourse and comments on the content we experience what Stern and colleagues (1998) would call significant moments of encounter. Needless to say, since then every once in a while the phone, now a character in the text to be analysed, announces itself spontaneously to demonstrate its technological wisdom.

Empty stage

There are some patients who do not bring dreams and who tend to monotonously and endlessly recount the events of their daily life. They give the impression of living in a two-dimensional world where everything is grey and concrete. They seem to have got lost inside reality. At the same time they are extremely fragile and suffer when any attempt is made to introduce new developments into their desert-like landscape. Their words are empty, they are pure sound, they resemble a dirge and are devoid of any emotional resonance. Emotions are not allowed in unless on a Lilliputian scale, and proximity is not seen for what it is but as a threat. Ideas are deployed more for their sensual packaging than their symbolic meaning. There are no stories and no characters, and if any do exist, they are not exactly engaging. The stage is desolately empty.

One senses that the patient has put up barriers to protect a wounded or otherwise fragile self. In this way he maintains an illusory sense of continuity that is unaffected by an awareness of others as separate from himself. As a consequence, the analyst too is drawn into a timeless world, a world that is frozen, fixed. He feels isolated, just like the patient. And, again just like the patient, he may have recourse to transformations in hallucinosis, pathological projective identifications, autistic transformations, extracting himself and withdrawing from the situation into the world of his thoughts. Sometimes he can experience intense boredom, to the point of feeling real discomfort tinged with persecution or claustrophobia. The overriding feeling is, in short, that the analysis is lifeless, hopeless, because it lacks true dream-images, lively images to convey emotions. These are patients who use mechanisms similar to what Meltzer *et al.* (1975) term dismantling, which is a way of losing the consensuality of the senses, letting each of them go away on its own, and binding oneself to the stimulus offered by one's own words; it is a way of defending oneself against the hypnotic charm of the object that brings together the scattered fragments of the ego, but which is also experienced as the monster that might swallow them up.

In these situations we must practice the art of patience and resign ourselves to the very slow, minimal changes that occur, if they occur at all, over the course of years. As with the 'facilitated communication' that is used with autistic individuals, the analyst must keep up constant contact so as to support, enhance and strengthen the patient's fragile narcissism. Prudence becomes the order of the day because the patient's need for stasis must be respected. It is well to pay more attention to the patient's hypersensitivity (which he protects behind a shell) so as to register every little movement even where there is no movement, to sharpen our gaze so as to make out growth where there seems to be only arrested development, offering an advance in trust when scepticism would seem the only sensible attitude to take.

The puma

I see Daniela once a week. She's always on time. She puts her bag on the ground, she sits straight in her chair, her head tilted slightly to one side, the expression on her face shy and elusive. A meek girl with a melancholy air about her. Then she sits in silence for three quarters of an hour. I try in various ways to get in touch with her, but without success. I resign myself to silence. Pure Beckett, I think. I know that sitting like that also helps her: she makes me a witness of her suffering and yet in the meantime she becomes a little more integrated thanks to the space I give her by receiving her in my room and symbolically accommodating her in my mind.

The weeks and the months pass. One day, as I am seeing her to the door, she turns around and I notice that her orange bag has the 'Puma' logo on one side. I feel I can see a little light in the darkness. Somewhere inside her, I think, there's something primal, perhaps something fierce, angry. Sitting still and in silence is a way of hemming in the puma (explosive emotions) that she may have inside her. This time, however, she has found a way to let me know. On the other side of the bag, I later discover, there are two childishly drawn dogs snuggling up to each other. Later, there will be occasions when these will accompany the two small red Pumas that form the logo for the well-known brand of tennis shoes (!). They almost seem to signify her gradual acquisition of some minimal quanta of awareness of emotional ambivalence: two tiny red pumas, one on each shoe, flanked by two large frolicking puppies. Then she changes bags, and this time the word on the side is *légami* (or *legàmi*) ('tie me up' or 'bonds'). Then she brings another bag with camouflage patterns and colours: 'struggle, danger, lurking, hiding …' – I think to myself.

There's more: it's something I didn't realize right away, but next time I notice the repetition of the word 'energy' (in small letters). I picture the sense of psychic fragmentation Daniela is telling me about in this way and which deprives her of strength – the strength she actually has. Otherwise she would not be able to pass all the difficult exams she has to take at university. In short, I begin to create my own images of Daniela's inner world, but also of the emotions that are secretly activated in the field of the analysis. At the same time, I see that we have found a way to say something to each other that cannot yet be expressed in words. Later came the moment when we started talking, with tact and delicacy: 'Is the bag in the mood for pampering or guerrilla warfare today?' For a long time, however, the silence was necessary to keep at a tolerable level the tensions that arose at every session. The sense of helplessness and frustration that I felt must be the same, I said to myself, as that which Daniela felt. All I could do was register my emotional reactions, and the images that went through my mind; in other words, I had to remain receptive and ready to dream her undreamt or interrupted dreams.

Kaa

After a session during which I had been struggling with my usual feeling of boredom, futility and frustration, I accompany Elena to the door. I watch her take her long scarf and start to wrap it around her neck. Out of sheer clumsiness two or three times the scarf slips out of her hands and each time she puts it back over her head and it is as if the scarf had a life of its own, and I 'SEE' a snake twisting around her body. Suddenly I get a clear idea of the obsessive, sterile repetitiveness that constrains her thoughts into tight spirals. Then, in the space of a moment the snake becomes Kaa, the character from the Disney movie; I am reminded of the books I used to read as a child and the child who lives inside her, both in the sense of something not yet developed and in the sense of a nascent desire to play. It is difficult not to think of original sin, of the serpent in Eden, the Garden of Earthly Delights, of desire. The dream-like flash of the snake, in short, opens up a whole range of scenarios and possible narratives.

This reverie can be seen as a transformation of the emotional field in which both parties are immersed. A character makes its fairytale appearance. Something brings meaning – at last! – but above all, boredom suddenly vanishes and I feel a sense of wonder, interest and relief because I think that something is coming alive between us. A series of scattered elements, like the crazy pixels on a television screen when the reception is bad, are organized into a meaningful configuration, into a good shape, the right word or image that contains/dreams the experience and brings it alive. Successful symbolization should be seen, in fact, as intersubjective and not as something that belongs exclusively to the analyst, and, as Pozzi writes (2003), it can be considered a preconception, also in the patient, of a form of vitality and creativity.

Bad girl

While listening distractedly to Laura, I fleetingly glance at the clock that I keep on the table. The minute hand is almost at nine. Time to finish, I say to myself, and so I close the session. Only later, when she's gone, do I realize that I have shortened the session by ten minutes, and that the timetable pattern I was thinking of – that is, a full-hour session that begins and ends with the minute hand at nine (or at 45) – actually applies to the next patient. I had behaved *badly*. For some time, however, we had been repeating the idea that Laura was too good. By superimposing the next session, which belonged to Irene, a really 'bad girl', onto Laura's, and thereby perhaps making her angry, I was unconsciously striving to provoke a side of her that was split off but which I had felt an intimation of somewhere. The involuntary act of encroaching upon the setting – what Lacan would call *ponctuation* –

took on the meaning of an emptiness that would serve to give back a sense of fullness. The chiastic crossing of Laura and Irene, and their two timetables, enabled me to see each in a new light.

The incident was repeated more than once, and each time I felt embarrassment, and a little disappointment. Of course, the 'bad girl' dozing inside her woke up and made herself felt, becoming a character in our conversations. The result was that a rather boring and sterile phase of the analysis gave way to a more lively and productive phase. Somehow we found a way out of the sickly sweet atmosphere of collusion we were locked inside and managed to construct a space of representation for what later proved to be an intense unconscious anger towards an internal object that alternated between being controlling and intrusive on the one hand and distracted and indifferent on the other.

Parameters

With patients who make 'casting' difficult one can sometimes get somewhere by intentionally introducing certain parameters into the way the analysis is conducted, in other words, *ad hoc* or permanent technical variations, or by making good use of accidental variations.

One stratagem that can sometimes prove useful is that suggested by Winnicott and explained by Bollas (1999): occasionally one can lengthen the sessions, or one can ask the patient to stop talking and to listen to the silence. In some cases, the analyst's silence may provide that atmosphere of tenable frustration which gives the analysand the opportunity to listen to himself in a different context from usual and to ask new questions about himself, as when in a Lynch movie reality gradually begins imperceptibly to take on a dream-like colouring.

Other times, the primary purpose is to 'put the patient to sleep', to cure the session of its insomnia, and thus to induce the hypnoid state that promotes free association: dimming the lights, cutting out noise, singing a lullaby – 'bathing the patient in words', in short – and, reciprocally, being receptive to the sensory side of the idea of reverie (Ogden, 2001).

With psychotic subjects, and often with adolescents, one can sometimes overcome the inhibition that prevents self-expression by asking the patient to draw, or to write notes between sessions, or even to speak of the blog they keep on Splinder (an Italian social networking site). In other cases, one can try to change the frame of the exchange by suggesting that the patient pretend that what has just been said is the story of a dream or a film seen at the cinema, or that he should say the same things as if he were talking to a close friend or as if it were the friend who was speaking, or the immigrant domestic help, or any other character. In this way patients can be helped to break away from the defences erected by intellectualization and abstraction and to get in touch with their more lively emotions. The domestic help, or whoever, thus becomes a fixed character in the analytic field.

The fact is that there is never a lack of possible actors, even when the patient is absolutely silent. Nor is there a lack of roles or emotions. They are supplied by the transference script and by the stage of the setting. What varies greatly, however, is the degree to which a certain actor is suited to play a certain part and how willing he is to do so. At this point the analyst can shoot scenes with a candid camera, or he can try to persuade the actors to act. After all, a transference interpretation is a way of making the actors play certain parts, but as with a candid camera, it can be experienced as an irritating and unpleasant intrusion.

A typical situation is when the whole analysis risks being conducted on the basis of a lie, or a 'paramnesia' (Bion, 1978). This is the case of psi-somethings in formation. The two (apparent) opposites of the psychotic patient and the pseudo-normal patient sometimes meet in a denial of reality and in a sort of psychic functioning characterized by negative reversible perspective (-RP). Both ask for specific rewards, one explicitly, the other without asking for anything.

It should come as no surprise that a therapy situation can generate such violent anguish. After all, every session is like the tragedy where the spectator gazes at his own death (end, *télos*) even though he is never actually able to see it – as reflected in that of the characters. As Benjamin (1955) noted, it is only death that gives meaning to a story. We all spend our entire lives engaged in the paradoxical task of giving meaning to a story whose ending is unknown; all we know is that there will be an ending. One can understand why Bion sees analysis as a kind of theatre of cruelty, where what is staged is fear, pain and ferocity. Narration in analysis, however, does not only have this meaning. It is true that a character's entrance on the stage gets the narrative going and hence introduces temporality and absence into situations in which they arouse great fear in patients whose overriding imperative is survival. However, care should be taken to avoid that this arrival is perceived as too abrupt or experienced as traumatic.

It goes without saying that supervision may sometimes open up new creative possibilities for a deadlocked couple, who, for example, find themselves in mutual and complementary identifications that are at best reversible. Here it is important to break away from binary oppositions and to generate multiple perspectives that form the basis for mutual recognition. This is part of an ongoing, dynamic process of negotiation of meaning. Aron (2006) gives a nice example: a colleague told him about his problem of feeling dislike for a patient who had expressed his sense of excitement at watching the tragedy of the twin towers in New York. But, in my opinion, the most remarkable thing about Aron's article is that he manages to re-signify what for the analyst and his patient appeared to be merely a material event by interpreting it as the externalization of internal destructiveness due to a chaotic and violent primal scene, but without ever resorting to what Ferro (2009) has called 'transformation into dream'. This shows that the field vertex is not something new and incomprehensible but rather a more rigorous version of the oneiric paradigm of analysis – the most coherent and radical development of that paradigm.

At any rate, a third point of view, or the point of view of a third party, is what can enable therapy to evolve, and this often has to do with the possibility of finding the right actors for the characters and stories that are being told:

> As a supervisor I often feel that my job is to push the analyst to overcome the limits of his skills, helping him/her to feel freer to accept the most varied identifications and positions in the relationship, which, in return, since the analytic dyad is a complex system, encourages the patient to interpret new roles [...] it is essential for the analyst to be willing to take on all the patient's multiple unconscious identifications: with victims and terrorists, with rescuers and witnesses.
>
> (Aron, 2006, p. 350)

In the same article Aron discusses several other techniques that can be used to create a scene or an analytic space in the proper sense of the term. For example, if at times the analyst feels free to express his doubts and admits that he is experiencing a conflict regarding the way he should conduct himself vis-à-vis some fact of the analysis, this may direct the patient into a dimension of ambiguity and creativity. By having the character of the analyst come on stage in a new role, self-disclosure creates a third, or alternative, space that fosters self-reflexivity, and thus mentalization. Of course, from the point of view of the analytic field, self-disclosure is still constrained by the law of the setting and of the oneiric in the session, so it is not so much a question of fragments of the analyst's private reality breaking in on the scene but arguably more like the arrival of a new type of unconventional, perhaps Brechtian, actor, in other words someone who is very conscious of his role.

Another path the analyst can take in order to cope with 'impossible' situations is to rely more on his own emotional reactions, his physical sensations and the images that come into his mind. A further possible approach, similar to Pozzi's (2003) descriptive infant-observation-like commentary in her treatment of Johnny, a twelve-year-old boy with Asperger syndrome, is the analyst's observation of his/her flow of associations, which go to form a constant, though unexpressed, commentary on what is happening. At times, however, elements of this stream of consciousness can be verbalized, or quite simply one can describe what one sees or conjecture what is happening, as the psychologist played by Bruce Willis does in *The Sixth Sense* (1999) when dealing with a boy suffering from mutism.

In a certain phase of the therapy, Pozzi describes how she had to resort to a further modification of technique. She began talking to an imaginary companion of Johnny, which enabled her to arouse his curiosity and to bring him out of his autistic withdrawal. But let us see what Pozzi says about Bion's concept of consensual emotional experience and common sense:

> For Bion, a 'common sense' is an essential mental act 'which apprehends objects in their multifaceted aspects as opposed to neuro-physiological events' (Meltzer *et al.*, 1975, p. 13). However, for a common sense to develop in Bion's terms, the nursing infant has to have an experience where the senses come together in a gratifying and containing feeding situation. Andersen (1992) wrote about this in her intensive therapy with a 3-year-old boy with autistic features. She referred to a good feeding situation, where the baby is held by the nipple in the mouth, by the flow of milk in the stomach, by the eye contact with the mother and by the physical holding of the baby in the mother's lap. These sensory

> experiences, simultaneously co-ordinated, develop the cohesion of a psychological common sense and a sense of oneself as a recipient of those profound physical and psychological experiences. For Bion, common sense implies that the senses are in harmony and support each other, as we can imagine they are in the good experience of the baby at the breast (1992, p. 10).
>
> Johnny did not seem to have achieved a harmonious co-ordination of senses as a small child and now he could not perform adequately two activities at the same time, such as hearing and seeing or talking and hearing, without much anxiety.
>
> (Pozzi, 2003, p. 1345)

I have quoted at length from this excellent article by Pozzi not only because it explores in depth the quotation from Bion at the beginning of this chapter but also because it refers us to the scene of the 'sacred conversation' between mother and child and thus cross-references with other chapters in this book, two on the meaning of aesthetic conflict (Chapters 5 and 6) and one on the metaphor of the text in Freud and Bion (Chapter 8).

In fact, after having written this chapter, I wondered if there was something that might unite the vignettes I had chosen to illustrate my proposition. My idea was to clarify, above all to myself, which factors (primarily, experiences) I had more or less preconsciously selected, even before making them the focus of theoretical reflection, and which evidently I felt essential to casting that stood any chance of success. I realized then that once again I had come close to the area of aesthetic experience. I think that some elements stand out: the effect of pleasant surprise, the context of fiction or play, the lively and almost immediate feeling of a broadening of experience and the creation of meaning; all features which form part of *aesthetic experience*.

When an actor presents himself for a casting audition and proves to be good at acting a certain part, something revelatory occurs. One experiences the effect of truth that only certain dream images possess – on account of their presence and vividness, qualities which outside dreams, and in the best cases, we can find only in art that moves us. The circle is closed, and as usual the casting metaphor proves to be more than a mere metaphor; rather it is something that leads us to the very heart of the matter. That is to say, it reveals the meaning of the most felicitous moments of analysis, namely how it feels when a selected fact comes along and as if by magic brings order to chaos.

5

THE EQUATION ANALYSIS/PAINTING AND THE AESTHETICS OF THE REAL

Sic aequo geritur certamine principiorum
Ex infinito contractum tempore bellum.[1]

(Lucrezio, De rerum natura, II, 573–574)

The structure of experience, the secret of relation between subject and object, can be, for Nietzsche, at most 'an *aesthetic* relation ... a suggestive transference, a stammering translation into a completely foreign tongue' (1873, p. 58). Man is 'hanging in dreams on the back of a tiger' (ibid., p. 54), and every piece of knowledge is self deception and 'fiction'. Men's eyes 'merely glide over the surface of things and see "forms". Their senses nowhere lead to truth; on the contrary, they are content to receive stimuli and, as it were, to engage in a groping game on the backs of things' (ibid., p. 54). So, for Nietzsche, the lie – understood in an extra-moral sense, i.e. theoretically – means the complete oblivion of the metaphorical nucleus of language and of its poietic character. For Bion it is no different: the lie gives birth to the subject. It is not the Cartesian 'I think, therefore I am' but rather 'I lie, therefore I am'[2] (Grotstein, 1981b). Only false thoughts presuppose a thinker, whilst true thoughts already exist before him. How can we interpret this paradox?

The beauty of a rose

When a living organism becomes more complex and differentiates itself from the inorganic, it clashes with the real and has to fight to evolve. The subject continually needs to build itself up. This can only happen if it manages to *feed* on the real,[3] or find a point of balance between assimilation and accommodation, similarity and difference. Radicalizing Meltzer's original concept (Meltzer and Harris Williams, 1988) – which anyway is only a reformulation of some of Bion's surprising statements – we can define this struggle as an 'aesthetic conflict'. Thus the sensible roots (in Greek the word *aisthesis* means 'sensation') of (conceptual) thought are brought into the foreground, that is the fact that the various forms of experience are met aesthetically, in other words are both 'sensed' and 'invented' (Borutti, 2006). Appreciation of beauty and ugliness can be traced back to this conflict, insofar as it is the expression of H, L, K and links, which mark the *distance* from the real. 'The beauty of a rose – Bion writes – is a phenomenon betraying the ugliness of O just as ugliness betrays or reveals the existence of O' (1965, p. 140).

The aesthetic conflict is the *encounter/collision with the real*, reflected in the vicissitudes of the emotions and feelings that echo it. Pleasure is felt as something positive because it corresponds to everything that reconciles one with the real, annihilates conflict, restores a condition of harmony and for this is in relation with truth, 'O', God, the divine, Ultimate Reality, the thing in itself, infinity. Displeasure, on the other hand, is a synonym of difference, dissonance, constitution of identity, resistance and – in this sense – a lie. At their peak, both dissolve the subject[4] either in a nirvanic or ecstatic state of undifferentiated reality[5] or in the falsity of delusion and hallucination. From a position of absolute truth or reality, which is now no longer connected to the symbolic, these lead to an intolerable laceration with the real. Maximum differentiation thus corresponds to maximum alienation. To ex-ist, therefore, the individual must come out of/be other than a self-as-real that he actually continues to be part of, albeit at a different level of organization. That is he has to 'lie' whilst not distancing himself too much from the real he needs for his own self-poiesis.

From this paradoxical vertex 'true' thoughts move in the direction of the drive towards death, entropy, return to the quietude of the inorganic. False thoughts, intended as dissonant or fictitious, on the contrary, gain the vital gap of subjectivation. In the aesthetic conflict the α-elements are the product of the friction that O opposes to the person. The α-elements are reality-truth-beauty data assimilated in a way that is idiosyncratic to a person; *fake*, because personal, reality. That is to say, the thing-in-itself is caught subjectively. To think means creating subject-specific *carriers* to transfer and metabolise primitive sensory impressions and protoemotions. Each of them is a symbol, the way in which an individual gives shape (aesthetically) to experience. It is the necessary fiction, as in Heidegger's (1950) famous image of the vase, to surround the vacuum of the real. It is something that fills an absence, stands for something else, and is therefore *false*. It works on the basis of internal laws of relationships by similarity and difference.

In the ontological epistemology of Bion, the α function, like the imagination for Nietzsche, is the device for constructing symbols, or the 'lies' necessary for facing up to the real. Before becoming an internal function of the individual, the α function is the mother's reverie, which consists in a way of adapting the real of the mother-as-world to the needs of the child. This makes the aesthetic conflict tolerable. Thus the α function comes to be an essential variable in the opposition of meaning and being, between symbolisation and non-symbolisation, between the capacity and the incapacity to dream O, between living and avoiding emotions.[6]

Now, in explaining the transformations to which the α function gives rise, Bion takes art as a model. In doing so he gives us the basis of an aesthetic, i.e. a theory of the origin and meaning of aesthetic experience. In *Transformations*, he explicitly and systematically gives the equation analysis=painting. Art is viewed as the preferred device for meeting with and transforming the real. I quote:

> I shall therefore assume that the material provided by the analytic session is significant for its being the patient's view (representation) of certain facts which are the origin (O) of his reaction ... I shall understand what he says or does as if it were an artist's painting. In the session the facts of his behaviour are like the facts of a painting and from them I must find the nature of his representation ... I hope to discover from the invariants in this material what O is, what he *does* to transform O.
>
> (Bion, 1965, p. 15).

Later he continues (ibid., p. 32):

> The artist stimulates a reaction in his public by his representation of the subject of his painting … The problem is the transformation that issues in an end-product, Tβ, which communicates an *emotional* experience, such as the artist intends to produce, in the greatest number of the people in whom he intends to produce it. The components of Tβ in this class of transformation are: emotional experience, precision of communication, universality and durability.

The psycho-analyst tries to help the patient to transform that part of an emotional experience of which he is unconscious into an emotional experience of which he is conscious. If he does this he helps the patient to achieve private knowledge.

If the sense of art lies in the induction of a particular emotional experience, the medium is neutral, provided it has these characteristics: *effectiveness*, *precision*, *universality* and *durability*. Conceptual art, for instance, is no different in this than figurative art. An aesthetic object does not exist *per se* but only in the encounter with someone who appreciates it. To try to fix beauty in permanent universal canons is like claiming to know O – so to speak – beyond interpretation. But the essence of aesthetic (and psycho-analytical) emotion lies elsewhere. Bion writes:

> If the emotion stimulated in the recipient of the communication is a *representation* of the emotion stimulated by O in the artist we may regard the artist's intervention in the chain of events as one that does not stop at the disposal of patterns of pigment on canvas, but extends to the emotional state evoked in the individual, or group, and to giving durability to the power to evoke emotion.
>
> (Bion, 1965, p. 33)

He adds in a note, 'Strictly speaking the interpretation *draws attention* to an *existing* emotional state; *but it produces the emotional state of awareness of an emotional state*' (ibid., p. 34, italics are mine).

This is the point: from a fictional experience[7] (the colours on a canvas, for the painter; the regulated inter-subjective field of the setting, for the analyst) is born a real emotion, which has the stamp of irony, anti-realism and self-reflection. *Art and psychoanalysis both aim to deconstruct reality in order to approximate the real. In this way they render the subject aware of the unconscious lying on which it is based. This process, then, is adaptive for it produces psychic growth.* Putting it another way, it is a matter of realising that the context of experience, its 'framework', is an unavoidable part of the process towards meaning.

Meeting the tiger

But we can say that Bion's epistemology meets aesthetics on a much deeper level, when it emphasises the extension of thought into the field of the negative. Indeed, Bion asserts that primitive thinking, which anyway I would consider along a gradient originating in proto-sensations or proto-emotions and from the 'groping game' of 'autistic forms' (Ogden, 1989), is born from experiencing a no-longer existent object, or, in other words, 'from experiencing a place where we thought the object was but it isn't' or 'no-thing'. Then he assimilates 'the breast that isn't there' or 'no-thing' to the geometric point: 'I am assuming that points were originally the space that had been occupied by a feeling, but had become a 'no-feeling' or the space where a feeling used to be (Bion, 1965, p. 121).

Taken to extremes, therefore, the aesthetic conflict lived by the infant and described by Meltzer between being in reverence and awe while looking at mother's eyes and the painful doubt about the insincerity of her invisible-inner world, between presence/absence, breast/no-breast, resolves in contrasting and *more elementary* emotions between things/no-things, contact/no-contact, sensations/ no-sensations. Indeed it is a matter of *rhythm*. This becomes explicit when, further on, Bion takes up the aesthetic metaphor again for the umpteenth time:

> The investigation must be directed to the elucidation of point and line as elements imbedded in the material of transformations in the media of all arts and sciences. In the poem it may be found in the long-short of rhythm; in painting it may be found … in the matter from which the construct is formed.
>
> (Ibid., pp. 125–126)

In a similar way, in *Dot, Line and Surface* (Kandinsky, 1968) resolves the image in temporality.[8] And Bion continues (ibid., p. 138):

> various phenomena, such as the appearance of a beautiful object, are significant not because they are beautiful or good but because they serve to 'remind' the beholder of the beauty or the good which was once, but no longer is, known. This object, of which the phenomenon serves as a reminder, is a Form.

So if the subject can be born of nothing but a *sustainable lie* or *in a private truth*, even if it can be raised to a level of consensuality, it is essential that the encounter/collision with the real should take place at a good pace, with good rhythm. A good rhythm of correlation with reality gives the sensation that lies at the basis of every aesthetic pleasure. Therefore it always contains within itself, at the point where pre-conception meets realisation, an element of negativity. And it is precisely this component corresponding to the sense of the caducity of things that Meltzer considers inherent to aesthetic experience, and which is adumbrated in the Kleinian interpretation of art as a reparative activity.[9]

The concept of rhythm returns in the definition of 'invariant': 'the invariant under psycho-analysis is the ratio of no-thing to thing' (ibid., p. 103). And significantly

> The same is true of every form of expression: it is accepted that there must be rules that are to be obeyed in verbal communication, or music, or painting, if the transformation of O is to combine the invariants in such a way that communication with others is effectual. These rules must be such that the no-thing is adequately communicated by a proper combination of the invariants. A work of art should satisfy by a proper disposition of the invariants to O, the no-thing (· or ——) and Tβ.
>
> (Ibid., p. 102)[10]

From this vertex, in short, art can be defined as a passionate thinking about Time, the rhythm of being, 'O', and it is in itself *a joyous time*.

For Bion, therefore, the negative dimension (what in music is the caesura of the pause), is intrinsic to aesthetic emotion, from the most elementary experience of the presence of absence (no-thing) to the mature sentiment of the finitude of all things.

In his reading of Bion, even Grotstein overlaps α function, dream and 'aesthetic vertex', to indicate how a person can know O. The real can only be dreamed of: 'What we believe we experience is a "virtual reality"... *Aesthetic, perhaps the most satisfying of the vertices,* constitutes the organic, living, changing/unchanging template of O' (2007, pp. 124–125, italics are mine).

But a reality can be called virtual only if it depends on form. If the formless O cannot be grasped directly, as it is *out there*, but can only be dreamed, oscillating between 'horror and beauty', this means that every representation is pretence or fiction, 'seeing as if'. *It is the product, within an analogical and differential system, of aesthetic-rhetorical operations of the dream-work driven by pleasure and based on pre-structures which have been selected in the course of phylogenesis.*

Summing up (very provisionally) this quick excursion into Bion's aesthetics, we can state:

a) Art, like psychoanalysis is a privileged vertex from which to meet the real (O), in that it is based on intuitive appreciation[11] of sensible, i.e. aesthetically significant, forms.
b) This encounter can take place thanks to the α function or rather the dream-work α based on the principles enunciated by Freud (condensation, displacement, considerations of representability and secondary revision); principles which correspond with the rules of the functions of language (highlighted by Jakobson as metaphor and, principally, metonomy).
c) Dreaming of O means constructing unconscious lies/fictions which are necessary to the subject because they protect from the trauma of the real and make possible psychic birth and growth.
d) The pleasure one gets from aesthetic emotion can be traced back to a happy *rhythm* of correlation with O. This is why it encourages the living system/being to grow, but intrinsic to this is a negative dimension. In fact, aesthetic emotion is at the point of balance between pleasure and pain, where the individual realises that reality is illusory, all things are transient, and representation has its limits.
e) The framework of the setting in psychoanalysis and the framing of an aesthetic object (an invented/constructed object, not a natural one!), which is specifically achieved by the social practices of art, makes both into effective carriers for 'seeing oneself', for self-reflection or for *dreaming a dream about the dream of* O and thereby arriving at a paradoxical knowledge, in as a much that it is true but private (Magrelli 2002; Civitarese, 2005, 2006a, 2007).

f) The aesthetic object is the product of a Tβ transformation that, remaining unsaturated because of its open or ambiguous formal structure, functions as a preconception for later realisations.
g) Once all these conditions are satisfied, there is the final essential element of *surprise*, a *perceptive catastrophe*, which renews the miraculous feeling of pleasure every time the object reappears (along with the pain of its mysteriousness).

This is the very pleasure of thinking.[12] Therefore it can happen that in the 'equal strife among the elements' which is life, psychoanalysis and art represent a possible opening to Being (at-one-ment/*reconciliation)* and even if only stripes on its coat, they nevertheless sometimes manage – Bion's image (1975, p. 112) – to come across the '"Tiger" – The Thing Itself – O'. Putting it another way, they manage to inspire a feeling of faith in being able to give meaning to the real.

6

AESTHETIC CONFLICT AND THE α FUNCTION

> [D]as Schöne ist nichts/ als des Schrecklichen Anfang, den wir noch grade ertragen.
>
> (Rainer Maria Rilke, *Duineser Elegien*)

> He alone can appreciate the art, who could comprehend the conversation of the painter, and share in his emotion, in moments of his most fiery passion and most original thought.
>
> (John Ruskin, *Modern Painters* (1843))

'In the beginning was the aesthetic object and the aesthetic object was the breast and the breast was the world': this is the 'new idea' that Meltzer (1986, p. 204) on his own admission borrowed from Bion when coining the concept of aesthetic conflict. At birth the child feels irresistibly attracted by the external beauty of the mother. However, it is also perturbed because it does not know what is hidden behind appearances; it senses that beyond what it sees she has an inner space that is opaque and inaccessible to it. For this reason it doubts the goodness of the contents she harbours in her inner world, and it sees the looming shadow of abandonment. Meltzer took this notion as the basis for a new conception of aesthetic experience that was already contained in embryonic form in his 1963 essay, 'On the social basis of art'. In this reprint of a dialogue with the writer and art critic Adrian Stokes,[1] he makes a comparison between sexual intercourse and the contemplation of art, commenting that there is a difference between masturbatory sex with a random partner and sex where contact with one's inner self is central, that is, if it is also an act of love. In short, he sees the quality of the aesthetic experience in adulthood, and also (more or less between the lines) the quality of emotional relationships as depending on the transference of the original aesthetic conflict:

> The viewing of art is an expression particularly linked to this component of the breast situation, that is, the feeling of looking and listening to the events going on inside the mother, of seeing either the intactness of her inner world, or conversely, of seeing the destruction that has been wrought there. It means an experience of allowing, in the first case, the introjecting of this goodness and intactness and, in the second case, exposing oneself to having destruction projected into one.
>
> (Meltzer, 1988 [1963], Kindle edition, locations 3958–3962)

Ten years after his first insights into the meaning of aesthetics, in 'On the apprehension of beauty' Meltzer attempted to put his theory on a firmer footing by tightening its relationship with clinical practice, developing further what had been sketchy in the previous text:

> I noticed that whereas the more healthy of my patients recognize beauty as a *donné* without uncertainty through a powerful emotional reaction, the more ill were very dependent upon social cues, formal qualities and intellectual criteria. Often their judgement appeared sound, and in some instances even served as the basis for successful careers where aesthetic judgement was quite central. Nonetheless it was clear that, due to the lack of direct and immediate emotional response, they were deprived both of the confidence in their judgement and of sincerity in their interest.
>
> (Meltzer, 1973, p. 225)

He adds: 'An experience of the apprehension of beauty has been split into its joyous and terrifying components parts' (ibid., p. 228). So, basing himself on vignettes involving two of his patients, he concludes: 'The apprehension of beauty contains in its very nature the apprehension of the possibility of its destruction. In Bion's terms, the present object is seen to contain the shadow of the absent-object-present-as-a-persecutor' (ibid., p. 229).

Meltzer returns to the subject in several other essays and at more length in a 1988 book written together with Harris Williams, *The Apprehension of Beauty*, which contains the 1973 article as the first chapter and in the appendix the paper written twenty-five years earlier. This brief account immediately shows that the aesthetic theme was central to the thinking of one of the most creative writers in the history of psychoanalysis.

For Meltzer, the way in which the subject has lived and relived the aesthetic conflict affects his ability to be moved by artistic beauty and in general to feel authentic emotions. If tolerated, the terror of uncertainty about the intentions of the mother stimulates mental growth and creativity and is transformed into a calm feeling of compassion in the face of the transience of human life and of all things. Indeed, we are not moved by beauty in itself but by its fragility, what at the most basic level we might call, using the language of Bion, by the 'no-breast' or, better, the 'no-thing', that is, the point-like perception of the absence of the object that gives rise to thought. Conversely, a person may lack aesthetic sense when the anguish caused by the difficulty of enduring the constitutive ambiguity of the object appears immediately and has a paralyzing effect; and, as we know, ambiguity is an essential element of any work of art. Failing to sufficiently integrate the emotional ambivalence that comes from this ambiguity means exposing oneself to potentially overwhelming emotions. Cancelling them, however, deprives the subject of the lifeblood of motivation and knowledge they bring with them.

In borderline patients, for example, the aesthetic conflict may take the malignant form of an aggressive negative therapeutic reaction and may follow an eroticized transference. Ecstasy and terror, which at the beginning of life were experienced simultaneously in the presence of the mother, are played out in two consecutive phases. These two phases are marked by opposite transferences and sometimes they follow one another rapidly and violently without passing through any spaces of transition. Criticisms expressed in an intensely paranoid atmosphere give way to harrowing manifestations of attachment, and later to requests for concrete rewards, and then the whole cycle starts up again. Not having an interior room spacious enough to contain overly intense emotions, the patient evacuates them and ends up poisoning the ties that should nourish him. He reverses the perspective he has on things in a static and absolute way. Each time there is a shift from idealization to denigration and vice versa. Continuing to present one side and then the other, both of which lack depth, he gives the impression of functioning in a two-dimensional way. Emotions are expelled or split off but not transformed into thought.

This pattern of brusque alternation appears as repetition on the analytic stage, precipitated by the extreme meaning that moments of encounter and separation, turbulences that marked the construction of the ego at its origin, have for the patient; just like the consequence of the traumatic imprint left by a failure to hold and an incapacity for reverie on the part of the mother (in the sense of caregiver) in the early stages of life. The child was not sufficiently reflected in her face to receive the confirmations required to become better integrated. Early vicissitudes remain in residual form as a great difficulty in tolerating frustration and basic insecurity about the other's ability to transform his states of anxiety. If, as Winnicott writes (1947), the end of the session expresses the analyst's healthy hatred, in these situations this hatred is felt as particularly hard to bear. The analyst's inevitable errors can take on the meaning of rejection.

The effects of an unresolved aesthetic conflict, however, not only manifest themselves in borderline and psychotic patients but also in neurotic patients and, as a character trait, in normal people. And, although to varying degrees, the emotional life of all of these can run dry. For example, as a way of protecting himself from aesthetic conflict, an intelligent person, someone who has not suffered more severe traumas, may turn to abstract thought rather than regressive defences. He 'cools down' his sensitivity and tends in life in general towards aestheticization. He tends, that is, to give what others see as excessive importance to the outward form of things. One senses that in this way he erects a barrier between himself and the others so as not to get too deeply involved in relationships. He cannot afford to feel 'warm' emotions because he would experience them as voltage spikes that might burn through a thin wire. So he switches off the 'electricity' and transforms the object into something inanimate. He only admires its surface quality. He makes it into a fetish, but does not love it. Rather, as in perversion, he uses it (in the case of a work of art, he feels gratified by its possession, and appreciates it most of all for its economic value). He pays a price for this: he feels a chronic feeling of emptiness and at the same time falls under its spell; he lives in a world that is not fully human, that is sterile and colourless; he feels numb. As in hypochondria the exclusive focus on the sensations of the body is an attempt to regain an adequate perception of psychical qualities (Bion, 1962), so in the compulsion to seek beauty and in the obsession with aesthetic judgment (which may also express itself in a career choice) he seeks to recapture the vital impulse of the emotions. This is ultimately the only way he can attribute a personal meaning to existence.

Abjection

Useful as it may be, the concept of aesthetic conflict presupposes a mind-body dualism (Sweetnam, 2007) which limits its heuristic scope. For this reason I suggest enhancing it with the concept of abjection. With her concept of abjection, Kristeva (1980)[2] arguably went even further than Meltzer in delineating the meaning of the more impenetrable and threatening side of the aesthetic conflict since she focused primarily on its sensory, bodily and pre-object dimension. I mention this here because it goes in the direction of 'backdating' the aesthetic conflict, a move I regard as essential if we are to come closer to a psychoanalytic theory of the aesthetic experience in art. Also for Kristeva, in fact, the 'nuclear' aesthetic conflict comes out not only on the more advanced level of what in Meltzer's original definition is rendered as the opposition between visible and non-visible, where it is assumed that the child perceives the mother as separate, but also on the most basic level of the process of constructing subjectivity *prior* to the development of the ego.

Abject means despicable, disgusting, contemptible, degraded, thrown away, and the word is used to talk about things that cause nausea, disgust, revulsion. For Kristeva, the feeling of abjection obscurely preserves something of what, on an archaic level in the relationship with the pre-object mother, was felt by a body that was separating violently from another body ('self-birth'). Abjection, that is to say, refers to the stage of individual development in which the child was neither subject nor object, neither totally other nor yet itself. At the primary narcissistic stage in between being and no longer being part of the body of the mother, the subject can only be born as such by being 'vomited', by being rejected and made contemptible. It is as if the infant first had to kill the part from which it was being separated and thus reduce it to the same condition as hair, nails and faeces.

Because of this state of being somewhere between the human and the inhuman, what later in adult life is typically re-experienced as abject takes the form of an organic fluid, vomit, pus, sweat, an open wound, and in its extreme form, the corpse or part of it; something that *was* but is no longer human, something both familiar and disturbing. All these elements bring us back mysteriously to that old experience. But following on from this, in Kristeva's theory the prototype of the abject can only be the mother's body, insofar as it is experienced as what one belonged to before *ex-isting*, before an ego was formed and one had access to the symbolic order, to the order of language and a separate identity.

The category of abjection marks the border beyond which the subject feels threatened because it comes into contact with impure elements, both material and spiritual. Sensitivity to the abject, and also to what is morally abject and which we must defend ourselves against, is essential for mental health. Without it, if one comes too close to the abject, one falls in turn into abjection, as signalled by the feeling of shame, which is both a defensive device similar to physical repugnance and a symptom of abjection as a condition of unhappiness.

Later on in individual development, and without there being loss of contact with the more undifferentiated sensory and bodily experiences – as demonstrated by our literally visceral reactions when faced with shocking situations – abjection becomes a moral condition. Abjection is when one has the sensation of living in a state of degradation, dishonour, humiliation, shame. The feeling of shame, which is a social feeling, refers to the other and to the feeling of not being recognized, of no longer being fully human or socially accepted, and therefore to a blurring of the usual distinctions between self and other, subject and object, human being and thing that structure experience – of course along a infinitely variable scale of intensity. In short, it is a sensitive index of narcissistic balance. Shame, that is, can be seen as a fever that signals to the subject a problem of distance from the object – too far away (when you 'die' too much for the other) or too close (when you 'die' by merging with the other).

Kristeva's concept not only has obvious affinities with the concept of aesthetic conflict (whereby the part played by the human body is less convincing), but also with Freud's concept of the uncanny (*unheimlich*): that which has been made abject may recur with the 'massive, abrupt eruption of something uncanny which may have been familiar in an obscure, forgotten past but now assails me as radically repugnant and other' (Kristeva, 1980, p. 2). Abjection, however, precedes repression, which is a symbolic mechanism that requires a pre-formed ego and a reflective consciousness, and can thus be regarded as *primal repression.*

It is significant that all three of these concepts are audacious attempts to penetrate the mystery of the aesthetic experience. The body of the mother as an abject and alien monstrosity, for example, is what we are shown with obsessive regularity in particular in horror films, including today's versions of the Sadean universe; and it is no accident that art, whether low- or high-brow, tends in one way or another to purify abjection; because it is impossible to rid oneself completely of the abject, all one can do is push it beyond borders, laws and taboos. Every time the abject rises up again, the feeling namely of being sucked into the deadly embrace of the black and powerful mother of our origins towards the non-being of the indistinct, being present at something that is reminiscent of the sharp cut of separation, at the place where the drama of the violent definition of the boundaries of self is played out. In fact, the abject does not only provoke a sense of horror, but also something closer to erotic attraction: abjection is a liminal space.

This is why Kristeva sees a link between abjection and aesthetic experience. The abject disrupts any kind of border, order, identity, system, margin. It is the trauma of being exposed to one's own death through the death of another, but through the minimal metonymy of insignificant bodily productions. Poetry and art in general, however, purify the abject: by immersing themselves in it they break all the rules of language, they reveal the arbitrariness of language and, finally, they first undermine it and then find meaning in the very place where the opposition between self and other becomes blurred.

The spectre of beauty

Luca is doing a doctorate in sociology; he is about thirty years old and has been doing four sessions of analysis a week for two years. He started therapy because he felt he was no longer capable of having a love life. He is always gloomy and angry for no apparent reason; he doesn't work or study for fear of being judged by others. He is afraid of disappointing people and being overwhelmed by a sense of shame; in essence he is afraid of seeing himself and being seen by others as 'ugly'.[3] Despite this, during the period when the sessions I talk about below were held, he met a girl on the Internet, Sara. The city where she lives is far away. At some point she confides to him that she has a tumour. *Immediately after this*, his emotional involvement becomes inexplicably violent, even though she is nothing more than a voice at the other end of the phone and a collection of (beautiful) photographs.

Thursday. A week before the beginning of the summer holidays

Luca sinks on to the couch. He has a face like thunder and he looks like he is doing battle with a set of distressing thoughts. Only after several minutes of silence does he calm down, like a child held in his mother's arms. Then he sighs a couple of times, and it seems he can only speak when I prompt him: if I make some inarticulate noise or change posture he takes it to mean that I am ready to listen to him. This same pattern of interaction is repeated at almost every session, and I think to myself that this could express his need to re-form a symbiotic bond with the object by snuggling into the 'womb' of the setting (Winnicott, 1956).

'As a child I used to spend long hours talking to my mother, it was as if we were in a state of fusion. I worshipped her. And then sometimes she would suddenly turn to ice. Other times, she would become the exact opposite. As high as it was possible to go, and as low. And there was no reason for any of it. The better I seemed to communicate, the more I moved towards a total inability to communicate. For me it is the experience of madness. Because whatever I say has absolutely no effect. I have no more words. I have no tools. And it is a feeling of death. At moments like this I feel as though I am dying. I feel as if I am moving from an ideal situation to being expelled. Such a strong, Manichaean vision is something terrible. The greatest pleasure turns into the greatest pain without any gradation, without any *intermediate steps*, because everything is a construct of the mind. If only I could see someone for what she really is, what she is really like … In the last few weeks I have become more and more isolated … And when I feel bad, time expands incredibly. Yesterday I told myself that I have to get out of this sociopathic predicament.'

Listening to Luca speak, I feel a certain amount of attention awakening in me and some reflections by Meltzer about aesthetic conflict that I read recently come to mind. For some time, in fact, I have been interested in this topic, and I am struck by the fact that what Luca says chimes in remarkably with Meltzer's descriptions: the relationship with the breast-mother as ecstatic adoration, religious awe, and fear/desire of fusion. The mother's enigmatic icy mood, which prefigures the loss of the mother and which reflects the dichotomy between the internal and the external, and between the visible and the invisible ('If I could see … what she really is…'); the unavailability of a transitional area (Winnicott also talks about a third area) between opposite emotional states, and thus of a mental space up to the task of withstanding change; the spatial symbolization (high/low) of the intermittence of the relationship, which suggests a dramatic oscillation between ecstasy and abjection; the conflict between pleasure and pain; consciousness of the 'sociopathy' of the relationship, which leads to an absolute and paranoid ('Manichaean') view of reality; isolation as a defence; the expansion of lived time; the fear of going crazy, and finally, the feeling of dying.

The fact is, I realize, that Luca has brought me back from my semi-stupor to a state of mental concentration and curiosity.

Saturday

It's Saturday afternoon and I'm at home. I hear the phone ringing, and when I look at the display I see his name. Somewhat surprized, I answer the phone, but nobody speaks at the other end. For a few seconds, however, the connection remains open and in the background I hear a hum of voices, like people gathered in a crowded place. I am a little troubled. I know that he is going through a difficult period, but I doubt he would call me just to hear my voice. It must have been an accident, perhaps a parapraxis, I conclude, and I try to remember what we were talking about the last time we met, on Thursday. Then I am reminded of the scene (a kind of cinematic topos) of the serial killer who calls his victims on the phone but never says a word. I had seen a similar scene not long before in a film entitled *When a Stranger Calls* (Simon West, 2006).

I imagine that in the void of the weekend Luca felt unconsciously impelled to make contact. Maybe he found himself too alone and having to cope with the 'experience of madness' and 'sociopathy' he had spoken to me about recently. I take mental note of the appearance of this disturbing character in the field or analytic third that unites us, not only in the consulting room but also at a distance (Ogden, 1997).

I wonder who the author was and I conjecture that he might stand for 'unknown' and potentially destructive emotions. As far as I know, they may belong to him, but also to me, or both of us (and I also think I'm going to have to keep these three points of view in a state of tension with each other).

Monday

'Oh, by the way, you haven't said when the holidays will be': these are his first words. I am pretty sure I had, Thursday this week, but I apologize and tell him again. 'That's all I needed!' he exclaims, 'Now that I'm *split in two* … Do you remember that the whole story with Sara began in a moment of solitude? Then it turned into a game. Then came the twist in the plot. The boyfriend I had imagined was the reason for her reticence was in fact a tumour that had come back after two years, after it seemed she had got over it, after chemo- and radiotherapy! The 'boyfriend' is death … Have you read Kleist's letters to his fiancée? Do you remember the part where he tells her he has found someone to die with? I fantasized a *birth in reverse*, a return to nothingness. I thought I had everything under control, that I could avoid all the unpleasant things of life.'

It is a sad story, I comment, the only thing you can do is help her as much as you can, be close to her. Then I think of the woman/girlfriend who dies repeatedly, like the mother who is dead because she is unknowable and/or insincere, and whom he carries within him. And I add that, nonetheless, the Kleist fantasy is a bit like constantly telling me about the mother who would turn to 'ice' in an instant and then he too 'died' together with her, and I wonder if that's what it is, that he was attracted to Sara because of her illness. I stop speaking, and my intention is to explore other possible meanings of what is going on with him, but then I realize that what I have been telling him is not true because it is not in harmony with his state of mind and is inappropriate to the situation. It is as if I had had to distance myself from something too distressing precisely at the moment when I'm about to go away and really scary phantasms are coming towards me. It seems to me quite clear now, in fact, that I have said something insensitive, perhaps merely the product of my intellectual sensibility, driven mostly by my theoretical interest; for a moment I realize I have misplaced the potential meaning of the mother, of 'Sara', of the boyfriend, etc.., as characters of the analytic field (Ferro, 2002a, 2006), that is, as possible carriers of the transference. In terms of 'therapy of the field,' Luca's answer could not be have been more explicit: '*I want to heal her!*' he says.

I am struck by this phrase, and I think it also relates to me (again, in Italian 'her' could also be 'you') and his need to 'heal me' of my transitional state of emotional closure towards him. I try to collect my thoughts. Luca says he feels split between bliss and coldness, just like his perception of his mother: lively and deadly, charming and Medusa-like. There is duality in the fantasy of the double suicide, death as the cancelling of all tension and the unconscious fantasy of regeneration and rebirth as a couple that will remain forever indivisible.[4] The analysis that supports him is also double, or ambivalent; and then, when he needs it most, it drops him: the analyst who departs ('parto' in Italian means both 'birth' and 'I depart/go away'; there is also an allusion to the absence of the object and the trauma of separation) and dies on him again every summer, just like the mother who, so to speak, was unable to dream him.[5] Then, finally, there is duality in the sense of something inauthentic or 'false', the 'technical' awakening of my curiosity about him at this point in the therapy. Over the years, I think to myself, taking refuge again in the reassuring world of history and material reality, Luca has sent away many possible 'girlfriends' – several relationships aborted or 'suicided' at birth – and somehow I connect this fact to the touch of aestheticization of death I sense in his reference to Kleist. The association may seem superficial, but actually it touches the deepest core of a conflict that, according to Meltzer, can be called 'aesthetic'.

The relationship with the mother was very tormented, both because the infant had initial problems with feeding and growing steadily, and because the mother also had to look after a younger sister. In retrospect, one can see that this must have been experienced as an unexpected succession of moments of heat and moments of frost. The resulting need for contact must have been, and continues to be, so intense and absolute that the slightest crack quickly turns an ally into an enemy, love into hate, beauty into death. Later, intelligence came to the rescue to drain the swamp of feelings, and a certain partial inversion of the α function left him with a set of convictions that are like Lego pieces left standing after demolition (the image is Meltzer's). Despite his sophisticated ability to make a case for them, these convictions are so uncritical that they are akin to transformations in hallucinosis; one such is the belief that women (the analyst, everybody) are 'objectively' the way they are (that is, unreliable).

But while these things are going through my mind, a distant memory returns. Years ago I once asked a friend for advice about a personal problem, but she didn't listen to me the way I expected her to. I had not felt welcomed or acknowledged. I can see that the re-emergence of this memory gives me an unexpected clue to understanding something of my lively experience in the session with Luca and my altogether rather aloof attitude. I conjecture that it could also be the sign of repetition in the transference of something similar that he experienced with his mother in his past and that he is reliving with Sara during this period in his life. Obviously, I do not see this fragment of my personal life story as a pure countertransference reaction and even less as a mere association, but rather, in line with an intersubjective model, as a reverie or a factor in the analytic field, a construction in which both members of the analytic pair participate unconsciously (Ogden, 2001). I remember that in order to emerge gradually from the grey atmosphere that had been created in my relationship with my friend, I had had to go through a slow process of emotional work.

The memory of that episode, which I had suffered directly, now appears as a slightly painful but authentic way of tuning in to the insincerity Luca suspects in his mother, in me, and in women, and ultimately in everyone else; at this point, it also appears as a way of experiencing the truth of the concept of aesthetic conflict, the focus around which my interest in Luca had awakened, not just 'in my head' but also inwardly. What I had suffered then as a result of an episode altogether insignificant, when compared with the problems Luca faces, resurfaces in the context of the sessions as a kind of unconscious work. The purpose of this work is to solve the problem of this relationship in the present, namely how to get back in tune with him; more generally, the goal is to enhance his ability to think; or, to use Bion's concept of container/contained, to make richer and more complex his mental contents and to make the container bigger and more elastic. As Ogden (2005) points out, both these terms are to be regarded as processes.

This work, which can be described in general as the ability to dream or in this particular case as reverie, gives me the opportunity to switch from routine listening to a more empathetic kind of listening. It is the expression of a personal change experienced there and then with the patient and now suffused with emotion. In other words, inside me the split between intellect and emotion that Luca suffers from has been temporarily repaired (but one could also say, the split between surface and depth, or between content and form, between the symbolic and the semiotic), and on the basis of the concept of aesthetic conflict this can be seen as a defence against the unbearable ambiguity of the object. In the light of this interactive sequence, the interpretation that I gave him and which left him deeply unsatisfied appears to me *a posteriori* as dictated by a sense of necessity.

On the one hand, it is the virus that infects the field but which at the same time also represents a prerequisite for the therapy; on the other, its defensive meaning appears clear to me. I may have withdrawn from the relationship, I realize, and made myself less permeable to what the patient was saying to me because I was overwhelmed by a burden of responsibility that right now is difficult for me to endure. All the while I continued thinking about Sara, his mother and Sara's boyfriend as real figures and not even as dream characters of the session. For example, could the 'girlfriends' he always rejected stand for the aborted occasions of contact in the analysis? Were the figures of Meltzer and Kleist derivatives in the analytic field of an unconscious collusive pact based on intellectual accord and mutual admiration?

At this point I have the impression that something valuable for the analysis has happened, as occurs at those happy moments when I rediscover the profound sense of beauty of the method invented by Freud and I feel gratitude for its having made my life fuller. Reinvestment in theory, analytic technique and patient go hand in hand; I re-discover the inner motivation to do this work and I find my way out of a sense of routine that inevitably over time tends to level out meaning. Instead, completely by surprize, things regain meaning, harmony, perfection. How else can this experience be described if not as 'aesthetic'?[6]

Wednesday – penultimate session before the holidays

His first words are: 'Yesterday you almost lost a patient. I say that just for the record. I was driving with my mother in the car. I ended up on the wrong side of the road. I almost landed in a field. I heard her scream. She was terrified. I managed to get back on to the right side of the road just in time. Only later that evening did she say to me: 'Do you realize what you did?'. No, it's not that I didn't realize! It's just that I almost fell asleep.'

And I think rather sorrowfully that *this incident was almost like a double suicide*, and how any failure in tuning or recognition in the session can represent a 'double suicide', and also that he may have sensed something of my 'terror'. 'It happens to me sometimes,' he says in an almost euphoric a tone of voice, 'that I pass from a reflective, meditative state, from a moment of high concentration to sleep …'. I associate falling asleep with the 'absent-mindedness' that had produced the strange phone call, which I now see as a cry for help. *I tell him what happened, and ask him if he had by any chance tried to get in touch with me on Saturday*. 'But … that's incredible,' he says, 'this thing with the mobile on Saturday, because … you are not the first.'

Of course, he is referring to the list of names in the phonebook on his mobile phone, but I seize the opportunity and, infected by his light-hearted mood, I reply: 'SO I'M NOT THE FIRST?'. Luca replies, seriously: 'NO.' 'Ah … so I'm not the first …'. Then he grasps the play on words, smiles, and a moment later the field 'breathes' and returns to the level of play. '*No, there is a woman before you!*', he resumes (and it's almost like he's giving me a lesson on transference!). And I reply: 'Oh'. 'Really weird,' he says, 'because I always put on the *lock*. But I agree with my unconscious, of course. It could not have chosen a more appropriate person.'

He tells me he was attending a university conference on sexuality, where he met a girl who had approached him in a very seductive way but whom he had coldly turned away. He had explained to her, among other things, that he regarded cultural relativism as the cancer of knowledge. He adds that this is what always happens to him, and that for some time now he has stopped being able to view sex as detached from feelings, that he is no longer able to let himself go, and that in recent years he had broken off many possible relationships because every time there was 'something imperfect'. But then, unexpectedly, along came Sara. At first it was just like a game but then it gradually became something serious, especially after he learned about her disease. At first, *the deciding factor was her beauty*. He has always had, he explains, the fantasy of saving 'a beautiful girl in distress', and that for him this is a test that presents him with many obstacles '*because her extraordinary beauty makes me uncertain*', but that he has to face her and that in the end there will be a great prize. He feels '*irresistibly attracted*' to this thing. 'It's possible to truly get in touch with someone, though, and to overcome the obstacle,' he concludes, 'And then you're where no one else can ever have been because *you have gone beyond appearances, beyond outer beauty*. BUT STILL THERE IS ALWAYS THE SPECTRE OF SUPERLATIVE BEAUTY'.

Thursday – the last session before the holidays

'I could have done without that now ... the end of the analysis. I have to resolve this thing inside me, or else I'll go mad. I have got myself into an amazing situation, and I don't know what I'm trying to get out of it. She's dying.' I ask him how Sara is, if there have been any developments. 'She mentioned something ...,' Luca says, 'but then she didn't go into it any further, although she has given me to understand that there is little hope. All in the space of a few days. It's all so random, and the whole thing has become something immense. I could easily be haunted by a *ghost* for many years to come. And even if she survives, she's got a *horrible* journey ahead of her. The other day I was almost on the point of killing myself, because *I can't sleep* properly. It's the same with her, she sleeps at most two hours a night, what with all the pain. Sometimes, when she speaks ... Yesterday she said a month, two months, three months ... I find myself – against all logic, against all common sense – investing in something that was completely wrong from the start. Before she enters the final phase we want at least to say hello to each other in person. For me, he told me, *her* death will be the beginning of something new [*for the first time since starting the analysis he breaks down in tears*] Well ... it serves me right.'

I give a hint of an interrogative look. '*I let myself go*,' he replies. 'It's just that people who are not used to letting themselves go always do it at the wrong time and with the wrong person ... I can no longer distance myself from things. I have entered the deep pain of grief and it's eating me up inside ... The amazing thing is that she is worried about me ... It could take me days to explain why I was suddenly so impressed by her. AND IT'S ALL PERFECT. ALL SO PERFECT, IF IT WEREN'T FOR THE FACT THAT SHE IS GOING TO

DIE, a punishment! Like a tortoise that after years puts its head out only to have it cut off at one fell swoop. And all she does is to thank me and tell me that, even if it's the end of life, in me she has found the person she had been looking for. And if she has to go, she's going to go happy. She has this distant look, and she makes me see this elsewhere that is really distressing. IT IS THE VOID.'

Fading

I have recounted a fragment of Luca's analysis not only because I think that it can be interpreted in terms of the concept of aesthetic conflict (and, after that, of abjection), but also because on the one hand it confirms its heuristic character, and on the other can serve as a starting point for highlighting its limits. Of course, this clinical material is also an expression of more advanced conflicts. Psychic development unfolds on various levels and obviously these different levels interact and overlap. In my comment on the Thursday session I listed a number of things that prompted me to prefer the perspective offered by Meltzer's theory. I do not intend to go over them again here, but there are other indications of a basic narcissistic transference (Godfrind, 1993): Luca has completely given up the prospect of having a love life; when he does try to overcome this block, he binds himself specifically to a woman under real threat of death; his reaction to the episode is so unrealistic as to suggest, as a possible key to understanding, Green's concept (1983, p. 155) of the 'affective hallucination of the dead mother'; he experiences the approaching separation from the analysis for the holidays as extraordinarily painful, as if it stirred up the 'undifferentiated and non-solved parts of the primitive symbiotic links', the part of the personality that acts as a 'frame' for the ego (Bleger, 1967a, p. 514).

My hypothesis is that he relives in the transference a relationship with a maternal object felt to be dead and a bearer of death. The idea of the double suicide originates from the fantasy of denying any separation and reaching a point of absolute oneness with the object. Such extreme intolerance of separation leads me to think that there is a fundamental wound, a gap in his feeling of self-continuity, an emptiness at the heart of the primitive constitution of his subjectivity – all this, however, in a person who in other areas is mature and fully grown. My reverie of the killer in the film and my personal memory also point in this direction, because both evoke situations of death, either physical or mental. What I see as equally important is, on the one hand, the insistence on the beauty of the object, which is reminiscent not only of the concept of aesthetic conflict, but also of Tustin's 'unbearable ecstasy of at-one-ment' (Mitrani, 1998), and on the other, the emphasis on flaws that are inevitably present. In its almost obsessive quality, this insistence takes on meanings that go beyond the Oedipal plane. This, in my opinion, is true of the tug of war with death that Luca engages in through his relationship with Sara, and the fantasy of the body-corpse of the mother.

One might ask how clinical practice may help us realize that a patient is above all reliving memories, evidently implicit memories, of these first stages of life. My impression is that these primordial memories re-emerge in the various rhythms of the analysis as a kind of aesthetics of the relationship, albeit under the guise of apparently more mature conflicts. For example, they come out in the way in which the patient uses the analyst in the transference and in particular in the way he experiences the 'institutional' aspects of the setting, those aspects that go to define the deepest and most silent layers of identity.

To take the theoretical perspective that I find most useful for an understanding of what happens in the therapeutic relationship, the central theme of this vignette is the *fading* ('*fade-out*') of the object, to use an evocative expression introduced by Barthes in one of the entries to *A Lover's Discourse: Fragments* (1977) (and also in *Le discours amoureux. Séminaire à l'École des hautes études*, 2007). With this term the French writer indicates the critical moment when the lover feels his desire for the object of his love fade. It is not a voluntary turning away, a betrayal, which would give rise to a clearly Oedipal jealousy. It is rather an emptying, a fainting, for example, into depression ('It is mourning for an object which is itself in mourning' (ibid., p. 163). The mirror mists over, the gaze of the other stops reflecting. The subject sees its desire for the desire of the other frustrated, that 'desire' that Hegel (1807) sees as the foundation of recognition and thus of self-consciousness.

The context of the vignette is dramatic, but the analyst has a duty not to lose sight of the specific nature of his listening and to keep to the objective of attuning himself to the analysand's unconscious communications, and not only to understand him on the level of instinctive human sympathy. The concrete prospect of the interruption of the analysis for the summer, my being away in the sense of being absent-minded, as if I were already elsewhere ('on vacation') in my mind, and therefore my diminished receptivity and capacity for reverie make Luca go through an experience of *fading*. He relives his original illness, his reason for requesting the analysis, both in his relationship with Sara and in the disease ('cancer') of the analytic field. If I want to get back to being truly present and alive as an analyst, I must first lose and then retrieve a view of the facts of the session from the perspective of the dream of the session or of its transformation into dream (Ferro, 2009), and go through an intimate elaboration which is at one and the same time conscious, preconscious and unconscious.

The memory-reverie of the scene from the film, which in the context of this clinical vignette takes on the meaning of a sort of overture – and it is the feeling of strangeness-killer that appears unexpectedly when Luca senses that the other is moving away – and then that of the episode of misunderstanding with my friend lead me to relive the emotions of the past, when on a smaller scale I suffered the same disappointment at not feeling more invested by the other's desire and consequently mortified. Since, however, these emotions are 'in unison' with the patient's mental state – to which I myself have contributed – we can regard them as coming from a double unconscious identification, so to speak, with the killer and the victim, and leading to a transformation of my emotional state in the session. At this point Luca responds symmetrically to my 'aesthetic' experience, starts to 'feel' again, manages to *go beyond beauty reduced to aesthetic judgment*, and can weep for an old pain that he has always hidden beneath layers of intelligence, cold sensitivity and clear-headed but inconsolable irony. Luca's intelligence has led him to choose aestheticization as a way of safeguarding himself against emotions. In order to be able to keep the bond with the object at a manageable level, he has exaggerated the value of beauty, and emptied it of its deepest meaning. In short, he has deprived himself of the capacity to love.

So when he says 'I cannot let myself go', he is expressing in a condensed and nicely ambiguous way the idea that really it is not the others who are letting him go, but he himself, and at the same time he admits he does not want to do so, that he is struggling against his illness. It is as if he were saying: 'I cannot let myself be involved in an intimate relationship with a woman because I would immediately let myself go.' Any decision, therefore, is taken earlier, at the very moment he gets involved in an emotional bond. The eclipse of the object is already inexorably foreshadowed by the act of giving up his defences, which, whatever the cost, is something he cannot risk. In numerous paintings by classic artists, beauty and the spectre of death go hand in hand; likewise, in his mind so too do attraction and loss. In these sessions, however, a transformation occurs. Luca can be moved, and he goes from 'I cannot let myself go' to 'I let myself go'.

In telling the story of the conference he re-dreams – as it were, *live* – what we are experiencing as something that surprizes us, but which for this reason he also experiences as an insidious attempt at seduction. So Luca 'films' – again, live – my intervention designed to lighten the emotional atmosphere – when I ask him with a hint of humour, 'So I wasn't the first?', and does not trust me. For him, investing in another woman (in the analytic relationship, another person) after the first (the mother) is a pernicious form of cultural relativism (to be translated, of course, as a mournful relativity of emotions) that amounts to a 'cancer' (his girlfriend, any girlfriend, as a vital risk). The tumour is the ice-mother as an internal object, and any other relationship is a metastasis. Luca laughs at sociologists, at himself, and their claim to make sense of the irrationality of passion through logic. And the fact that it really is a cancer is confirmed rather than denied by the attempt at control and the distancing from emotions which is the source of the veneer of irony with which he covers things. If he let himself be seduced, this would correspond to perceiving something vital in the analyst; it would amount to accepting the invitation to engage in greater emotional intimacy, to dare to experience the excitement that would make him feel alive but that would be acceptable only after sufficient experiences of being calmed down and contained.

Luca, one can conjecture, suffers a breakdown that's already happened and continues to happen and which he projects into the future; it is the deathbed expression 'I feel that I am dying' (Winnicott, 1974) or Bion's 'nameless terror' (Bion, 1962). However, after this period when he relived the aesthetic conflict at its height, both with Sara and in the transference, it is as if he were now better able to tolerate his mourning for the transience of the object and of all things, and, finally, to realize that there is someone who cares for him and keeps him in mind. At least this unrepresentable old state of extreme pain akin to the agony of death (what he calls 'the void') can now be staged and retold. For this reason, in the economy of these sessions, I would read the near accident and the character of the tortoise that sticks its head out of the shell only to be beheaded in the same way as Quinodoz (2001) reads what he calls the 'dreams that turn over a page', that is, as a dramatic depiction of self and of the conflict that seemingly falls outside time, with a time lag, after a process that has evolved but which precisely for this reason indicates a new capacity to give meaning to what had previously not been thinkable.

The analysis is giving Luca the opportunity (not totally risk-free) of re-living the original catastrophe of his life, the trauma of the irresistible and chilling beauty of the mother in a protected area, within the supportive framework of the setting and the rhythm of our sessions (but also thanks to their arrhythmias, such as my distraction, a kind of extrasystole of the relationship). The more alive the wound caused by the *fading* of the object, the more it is necessary to emphasize its beauty and imperfection as two irreconcilable factors. As never before, Luca is moved by himself, by the drama of Sara's disease, and by the analysis that 'dies' for the summer. For a moment he emerges from a superficial and aesthetic way of feeling. But the vignette also shows that the precondition is that I too manage to extricate myself from the superficial aesthetics of interpretation (my interest in him was at first dormant, as if I were distancing myself from a sense of death, but was then aroused by a narcissistically oriented drive; and, finally, I had to take on his unthinkable emotions 'in my flesh') when my reverie-memory gave us the chance to live through an experience of unison and recognition.

This, one might say, is the point where I participated in his interrupted dream (Ogden, 2005). From the technical point of view, I achieved this result by doing little more than adding 'punctuation marks' which lent a minimum of rhythm to what he was saying, but without interrupting him. I use listening as the mental notebook which gathers up his most secret and painful thoughts and then ties together the threads of meaning in the silent weaving of a progressively more cohesive fabric. In this way I try to tune in to the most primitive ('musical' or sensory) aspects of communication. My aim is not so much to translate a hidden meaning (which is what I do in my somewhat inappropriate interpretation), but rather to ensure the gradual development of a narrative competence of the mind and an ability to give meaning to experience. One can also see the game of immersion/interactivity, which is very similar to the way we live aesthetic experience (Ryan, 2001; Civitarese, 2008a), through which I play my part in the theatre of analysis.

A calming rhythm

Sensoriality

A certain amount of conceptual vagueness is unavoidable when investigating complex psychic phenomena, especially when they involve such early stages of life. Remarks of this tenor are to be found scattered throughout the work of Freud and Bion. Moreover, to the latter, as we saw in Chapter 2, Meltzer attributes an active search for ambiguity. I regard this premise as necessary so as to avoid giving the reader the impression that I am claiming to reveal the ultimate meaning of aesthetic experience in art, which no theory, whether psychoanalytic *or not*, has shown itself capable of doing. However we can approach this meaning, even though much of our understanding is bound to remain on an intuitive level.

A second premise will allow me to link up with the discussion of clinical material before going on to a more speculative plane. For Bion, only what one lives in the present with the patient can come close to a sense of truth. It is not enough to review history – and this is true even when we do so through the lens of transference/countertransference, concepts that are the result of more static caesuras between past and present, analyst and patient etc. (Bion, 1977a). What is needed instead is for the analyst to be involved as a person in the creative dimension of the analysis. Bion repeated this in any number of ways and on all possible occasions. Only then is lived experience in the present of the session – which is potentially the most transformative type of experience – a reliable gateway also to the reconstruction of the past and towards an idea of the patient's intrapsychic organization. Reconstructing the patient's past helps increase a sense of self-continuity, but one cannot consider it the main therapeutic factor: for Meltzer it is just a 'by-product' (1984, p. 145) of the psychoanalytic process. Often, when new memories become available, it is because the bets have, so to speak, already been made.

We have seen from Luca's history, his present life and a 'sampling' of the therapeutic relationship, that he presents character traits and clinical symptoms which fit the context of aesthetic conflict as described by Meltzer. In the 'exemplary' fragment of analysis examined above, I think I have shown sufficiently that the key factor that led to a change in the patient's ability to integrate his emotional ambivalence towards the object and to be moved by beauty – implicitly, to begin to mourn a fantasy of fusion with the object – was the analyst's recovery of his capacity for reverie (which can be seen as a conscious expression of the underground work of the mind's α function). This event modifies the analytic field even though the analyst does not intervene with explicit interpretations, if it is true, as maintained by Freud, that communication from unconscious to unconscious is always at work. At this point it would seem safe to infer, as an explanation of his psychological distress, that the patient had not sufficiently internalized this function in his primary object relationship.

I now propose, by way of hypothesis, to generalize this principle to construct a model of what happens when the subject is unable to resolve the aesthetic conflict and defends himself against it with aestheticism. One might suppose that the same causal agent intervenes whenever we are faced with the clinical pictures described by Meltzer: what in the worlds of history, external reality and analysis make untenable the aesthetic conflict is insufficient permeability to the child's (the analysand's) projective identifications, a lack of reverie on the part of the mother (and of the analyst in the session). And on the metapsychological level: his difficulties in making available his α function in the relationship, hence his mental absence. This would put us in the presence of a psychopathological situation not without its specificity and which is different from the outcome suggested by traumas that are either different in nature or, if similar, larger in size. This is not surprising, but theorizing in the abstract is very different from founding a model on a convincing empirical basis – assuming, of course, that our clinical 'demonstrations' have some value.

Now, I am not saying that Meltzer fails to put to sufficient use the concept of reverie and α function in relation to artistic creativity and the symbolic faculty of the mind. However, it seems to me that none of Meltzer's clinical examples demonstrate such a convincing link as that which comes out in the case of Luca and is reconstructed from the lively relational game of the analytic couple. Indeed, despite his theoretical model, these examples seem to be inspired more by a one-person rather than a two-person psychology. Moreover, even if the concept of aesthetic conflict has become a mandatory reference when it comes to the psychoanalytic theory of aesthetic experience, it still throws up at least two major difficulties: on the one hand, it does not explain what differentiates the nature of the aesthetic experience from what takes place in the 'artificial' sphere of art, a point that has been surprisingly neglected in psychoanalytic literature; on the other, paradoxically, it fails to offer an adequate representation of the aesthetic conflict in relation to the phases of life during which the child is in a state of fusion with the mother. I want to focus primarily on this latter point, because it is essential to an understanding of the deeper meaning of aesthetic experience, *the enigma of form*.

The same criticism – namely that Meltzer and Williams based the aesthetic conflict on a mind-body dualism – is levelled by Sweetnam:

> For Meltzer and Williams, the aesthetic conflict occurs between externally perceived (physical beauty) and internally unknown (psychic) reality; the theory hinges on the implicit and at times explicit [...] idea of psyche–soma separation. But the creation of beauty cannot be reduced to the letting go of projections and increasing internalization of good object experience, or to the notion of inner conflicts in these areas.
>
> (2007, pp. 1498–1499)

The observation is insightful and can be interpreted as follows: it is as if Meltzer were describing a child who immediately, at birth, has a functioning ego and is separated from the mother. Likewise, it is as if he did not take sufficient account of the fact that an integrated self is an achievement. The 'videocentric' image of the child who stares into the eyes of the mother and asks himself questions about her intentions suggests that it is already developed, that it has already left behind the state in which the self is not differentiated from the non-self. But only access to language (the symbolic) marks the full achievement of this goal. At this stage of life, however, 'the good (psychological) environment is a physical one' (Winnicott, 1949a, p. 245). At birth, as Freud writes (1926), there is no object, so no object can be lost, and also: '*the information of one's own scream* serves to characterize the object' (1895, p. 366). He is echoed in this by Bion (1962, p. 34): 'In this imaginary situation the need for the breast is a feeling and that feeling itself is a bad breast; the infant does not feel it wants a good breast but it does feel it wants to evacuate a bad one.' Building on Bion, Ogden describes psychic birth in similar terms:

> The breast is not experienced as part of the mother's body that has a particular (visually perceived) shape, softness, texture, warmth, and so on. Instead (or more accurately in dialectical tension with the experience of the breast as a visually perceived object), the breast as autistic shape is the experience of being a place (an area of sensation of a soothing sort) [and this seems to me a good, though partial definition of an aesthetic object] that is created (for example) when the infant's cheek rests against the mother's breast. *The contiguity* of skin surfaces *creates an idiosyncratic shape that is the infant at that moment.* In other words, the infant's being is in this way given sensory definition and a sense of locale.[7]
>
> (1994a, p. 174, my italics)

All these authors, as we can see, express the paradox of an object that is there but not there yet, which is not seen as having its own existence, and yet … is about to be.

At birth, identity coincides with 'an area of sensation of a soothing sort', with the space delimited by the tensions that are generated at the interface between contiguous surfaces both fused and distinct or dialectically interrelated – in fact, a contact barrier – between raw impressions and impressions that are already tactile, olfactory, visual, *proto*forms etc. Identity is negative and differential, it is made up of relations, it is itself only to the extent that it is none of the other elements of reality that are contiguous with it, but it does imply them all. In this sense it is a potential identity and not simply given, already divided at the origin, a field of possibilities.

We are in the area of what Kristeva (1974) calls the *semiotic*, the pre-representational and pre-reflexive area where meaning is produced sensually, from the materiality of the body, prior to symbolic language. It is a 'psychosomatic modality of the signifying process [*signifiance*]' (ibid., p. 28) as opposed to 'meaning'; a modality that is not destined to disappear even when one can speak now of fully established subjectivity. It is the thinking that precedes thought, the effects of meaning that foreshadow the realm of semantics, concepts and syntax. The question becomes clearer only if one thinks of the mother-and-child pair as a single system. Then it becomes clear that the symbolic is immediately conveyed by the mother but that it is immediately proper to the child (of the dyad).

At this stage it is the mother-environment, and not the mother-object, that intervenes to promote the development of the child, as

Winnicott has so splendidly explained. Thanks to her capacity for holding and reverie the mother gives birth in the child to a feeling of existing and of having a first psychic space. She provides an enveloping surface – a first psychic skin (Bick, 1968) – through the language of caring, a language made up of *sensations that can only structure the mind if they acquire meaning by being ordered rhythmically*. She carries out for the child a conscious, preconscious and unconscious psychological process which gives meaning to its nascent forms of vitality. She 'dreams' it and lets it share this dream, translating it for the child into visual, tactile, auditory, olfactory, gustatory and kinetic forms. From the interaction with the mother the child's initially indeterminate and amorphous flow sensations and emotions receives its first cadence, breaks, joints, gaps; the rhythmic repetition of sensory-motor patterns produces configurations and schemas that give shape to experience and an early sense of continuity to the body.

This is why at the centre of the clinical aspect of the aesthetic conflict lies above all pain at the partial failure of the mother-as-environment, the mother who helps the mind to settle in the body (*in-dwelling*), favours early integration or 'psychosomatic collusion' (Winnicott, 1974) and supports the process of ego-building. It is the mother who must provide a stable and peaceful setting for the psychological development of the child: from this point of view one can say that my interpretation was 'disruptive' (dysrhythmic) on this level, which is the opaque, bodily, 'institutional' level, the so-called meta-ego (Bleger, 1967a).

I would thus suggest that if, according to Meltzer, the aesthetic conflict is already present at birth, it should be described somewhat differently from the way he did (although there are some passages in which he speculates on the feelings experienced by the foetus in the womb). The aesthetic proto-conflict is played out at the elementary level of the process of the construction of subjectivity prior to the stage where the self is integrated and the Ego already functioning. It is already present in the state of psychological immaturity and 'double dependence' of the infant (Winnicott, 1945; Girard, 2010) and, as Likierman writes (1989), is intrinsic to the activity of perception itself.

At the beginning of life 'aesthetic' pleasure is the feeling of evacuating a bad breast, not in a conscious relationship with an object distinct from oneself, because there is as yet no real self-reflexive consciousness, and only later will it be experienced as the positive feeling of being connected to a separate object. For this reason, in the first phase the aesthetic conflict has as its theatre only the body and the senses. *It continues, then, throughout life to unfold in the same pre-symbolic and sensory (semiotic) way* with regard to the generation of experience which Ogden (1989), building on concepts developed by Meltzer on childhood autism, called contiguous-autistic. 'Psychosomatic collusion' is not achieved once and for all, but must be continually re-gained. Subjectivity is a fluid, dynamic process that is always in progress.

The question that needs now to be posed again is the following: what entitles us to move away from abstract speculation and to establish a link between the aesthetic conflict that is played out in the mother-child relationship in its extended sense (and indeed even more radically than I have argued here) and aesthetic experience in the contemplation of art? Well, as we have seen, hypothetically this relationship can be established starting from a clinical observation: namely, Meltzer's valuable observation that I mentioned at the beginning of the chapter and that I 'tested' in my personal clinical material. Logically, if the patient reacts to an object of art in the same way as he reacted to the beauty of the mother and continues to repeat the same pattern in his emotional relationships, *one can conjecture that in the object of art potentially similar stimuli, the same harmony of forms, the same rhythm of sensation and the same music all concentrate*, that it is, in short, the equivalent of a mother holding and dreaming her baby who by doing so helps him to supplement his self and guides him every time out of chaos and towards order.

In his article 'Primitive emotional development', Winnicott expresses a similar insight. Having emphasized the 'normal' existence of moments of non-integration even in adult and mature individuals, he goes on to write: 'Through artistic experience we can hope to keep in touch with our primitive selves whence the most intense feelings and even fearfully acute sensations derive, and we are poor indeed if we are only sane' (1945, p. 150). The concept of sublimation would not be able to account theoretically for the primitive pleasure when the body and not yet the mind is in the foreground, and so 'there is no repression or repressed unconscious' (Winnicott, 1949b, p. 181). It is related to content and not to form (Wright, 2006). The theory of sublimation and the theory of reparation that derives from it do not take sufficient account of the prehistory of the aesthetic experience, of the proto-aesthetic conflict that the subject (which is not even, or not fully, a subject) experiences at the stage where it is merged with the object, nor the intersubjective dimension in which it occurs. For this reason Meltzer's theory of aesthetics can be considered a useful critical revision (or, from another point of view, an extension) of the Freudian theory of sublimation.

The aesthetic experience continues to help the subject on different occasions throughout his life to find a fuller sense of consonance and contact between mind and body. *With the felicitous play of its forms, which are constantly swinging from moments of non-integration to moments of integration, even before and perhaps even more than satisfying the impulses of the Id, the aesthetic object (which expresses the artist's reverie) sustains the ego.* The order of the semiotic is, in fact, closely linked to the emotions and the body. As Butler notes authoritatively (1990, p. 119): 'In its semiotic mode, language is engaged in a poetic recovery of the maternal body, that diffuse materiality that resists all discrete and univocal signification.' Barthes adds: 'The writer is someone who plays with his mother's body' (1973, p. 37).

The deeper meaning of the aesthetic experience in the contemplation of art could be briefly expressed as the (re)living of the felicitous oscillation non-integration ↔ integration on a pre-symbolic and pre-reflective experiential level. Only thus can we explain the absolute importance of form in artistic expression, and the fact that arguably the most moving art forms are dance and music,[8] not for example painting, which works through sight, the most intellectual of the senses. When successful, the aesthetic object is the means whereby the artist transmits to the spectator who contemplates his work his reverie translated into the primal language of forms and feelings, which thus contains his anxieties and helps him feel more integrated. Hence perhaps the sense of well being that comes after a moving evening at the theatre or a visit to a beautiful art exhibition.

For this reason, in my opinion, the concept of aesthetic conflict can fulfil all its heuristic potential for a psychoanalytic theory of beauty only if it is brought back to the molecular, psycho-somatic, properly 'aesthetic' level of the construction of subjectivity – corresponding to moving from the figurative art of Piero della Francesca to the monochromes of Rothko. I am referring to the extreme level of visual resolution that Bion achieves in *Transformations* (1965) when he makes the 'impossible' attempt to mathematize the birth of thought.[9]

In the context of the aesthetic conflict, however, the concept of beauty can be misleading, insofar as it refers to an already complex psychological experience, whereas from another point of view it is nothing other than the natural extension of the experience of 'pleasant' or soothing sensations experienced by the subject in the initial state of relative non-separateness from the object (Winnicott's 'primary identification', 1956) and prior to that by the foetus in the uterus as 'proto-aesthetic' sensations (Meltzer and Harris Williams, 1988; Mitrani, 1998), and which have a precise function in regulating the homeostasis of the body. Likierman writes (1989, p. 133): 'the initial reaction of our sense impressions to the world is the primitive predecessor of all our later experiencing of beauty, and also of later artistic creativity. The earliest aesthetic experience is sensation-based.'

To grasp the full significance of the concept that Meltzer has, at the cost of some abstraction, taken from Bion, it is necessary therefore to emphasize the term 'aesthetic' as a sensation – as suggested by the word's etymology (*aísthesis*) – and to reduce the concept of beauty to its zero degree, that is, to reduce the aesthetic conflict to a conflict of feelings. A second etymological 'reduction' might also be useful: 'beautiful' comes from 'good' and even earlier has the meaning of 'suitable', 'appropriate', 'beneficial', 'convenient', 'serviceable'.

Starting from this set of synonyms, the primitive sense of 'beauty' could be traced back to the way in which the mother-as-world (the mother-environment, an environment that also includes the father and/or any substitutes for parents and which at the beginning of life belongs to the sphere of infantile omnipotence) is perceived as 'beautiful.' Because the mother who is capable of reverie – or in the terminology of Winnicott, who is experiencing a state of 'primary maternal preoccupation' and is able to provide adequate holding – adapts to the needs of a child who is still in a stage of non-integration and immaturity of the ego, and satisfies the child's need for psycho-physical balance and accompaniment in its development towards the earliest forms of subjectivity and consciousness of self.

In other words, the notion of aesthetic conflict proves to be more productive for a psychoanalytic theory of aesthetics only if it is brought back, 'this side of the pleasure principle', to Bion's radical social theory of the birth of the subject. At the heart of this theory lie the concepts of projective identification as a primitive form of communication, maternal reverie as a willingness to receive it, and the α function as the capacity to transform. Bion's theory of thinking, described by Grotstein (2007) as an 'ontological epistemology', is also a kind of aesthetic theory insofar as it expresses a philosophical obsession with reality, with 'O', with the thing in itself, and focuses on how contact with the non-self to which practically all these concepts dimly allude happens on the molecular level.

When an experience of tuning is produced by building a harmonious, *rhythmic* contact, thought comes into being and a sense of self is nurtured. The subject feels reconciled with the world, finds a happy balance between identity and difference, and experiences sensations perceived as belonging to the realm of beauty, in other words closer to 'O', the truth (where, with Keats, as quoted by Bion, 'Beauty is truth, truth beauty'), not a truth that emanates from a transcendental entity but the intimate dialectical concord with reality; a truth, it goes without saying, which is such because it satisfies requirements selected by the evolutionary process for the biological survival of the individual and the species.

An emanation of 'O', what Heidegger refers to as the thing (*das Ding*) (1950), Being – these are the β-elements which act as intermediaries between them and subjectivity at its appearance. The β-elements record the flow of interactions between subject and the real, the din of the *struggle* and the *work* necessary to extricate oneself from, and transform, the indistinct texture of the real. But for there to be an increase rather than a loss of organization, these need to be assimilated. The construction of the subject, therefore, takes place in a field of forces in conflict with each other, which we can also describe as a conflict between truth and falsehood in relation to 'O' or, in Piaget's terms, between assimilation and accommodation.

But then the 'nuclear' aesthetic conflict is between a non-symbolic and a symbolic area, between β and α, and is expressed not only on the most advanced level of what according to Meltzer's original definition is already present in the opposition between the visible and the non-visible – the scene of the child's eyes fixed on the mother's face that is depicted in many paintings as a 'sacred conversation'; of a child, therefore, who has already left a state of undifferentiation – but also on the more elementary level of the process of constructing subjectivity that *precedes* the development of the ego.

Let us now try to fix a *starting point* for a psychoanalytic theory of art: focusing on this plane of aesthetic conflict, reducing it to a conflict of sensations to bring it back to the dynamics described by Meltzer in terms of the visible/non-visible, helps us give an account of the importance, and perhaps the *primacy*, *of the sensory aspects of the communication we engage in with the artist when we contemplate his/her works*. One need only think, moreover, that undoubtedly the artistic languages that excite us most are music and dance, languages which are completely wordless or pre-linguistic, albeit not pre-cultural. *One might say that art is attuned to the more primitive levels of psycho-somatic integration*, and that it is a way of satisfying the need to *restore the body to the mind*, to return, that is, to that essential harmony of being and to put emotions once again at the centre of life and thought, even the most abstract thought. This is what the strands of modern psychoanalysis, neurobiology and cognitive psychology have only very recently, and on a theoretical level, started trying to do.

A hyper-abstract vision of this dialectic of the early development of the mind is present in Bion's theory of transformations, where he speaks, for example, of point and line, and then in more complex terms of the concept of projective identification. In its concrete interpersonal nature, projective identification can be regarded as the mature outcome of primitive tensions, and they are already elementary transfers created at the edges of the body (Mills, 2000). These are the boundaries that gradually define in the infant the surfaces of separation and connection where the first transformation from β to α is achieved, and the transition is made from protosensations to images. Here rhythm and the most primitive vibrations develop into the first sensations of having/receiving limits from the outside, being contained, and the α function, or that rudimentary α function that Grotstein (2007) sees as being present at birth, as the ability to shape one's experience.

The hypothesis suggested by the implicit aesthetic theory contained in Bion's thinking, illuminated *a posteriori* by Meltzer's concept of aesthetic conflict (and abjection), is that the core aesthetic emotion consists in a dialectical process of mutual recognition that passes through the medium of the aesthetic object, that is, by developing the capacity to give meaning to one's experience and to dream one's life (essentially, to develop the ego). Crucial to this process are the sensory levels of generating experience, those closest to the body and to the emotions. Only secondarily does the aesthetic experience seem to be attributable to the concept of drive sublimation, in other words, the gratification (by 'uplifting shift' Petrella, 2007, p. 1066)[10] of the needs of the Id. Art, in short, offers the unique opportunity to engage in a dialogue with oneself (but ideally with the other) which, when it is successful or when it is 'touching', helps the mind to grow.

If, as Rilke puts it, beauty is the terror that we can endure, it is also, as Homer says, 'the breast to soothe your troubles.'[11]

Rhythm

The psychic growth that in aesthetic experience originates from the tolerable recovery of the split-off parts of the self, that is, from a process that carries out a primitive synthesis of aspects not yet mentalized, is signalled to consciousness by emotion. The aesthetic object reveals us to ourselves, that is, it identifies in each of us some aspects that are perceived or intuited, if at all, only darkly. This helps us to transform emotions that are still in a state of chaos into thoughts and images. This explains the paradox of art, which at one and the same time illuminates something that we had and did not have inside us, or rather that we had but not in that form. The new form corresponds to the alphabetization of *quanta* of β-elements and is therefore something already known (as *proto*sensation, or which exists as a *pre-conception*) and as something new (as an image, idea, emotional pictogram, *realization*). All this amounts to saying that art transforms us. Ultimately, the pleasure we obtain from aesthetic experience, more than from drive gratification, or in anticipation of it, can be seen in terms of the dialectic of recognition, understood in its broader range of extension, that is, starting from the definition of the limits of the body.

Self-consciousness, going-on-being, depends on encountering the other's desire even before we perceive it as an object with its own existence, and at the same time on gradually internalizing this third intersubjective area that is created by the meeting of two minds, one of which is such only potentially. The aesthetic emotion occurs when there is an ideal point of proximity to reality and consists in a feeling of vitality, authenticity and truth. Truth as food-for-the-mind stems from the process of dialectical mediation that takes place between two parties. It is a measure of what is created and kept in a process of mutual negation (of what in falsely static and abstract terms is called unison, consensuality, empathy, etc.) It is a successful emotion, that is, a sense of tension that has been given a good form or rather, a fortunate moment, an effective cadence, a good rhythm.

This is a *second point* for our aesthetic theory: feelings become meaningful if they are ordered in *soothing rhythms*.[12] Time as a structure of experience, in fact, comes from the pain of waiting, the perception of space that precedes the appearance of the object, and even before that, when the object is not yet perceived as separate, from a play of identity and difference, regularity and variation, tuning and detuning. The difference comes about as dynamic negation (disturbance) of identity (of a state of balance): this is simply what the aesthetic conflict is if it is understood in the most radical way possible, that is, starting from the sensory pole of generating experience. Going-on-being (another of Winnicott's famous gerunds), and above all ex-isting, is going on with a self confused with Being, a self immersed in the natural world, that is, pre-human. It means apprehending the rhythms of the body and then, on the highest level, *thinking*.

If we then extend Meltzer's concept backwards to illuminate the idea put forward by Bion that had given rise to it – let me point out that this is my methodological proposition – it can be said that the aesthetic conflict stems from overcoming the early stages of non-integration and from the dialectic between β-elements, in other words, primitive feelings or emotions, and α-elements, between presentation (*Darstellung*) and representation (*Vorstellung*), between inability and ability to symbolize, between avoiding emotions and thinking emotions (Ferro, 2007). The inaccessible interior of the mother that disturbs the child is, before anything else, all the unknowable reality inside him/herself. But the decisive factor for the immaturity of the child and the most powerful ally for the outcome of the conflict is the α function of the mother – which must be thought of as that which promotes the aptitude of the mother-body-real-world to adapt to his needs.

Defining this relationship as aesthetic conflict has certain consequences: firstly, that it is a dynamic process; secondly, that for the development of thought what is at issue is the fate of the most primitive feelings and emotions; and finally, that a share of pleasure, first as a feeling to evacuate a bad breast prior to a real self-reflexive consciousness, and *only later* as a positive feeling of being in touch, as the happiness of singing-and-dancing, and then as drive gratification, is a key element in the successful construction of fully human subjects. In fact, until there is an ego and the attendant possibility of repression, sublimation is not even possible.

Returning to Bion, as I proposed to do, helps us understand that the aesthetic conflict is the result of an early rhythm which determines how the child still fused with the object first experiences the opposing pairs of terms tension/relaxation, ecstasy/evacuation, fullness/loss (and *only later*, as the child leaves the stage of narcissistic identification with the mother behind it, of presence/absence, intimacy/*fading*, tenderness/coldness, rapture/abyss, desire/indifference). The paradigmatic interplay of the two terms of these binary pairs is the same as that found in Freud's concept of *Fort/Da* (Freud, 1920). It is the rhythm which, prior to language, gives birth to the meaning and the sense of time. Rhythm is 'time itself become sensitive' (Fabbri, 2000, p. 128). The aesthetic conflict is thus an expression of the very dialectic of reality, that is, a logic of identity and difference (negation that simultaneously raises up and preserves, Hegel's *Aufhebung* [Kojève, 1947]) through which the subject emerges from undifferentiation. The time of being (the sense of self), which Luca experiences as dilating painfully, comes from the vital pulse that is expressed in the transition from one term to the other of the series of binary pairs listed above. This pulse is the origin of aesthetics, as Barthes (2007, p. 618) suggests in one of his dazzling insights:

> The sadness of a child who sees his mother move away and cannot help but be upset by the enormity of the tragedy that is happening to him. From there, [...] the idea of playing, of imitating this break, repeating it fictitiously to dominate it (as Freud would say) and find in the game of the spool the consolation of action, of power and of indifference (or even of aggression).
>
> The game of *Fort/Da* not only creates meaning – before any language – it also teaches rhythm, how rhythm and meaning are linked; this episode also arguably contains the origin ... *of aesthetics*.

Here in a few lines the brilliant French critic traces the same path that I have been following in this chapter in my attempt to review critically and enhance the concept of aesthetic conflict (taking a path similar to psychoanalytic theorizing about the nature of the aesthetic emotion in working back to hypotheses about the reconstruction of more primitive states of life: from sublimation to reparation, and hence to the aesthetic conflict). He describes a scene where the visual regime dominates (*l'enfant qui voit sa mère partir*), but which is already characterized by the infant's ability to perceive another separate from himself, and not only as a game of luminous sensations within an area of non-differentiation between self and object. It is the scene in which the subject – there is already an Ego – is captured, enslaved by the other and reduced to a state of alienation (*sidéré*) which embodies the wound of difference, the trauma of falling into the abyss that is the loss of the other and then the mystery of its inexplicable return. Then he moves back to the area of meaning that precedes language, towards the pre-symbolic (*avant même tout langage*), alluding to a phase of evolution of the subject in which there cannot yet be any ability to repair the damage done in fantasy to the object or to sublimate drive satisfaction. Lastly, he emphasizes the significance of rhythm, and it is only here, *where sensations and forms reign*, that the secret of the aesthetic dimension of experience flashes! A secret locked inside the extraordinary and unique opportunity that art offers, like the reverie of the mother at the dawn of life, translated at this stage into sensoriality, but also the level of generation of experience that corresponds throughout life to putting the seal on the formless matter of experience, and to soothing the anguish, what Rilke called 'the beginning of terror'.

Margins of beauty

In a psychoanalytic theory of art, therefore, the concepts of sensoriality and rhythm are central, yet they are still not sufficient to define the nature of aesthetic emotion. At least a third concept is required: the concept, namely, of frame or fictionality. The aesthetic object can only exist in a context of fiction. It can do without figurative or conceptual content, but not the frame that makes it an as-if object. When framed, any natural object is potentially an art object. This is what Duchamp demonstrated with his famous urinal, what Christo did with the Reichstag and the eleven islands of Biscayne Bay and what others have done with the body. These are, respectively, examples of so-called ready-made art, land art or body art. By frame what I mean is not only the frame of a picture, but in a broader sense also the environmental context, for example, a place designed for art exhibitions, and even the whole system of art in general as a social practice. An aesthetic object must have a 'beautiful' (that is, engaging) form, a fascinating rhythm – and one could use the adjectives 'true' or 'good' instead of 'beautiful' – but if there were no frame, it would still be equivalent to any natural object or artefact that is designed for another use.

Now, the 'frame effect' can be divided into three sub-effects which for the sake of clarity are worth discussing separately, although they are closely intertwined. The first two, which have I called *iterability* and *caesura*, act mainly on an unconscious level, and the third, *self-reflexivity*, on a conscious level.

Iterability

The fictional context in which the aesthetic emotion lies fuels *a sense of continuity of self*, which is reminiscent of the continuity of the mother's early care of the infant, because it makes it potentially into an infinitely iterable experience. And I use the term 'iterable' because, in addition to being a synonym of 'repeatable', the word belongs to both the language of deconstruction and to liturgy, where it has the fascinating meaning of administering or receiving the same sacrament several times. Just as the device of the analytic contract in analysis guarantees a timeless dimension, so too in art, which is the result of *téchne*, what cures the *fading* (*Fort*) is the 'guaranteed' reappearance (*Da*) of an object with both stimulating and soothing properties. In the same way as on the stage of the analysis the device of the setting allows the free mobilization of drive fantasies, so too in art – and in play, where however one has to consider that the libidinal gain is smaller and more narcissistic because what is lacking is the happiness of rhythm and the ecstatic attraction of the object – the sense of security, in other words the iterability guaranteed by fiction, which is equivalent to an individual's feeling of continuity of being, promotes the expression of emotions and fantasies that are potentially destructive to the civilized ego but which within the frame may find a form of containment and transformation (sublimation); it's like telling children watching TV during an unexpectedly cruel scene: 'Don't worry, nobody dies, it's all tomato juice!' The fiction also says: 'This will be yours forever, you will never lose it because it's true but it's not true.' The make-believe frame, in short, cures the desperation at the *fading* of the object and its 'soothing qualities', which the natural aesthetic object cannot do in the same way because it is by definition ephemeral. Paradoxically, however, as we have seen from our clinical material, full benefit from the new 'transformational object' (Bollas, 1987) that potentially any aesthetic object represents is only possible if the initial aesthetic conflict has left no incurable wounds.

Caesura

Nevertheless, continuity as iterability guaranteed by fiction is not everything. For it to be composed in a rhythm, there must be a caesura. Indeed, it is by delimiting the equivalent of the sensory, bodily movie made up of the images of the mind, that the aesthetic object helps to bridge the gaps or to increase their surface area. The frame is the caesura that separates and unites two worlds, inner and outer. So, every crossing of this threshold plays an intrinsic role in structuring and containing experience, it adds a building block to the structure of the inner world and continues the work of integrating the subject, amounting in all respects to a dialectic of recognition that starts from the desire for the desire of the other.

Similarly so-called markers in film introduce the scene of the dream or the return to reality; the same meaning is expressed by turning off or turning on the lights in the cinema, or by transitions from daydreams to more focused states of consciousness. These 'secret passages', if they can be maintained, mark the boundaries of the ego and thus participate in its construction. They create, in Khan's terminology (1974), the space of the dream, without which the dream itself would be a dissociated experience. They work, more or less underground, at maintaining the sensory floor of the ego (Ogden, 1989; Civitarese, 2006b), and continue to do so throughout life. Leaving one frame to enter another is an experience of being left (of leaving) and then returning to be held (of holding on).

The frame introduces the characteristic illusory dimension of the aesthetic emotion; it interposes a distance that at one and the same time is both a shield and a psychological proto-space. *Pure instinctual satisfaction, the pure possession of the object, such as is to be found in nature, is thus transformed through fiction into an intersubjective experience.* Just as the rhythmic sensations that originate in happy interaction with the mother constitute the child's psychic skin and the space where the child can experience the impulses of the Id. In this way the sensations transmitted by an object create the aesthetic equivalent of a psychical theatre by displaying the fictional frame that encloses them.

Self-reflexivity

Whenever we unconsciously perceive the frame, that which is at the margins of beauty, we are thus introduced to the world of the imagination and the symbolic (as if we were told: 'This is not true, or rather it is true, but in another dimension, in the world of psychic reality'), and we transform the absence embodied in the caesura into a representation. The containing function which comes from the make-believe experience and its reproducibility, or in other words from the artificial character of the aesthetic experience in art, thus intrinsically has a deep meaning because it reveals the *dialectical structure of the real*, whose very movement is different from consciousness of self, one's being dependent on another mind and on the other's desire, and not on a physical reality. But there is also a critical threshold beyond which everything becomes *conscious* and the individual acquires a mind and the ability to attribute mental states to others.

What is important is that at some point the background frame to the aesthetic object becomes a figure. As we have seen, the rhythm of the care provided by the mother-environment forms the background to the experience of a subject in the nascent state, the establishment of a psychological space, the sensory floor of the ego, the bodily frame which gives rise to metaphorical projections of concepts (Lakoff and Johnson, 1980). But as a rule we are not aware of this space-frame, which for the infant is the mother's womb, for the analysand the 'mother's womb' of the setting (Winnicott, 1956; Bleger, 1967b), and in thought is the 'mother's womb' of the as-if of perception because we see reality as given and not constructed. Art, on the other hand, displays it as fiction, as the device that makes representation possible.

Bion makes the point:

> If the emotion stimulated in the recipient of the communication is a *representation* of the emotion stimulated by O in the artist, we may regard the artist's intervention in the chain of events as one that does not stop at the disposal of patterns of pigment on canvas, but extends to the emotional state evoked in the individual, or group, and to giving durability to the power to evoke emotion. [...] Strictly speaking, the interpretation *draws attention* to an

> *existing* emotional state; but it *produces* the emotional state of awareness of an emotional state.
>
> (1965, pp. 33–34, my italics)

Just like the mother, art mediates between O and the subject, presents reality in doses small enough to be tolerable to an embryonic subject, showing its two faces: the object that both fascinates and terrifies. At birth, the initial integration of the psyche must necessarily be based on the body and can only correspond to the mother's sensory reverie, which is translated into variations in the rhythm of care and which, not unlike the setting in analysis, gradually leads one to discover the object and to lose one's illusions. Similarly, each time the aesthetic object resurrects the psyche; either it expands its space or it revives occluded and mortified areas. It carries with it the dream of O or of reality which the artist, by virtue of his creativity and sensitivity (reverie), has been able to dream and make available to others.

What gives the aesthetic object the character of a dream dreamed by the artist is precisely the frame, the fictional setting, 'the emotional state of awareness of an emotional state'. *It is through the frame that the relationship enters the aesthetic object, that which specifically serves to create a mind, a subject.* But, let me repeat, the specific nature of art lies in addressing *simultaneously* the psycho-somatic level of the integration of the subject. This is why it is reductive to focus solely on the intellectual content of an aesthetic object – the level of most Freudian aesthetic criticism – and not to include the sensory form. The highest ecstasy and the deepest fear, in fact, are experienced in the body and it is there that they are still deposited as dark memories. It is to that body, to our most immature parts, but for this reason also to the parts most capable of seeing the world as if for the first time, that the aesthetic object speaks. As Deleuze (1983) writes, this is where the happy rhythm of being itself becomes a feeling, a Figure.

Fort/Da

We could identify the meaning of fiction in art – and hence of everything that is an explicit but subtle metatextual indication of seams, edges, supplements, accessories etc. – as a function of holding or sensory containment as opposed to the second-degree container represented by the form of what is inside the frame (as an equivalent, instead, to the capacity to think-dream) and content-as-dream-thoughts (thoughts and feelings coming from lived experience). An aesthetic object would thus bring together the functions of mother-environment and mother-object, holding and containment – or, one might say, more primitive and sensory forms of containment and more advanced and abstract forms, more or less sensory levels of reverie. It is clear that there can be no absolute discontinuity between container and content, between frame and picture, since the containing function of the frame is active at all levels: the book is in a material sense a frame for the novel that it contains in its pages, the page for the paragraph, the word for its meaning, and so on.

The aesthetic experience is, therefore, iterable in the sense of repeatable as an experience of enjoying a work of art, and in the sense of reproducible in thought as in the representation (of the thing, the object), as a private liturgy for getting in touch with inner gods. The frame game sets up a clear tension between two worlds, the outer and the inner, each of which denies the other and is created in this destruction-that-preserves; at the same time it is also denied, or rather, it 'carves out' the inner world from the outer world understood as undifferentiated reality.

It is true that each time it is played the game of the spool involves repossessing a concrete object (sensoriality) and it is the active representation of the disappearance and reappearance of the maternal object (rhythm); but above all it is the emerging discovery of the disappearance of the mother *in* the spool, that is, the discovery of symbolization (fictionality). The child realizes that something can continue to exist in the mind as an image-memory in dream or in wakefulness, and beyond the visible, materially in another space, and also that an object (thing or person) that one perceives can never be possessed entirely because nothing is ever identical with itself and everything is just a stage effect, the result of an infinite series of metaphorical substitutions and, ultimately, the balance sheet of an infinite series of losses.

7

THE ANALYST'S INTERNAL SETTING AND ITS DISCONTENTS

We all know the definition of the *formal* setting of analysis. Also, after Bleger and Winnicott, we can no longer disregard its nature as an institution and, as such, the identity-creating basis of the subject, the locus where the psychotic parts of the personality are deposited, or its significance as a mother-environment. For the psychotic patient, Winnicott writes, 'the couch is the analyst's lap or womb, and the warmth *is* the live warmth of the analyst's body' (1947, p. 199). This observation can, in fact, be extended to include all analysands. In relation to this, Winnicott points out that the end of each session allows the analyst to express his (healthy) hatred towards the patient; it is a hatred we must both experience and tolerate together so that it becomes a factor that fosters psychic growth and is not an obstacle to it, which is what happens if it is denied. The formal setting, also known as the *external* setting, lays down the rules of the psychoanalytic game: the place where the analyst and patient meet, the timetable, questions of money, holidays, and so on. The setting has a certain ritual character. Etymologically ritual means 'religious ceremony', 'custom' or 'habit'. Generally a ritual has a group dimension, and serves to put the individual in contact with the gods, in this case with a person's inner gods.[1] It is essential that the rules are followed and that the setting is rigorous because it represents one of the most valuable tools the analyst has at his disposal. However, it should not descend into ritualism or become a fetish. Sometimes, having a 'classic' setting, the type of setting that is considered optimal for establishing the hypnoid atmosphere of the session, may for some be only the point of arrival, not departure, just as some analysands manage to free associate readily only when they are approaching the end of treatment.

Patients, of course, have their own idea of the setting, which does not necessarily correspond to the analyst's notion of the setting, nor can they necessarily adapt to it immediately. I am thinking, for example, of Carla: for several months the only place she could sit was on the floor. It took me some time to get her to use a cushion. Now we are at the point where we sit facing each other on two armchairs, both on the side of the desk where patients generally sit. Perhaps, I thought, she needed a while to test the elasticity of my setting, that is to say, my ability to 'hold' her and to 'carry' her infantile part. From a Kleinian point of view, in the abstract one might think that the various positions in the room corresponded to more or less habitable regions of the geography of the mother's body. After a few months I learned that she had a fear of high places and that she felt the need to establish contact with the earth, to be rooted to the ground. Then after a year an image became fixed almost obsessively in her mind, like a kind of dream flash: she saw herself as a child suspended in mid-air from the window of her flat on one of the top floors of a building by her sick mother, who was doing it as a punishment and a warning. Another patient, Anna, with a severe history of trauma, for a while seductively claimed the right to sit on my armchair. Yet another patient occasionally brings along Morgan, a big Labrador – and so there are three of us. A couple of times, upon seeing me standing at the door, it bestowed its rather embarrassing attentions on me. As she tried – for me, not quite promptly enough – to hold back these unattractive demonstrations of affection, by way of explanation she said: 'You must smell good today.' And I thought of a nascent, but already intense transference by proxy. Then there are those who need to say something in the corridor, and often these are the most valuable communications because they are less constricted in the role of patient that each assigns himself to perform. For Alberto, a young university student, the setting involves his inseparable girlfriend who spends the whole hour of the session in the waiting room next door. The two doors must be carefully closed, and Alberto speaks to me softly all the time, as if he were afraid of being overheard. Needless to say, the problem here is how to attend to the strong symbiotic needs that bind him to his mother and that subsequently led him to suffer from uncontrollable Oedipal jealousy. At regular intervals he transforms himself into a kind of Othello – he has already bid his 'farewell to arms', to borrow an expression from Shakespeare's famous monologue, by retreating back to his home and dropping out of work and university – every time he lends an ear to his inner Iago.

The internal setting

In addition to the formal setting, which, as we have seen, can be a bearer of strong psychological values and which it is at all events best to set up and maintain as soon as conditions permit, there is also the analyst's *internal* setting. Here, too, I would distinguish between two aspects, one *general* and one *specific* – on the basis of the pre-eminent model I use for work, which is an analytic or bi-personal field theory (Baranger and Baranger, 2008; Ferro, 1992, 2002c, 2006; Ferro and Basile, 2004). These two aspects together define the emotional availability and mental receptivity of the analyst, his ability to take on the patient's projective identifications (the most primitive forms of communication and pre/proto-symbolization) and to process them within himself before returning them consciously in the form of interpretive actions (Ogden, 1994b) or interpretations, and in various other ways even unconsciously, which inevitably means entering into complex sequences of enactment: in the language of Bion this would be called his capacity for reverie. General variables of this capacity include the number of hours of sleep the analyst gets (Bion, 1992), his own analysis, his total caseload over a certain period, his sense of his own limits,[2] his number of 'flying hours' as a therapist, his training and professional career, his satisfaction with his private life, his sense of pain and of existence, his institutional identity, his willingness to keep up with the conceptual and theoretical tools of analysis, and so on.

We come now to what I would call the 'specific' internal setting. But first I would like to point out that the external setting (*cadre* in French, *encuadre* in Spanish) has been conceived of as a theatrical space ever since Freud. Indeed, Freud writes that nothing can be overcome *in absentia* or *in effigie*. The battle against neurosis is fought in the combat zone of transference, i.e. of a neo-neurosis centred on the analyst and analysis, which is paradoxically true and false at the same time. But this virtual space, just like awareness of the *as-if* dimension of analysis, needs to be maintained also in the mind of the analyst and much more systematically than Freud did. From the vertex of the analyst's internal setting all the facts, events and topics of the analysis, if necessary even items of furniture, are seen in terms of the intersubjective field of analysis, the psychic reality and the transference (even if understood according to a model that I picture as extensive or as a fractal structure).

The basic principle, to borrow from an observation by the Austrian writer Peter Handke (1970), is that a chair on the stage, at the theatre, is a theatrical chair, a semiotic device. This radically anti-realist perspective seeks to, as it were, put in brackets the outside, current and past world in order to illuminate the inner and psychic reality (which, after Klein, we should think of as having its own extreme concreteness) that is expressed in the here and now, the dream of the session. There are two good justifications for this: first, because this is the only reality that concerns us as analysts and about which we can try to do something, and secondly because the here-and-now is the level at which our technique is most transformative. Besides, this concept is already implicit in some way in that of transference neurosis. Indeed, what is valued more than anything else in the relational situation we describe as transference neurosis are therapeutic factors such as emotional involvement and affective intensity (Reed, 1994).

After all, this view is simply the logical consequence of a line of development that runs like a thread throughout psychoanalysis. It starts from Freud's (relative) abandonment of theory of the seduction trauma, and his discovery of *Nachträglichkeit* and the complex notion of causality and temporality that this concept expresses, of primal fantasies and unconscious fantasies, and goes on to include the fundamental equivalence between dream and game decreed by Klein and then extended by Bion to encompass thought. For Bion thinking is dreaming, or in other words, symbolizing. In an even more explicit way, Grotstein sees knowing reality as dreaming it; that is to say, we can only approximate to 'O', or reality, or the thing-in-itself (in the Kantian sense) through operations of the α function (previously known as 'dream-work-α') and then of dream-work (condensation, displacement, figurability, secondary elaboration), which correspond to the principal tropes in rhetoric and linguistics: metaphor and metonymy. Nietzsche had already made the point: 'Our sensory perceptions are based on tropes, not on unconscious inferences. Identifying similar thing with similar thing – discovering some similarity or other in one thing and another thing is the primordial process. *Memory* thrives on this activity, and constantly practises it. *Misapprehension* is the primordial phenomenon' (1999, p. 68).

In every moment of our lives we transform the stimuli of the immediate context of experience, proto-sensations and proto-emotions or β-elements, into α-elements, into images that can be stored in memory or used to think and to dream. This is how the development of the emotional container – which is the strategic aim of therapy – occurs: a cloud of β-elements (in itself a proto-container) gradually acquires form and the various particles begin to be held together by threads of feeling that from being thin progressively become stronger. Why emotions? Let us return to Nietzsche:

> The most delicate sensations of pleasure and displeasure constitute the true raw material of all knowledge: the true mystery is that surface onto which the activity of the nerves, in pleasure and pain, inscribes its forms: sensation immediately projects *forms*, which in turn generate new sensations. It belongs to the very nature of the sensations of pleasure and displeasure to express themselves in adequate motions: the sensation of the *image* is created due to the fact that these adequate motions cause other nerves to experience sensations.
>
> (1999 [1872–1873], pp. 31–32)

As Grotstein puts it: 'The ultimate importance of feelings lies in their constituting our personal intersection and confrontation with impersonal O' (2000, p. 316). Emotions, therefore, express the immediate lived value in terms of pleasure/displeasure that any stimulus represents for the subject's survival, what happens every time we intersect with 'O', the real. The challenge facing the subject is having to order these feelings into a coherent picture that renders an adequate image of reality and makes it sufficiently predictable.

Similarly, the theory of therapeutic action that underlies the analytic field model, namely, enabling the patient to symbolize better, so that he can mature from a psychological point of view thanks to repeated experiences of emotional sharing, or unison, is nothing other than the development of a conception of therapeutic action that Freud also assigned to the present. Later, with Klein, the focus of therapeutic action became the modulation of anxiety in the here-and-now. Other factors lost ground accordingly: the value given to historical reconstruction and the (cathartic) effect of abreaction that was supposed to be related to it. And this is the point where, to pick up the first of the meanings of the discontent referred to in the title of this chapter, a series of criticisms of the bi-personal, relational or analytic field model of psychoanalysis converge. In essence, this model has been accused of devaluing the importance of history and thus even of neglecting mental pain; also, of being too 'good-natured' and not taking hatred, primary destructiveness and the death instinct into sufficient account.

Relational models, of which there are several very different versions,[3] are accused of focusing too much on the dual relationship between mother and child, and thus of minimizing the role of the third party, the father, in the development of the psyche; of not taking the Oedipus complex or drives into account, and of de-sexualizing psychoanalysis. All these objections, which are persistent, battle-hardened and sincere, and need to be given due consideration, can be countered with good arguments. With regard to the paternal function, it must be said that it is also present on various levels in relational models. First, at birth, in the two-party relationship it is a presence inside the mother's mind, which has another object of investment in addition to the child; likewise, the analyst is perceived as someone who has a private life, other patients, his own interests and so on. The third party/father as a separating element, as the law-bringer, the sense of limitation and reality appears, then, in all the inevitable (and necessary) moments of emotional disconnection or detuning that result from the absence of the other – and this is what also happens in the session between patient and analyst. He is present, finally, in the structuring function of the setting, which ensures a healthy dialectic between identity and difference, a rhythmic cadence of absence and presence, love and hate.

As for the past, we cannot escape it even if we wanted to, because there is no event – either fictional, in the setting, or imagined (*as if*) – that does not derive its meaning from the historical reality of life, both factual and internal. External reality, trauma, pain cannot be deleted; rather it is precisely when the unconscious psychic reality and the transference in its extended dimension are forgotten (as is reflected in the words of the patient, which can be regarded as always referring to the immediate context of experience) that there is a risk of retraumatization that goes beyond the inevitable and necessary. What an analyst can do, however, is simply to help a person find the best forms, and I mean this almost in the aesthetic sense, for those facts. The aesthetic emotion is indeed the model for the dream and the good form of experience. But to do this, as Bion writes, one should not be distracted by the facts. A patient of mine who had never had much to do with books has become an avid reader of novels. His absolute favourite is Dostoevsky. In the pages of the great Russian writer he re-finds his own personal torments and neuroses. There, both seem to him truer than all the facts of his life, which are often only, as it were, 'news items', that is to say, they have not yet been re-signified. But literature shows them to him in a new light. And the therapy is never so alive as when we talk passionately about the characters we find in books. These conversations have become for us a kind of playroom or dream space. It is, essentially, a question of working with adults as we would in a childcare setting (Ferro and Basile, 2006). An adult's words are his drawings. The facts of reality transposed into a drawing or a cartoon or a virtual reality environment take on meaning within the new frame, although inevitably they refer to other levels of reality or possible worlds in which we live (external, internal, past, present and future worlds inhabited by partial objects, whole objects, and so on). Bion writes: 'The past is not important, because you can do nothing about it: the only things about which you can do anything are the remnants, the vestiges of the past, of past states of mind [...] but it is possible to make use of these vestiges that are discernible in the present if we allow ourselves to discern them' (1997, p. 44).

And on the other hand, how otherwise would it be possible in child psychoanalysis to communicate with a child, to set off the complex interactions that allow him to gain access to symbolic thought and to cure him of his discomfort, if no reference is made to his personal archaeology? Are we sure that this interaction made up of rhythms and song-and-dance does not remain essential for the whole of life, along with our more mature abilities to make sense of experience? Since loss, separation and pain are always present, can we be sure that the subject is not constructed by moments of deep emotional communion? In essence, then, analytic field theory fully carries out the transition from a focus on contents to a focus on the container, although even here no clean break is imaginable. The shift in emphasis from *what* is meant to *how* it is meant has favoured open, non-univocal interpretations. The theory of dreams has undergone a similar shift. From being the translation or deciphering of a partly lost and therefore unintelligible content to be rescued from censorship, the dream is now of interest not so much by virtue of its content but because of how it works, its function as a symbol factory, and on account of the ambiguity and poetic richness of its text.

However, in my view the real explanation for the irritation felt by these critics lies elsewhere, and here I come to the second of the meanings of the term discontent. This is the subtle unease or genuine discomfort one feels when adopting a strictly field vertex, an internal setting. The wonderful title of Mazzacane's paper (2007) on killer contents speaks clearly. We should not delude ourselves. The analyst is very exposed. Every day he can be put harshly to the test, and for this reason he must bear in mind the critical point at which his relationship with a given patient stops being tenable. The more the patient suffers, the more he unconsciously transmits to the analyst his distress in the hope that the analyst will make it more tolerable. Another way of expressing the same thing is suggested by Searles (1965b), who says that the patient tries to drive his therapist crazy (but be careful, also to treat him).[4] While on the one hand the analyst's internal setting allows him more flexibility than the rigid professional superego of the analyst as mirror, on the other, it also entails taking on much more responsibility for how things go. Listening 'without memory and without desire', says Bion, means giving up a significant barrier against guilt and having to tolerate higher levels of anxiety.

Now, in the early stages of analysis it is even more understandable that this internal vertex becomes dark because, when the patient arrives, he already has a story to tell, which the analyst apparently has nothing to do with, and it is often a history laden with the pain, grief, traumas and violence he has suffered – the 'facts', in other words. It could be a list of symptoms that have been there for years if not all his life. There are then, even at a later stage, figures in his discourse that are difficult to see even from the perspective of waking dream thought or as characters in the analytic field. They can be characters from the patient's real life, sometimes unpleasant, violent, sadistic characters, whom it is hard to identify with or be reflected in hypothetically, and whom it is hard to see as signs of our functioning or dysfunctioning[5] (this may have been the case, for example, with the sick mother of the patient who sat on my floor; but shortly before this image surfaced, an increase in fees was probably the setting factor that brought hatred and aggression into the relationship). But when this happens, and every time one is amazed to see it, one instantly leaves the bleak fixedness of a frozen past and enters the virtual reality of analysis and its magic. Every time this happens, we rediscover the beauty, depth and extraordinary humanity of psychoanalysis and its method.

To put it another way: the internal setting manages to ensure the minimum conditions of representation, even when they are apparently missing. Let me mention here the fruitful ambiguity of the term 'rappresentazione' in Italian; it has the twofold meaning of mental representation and theatrical performance. It reconstructs a frame where no frame would seem to be present any longer, while still aiming at an ideal situation. Sometimes, as in Peter Yates' *The Dresser* (1983), a film about a theatre company that keeps on touring even though there is a war on, it means having to go on stage while the bombs are falling. In other situations it may be the opposite phenomenon that stops the performance, in other words, an idyllic climate that conceals the collusion that helps to avoid pain and hatred: you get lost in the show, like when you get the impression that everything is running smoothly.

In fact, it is precisely the opposition between outside and inside, and between past and present that needs to be rethought. The frame of the setting is neither entirely external nor entirely internal. Its position is ambiguous. It is both external to the image, and yet it is effectively part of the representation. It belongs simultaneously to two worlds. It is the threshold between them. What it excludes is as important as what it includes in the space it delimits. The parergonal status of the frame deconstructs the more obvious and more entrenched conceptual oppositions. It closes itself off to the world and opens up the space of fiction, but in doing so it shows that every representation pre-supposes a limit, a perspective, a vertex. The words themselves, after all, are frames for things. Case history, therefore, is not (ever) only case history, the history of the patient's life 'before' therapy, but also the dream that he is dreaming during the session. Among other things, also the story of a dream can (perhaps) be more of a narrative derivative (Ferro, 2002c) of waking dream thought than the story of an experience had during sleep. Everything depends on the frame, namely whether we assume an internal or external point of view to it. Transference is ubiquitous and immediate, although of variable intensity. One need only think of the infinite possibilities of organizing the narrative of his own life that a patient has from the very first session. There is no other constraint than the transference. Even when he speaks of 'facts', the patient means indirectly how he perceives himself, the analyst and the emotional quality of their relationship. Let me now briefly refer to some clinical cases.

Clinical examples

Wild Swans

In one of the first sessions Sara tells me that she has read a book she really liked: *Wild Swans*. I had read this book some years earlier. It is the story of three generations of women living in a family in China from the fall of the Manchu Empire to the present day. She talked about being struck by the description of the custom of making girls who would later become concubines wear tiny shoes to shape their feet. This was a way of attaining ethereal beauty, but at a high price. When they walked, these women gave the impression of swaying like reeds (in the book: 'like a tender young willow shoot in a *spring breeze*'). 'Very poetic, but how much suffering!' she exclaimed. Which life forced into shoes that were too small, I wonder, is she talking about? When I see them floating, she continues, sometimes wearing a white mask of greasepaint, which gives the idea of affectation, they seem to be somewhere in between a doll and a geisha, but not much like a real woman. Here, perhaps, I think to myself in terms of the internal setting, is what Sara is saying: she could have been expressing the fantasy of being 'forced' into a preconceived role. She is asking for something different from what possibly happened to her in the past in her family life: she does not want to be shaped according to my more or less conscious expectations, and if anything, she wants to be helped to become more like a real woman, and a little less like a doll or a geisha.

The diet

What would you like to change about yourself through analysis? I ask Stefania. My mother! she replies, with charming spontaneity. And indeed, in the early stages of therapy she dwells on her mother's behaviour, which she describes as intrusive and unbearable. A nineteen-year-old student soon to be taking her A-levels, Stefania surprises me with a sort of *belle indifference* to the many extra pounds that weigh her down. Later she mentions her past diets, each of which failed, as well as the continued pressure from her parents to find a solution to the problem, which has been going on for as long as she can remember. Almost in reaction to her indifference, I find myself losing interest and dozing off. After the first few months during which I struggle to feel involved in the relationship, perhaps we come to understand something of the possible meaning of her malaise. Stefania's problem has always been how to make herself visible to others. Her father is an archaeologist, a sort of Indiana Jones always about to go off to some exotic destination, and when he is at home he usually reads the paper while she talks to him. Although her mother is more intrusive, Stefania experiences her as equally impervious and as someone firmly entrenched in the concrete world.

Stefania then decides, perhaps for the first time in her life, to deal with her weight problem and she addresses it with a motivation that she feels comes more from inside her. Initially she makes some progress. This may mean that the therapy has taught her that in order to feel alive she has less need of the symptom. Accordingly, the sessions become more lively. I begin to *see more of her.* Emotions appear that previously she only told me about via images of dangerous animals that her father met on his adventurous travels and that she herself had seen on the few occasions when she had accompanied him on his travels around the world: scorpions, snakes, spiders, and the like. Now it's jealousy. She can still not take responsibility for it, but she projects it ever closer to her, on her boyfriend; recently he has started to worry that if Stefania becomes any prettier, other men might start courting her! A sort of pact of denial which forms part of the basis of their love relationship begins to show cracks, I'm thinking, just like the pact there perhaps was (or still is) at the beginning of an analysis one has started more under duress than out of personal desire.

The fact is that her parents have stopped asking her constantly to step on the scales (it occurs to me, when she tells me this, that babies are put on scales to measure how much milk they have drunk). Now they are more interested in the rest of her life, her plans, what she's going to do after she leaves school. There is some fresh air. Stefania has the air of someone who has started to grow. To help her grow, however, I first had to discover myself in the role of a mum unable to dream and of a dad-who-always-reads-the-paper, and for a long time I had to to tolerate boredom and frustration.

A 'tough cookie'

She's one 'tough cookie' behind her slender beauty: this is what I thought to myself at my first meeting with Teresa. Therapy started a month ago. Twenty-six years old, first-class degree in medicine, the only child of two reasonably united parents. Her work in a hospital brings her into contact with some serious haematological diseases. Sometimes when she gets home she cries to relieve her tension. This suggests that she puts her own suffering into the suffering she sees at the hospital, and which she seems easily upset by (the books tell you everything, but they don't prepare you for the emotional impact! she exclaims).

Teresa has requested analysis in order to be able to do her work; but the other reason is that she wants to understand herself. Above all she wants to understand why she has such unsteady relationships with men and why she is so tormented by jealousy. There is also the fact that in the past three years she has also suffered several bereavements, which have forced her to face up suddenly to loss.

The immediate impression she gives is of a determined, clear-headed, bright girl. I also say to myself that sometimes you have to wait a long time to understand the true meaning of a request for therapy. It occurs to me later that 'tough' can also mean challenging or difficult. But I also had the fantasy: 'This is someone who can go far.'

She is going through a period of crisis. Sometimes she has 'catastrophic' quarrels and outbursts of anger that surprise her as much as anyone else. Her boyfriend, like everyone else, finds it hard to see her fragile side. To him and to the others, in fact, Teresa appears strong and able to withstand everything. But she feels the need to rearrange the pieces of her life. Her investment in the therapy is immediately intense – last Wednesday, I missed it (you) so much, she says, that I started to keep a diary.

That's already two significant different 'diffractions' of the transference: I find myself taking the role of the rather uncaring boyfriend (who will have to become caring), but also, I have already become her 'dear diary' which she relies on to express her innermost thoughts.

New technologies

The setting has no value in itself. Its only value is that it has to serve a certain function, namely to enable the analytic field to establish itself and to promote the exchange of states of reverie. This exchange fosters the ability to dream the undreamt dreams (metaphorically speaking, night terrors, in the case of psychosis) or the interrupted dreams (metaphorically, nightmares, if we are dealing with non-psychotic disorders) of the analysand (Ogden, 2005); that is, the ability to grasp the unconscious movements and tensions that come alive in the relationship. In this way it is possible to encourage changes that enable psychic growth to resume where it had left off, a process that can be regarded as analogous to somatic growth. If the setting had an absolute value, it would be a kind of fetish and would involve the same type of partial denial of reality that Freud thought lay behind perversions. However, without a sufficiently organized and reliable setting, the analytic field is not even established, or it comes into being too unwell and incurable.

Sometimes, the setting itself can become a character in the field. Films can be about their own making, for example, Fellini's *8½* (1963), or Truffaut's *Day for Night* (1973). The film of analysis always has this self-reflexive or metafictional character, but without a screen, whether it be a sheet or a section of white wall, and an apparatus for projecting, nothing would be possible. Of course, we can watch a movie on TV, on a low- or high-definition screen, LCD or otherwise, at the cinema or on an iPod, but it is always necessary to have some kind of apparatus for projecting the images exposed on the film. The extreme case would be putting the film up to the light and examining it frame by frame. That's what sometimes happens in analyses in which the patient's ability to dream or to symbolize is severely limited, for example, in the case of autistic disorders or in the autistic areas of neurotic personalities. This too can be useful.

So the systems may vary, and each may correspond to different levels of immersion (emotional involvement, intimacy) and interactivity (that is, the ability to interact and modify the field with interpretation). However, each device has its own aesthetic impact (which one needs to be aware of) and specific effects. For our purposes, the best cinemas I know are those where there are gently sloping rows of comfortable seats, with Dolby surround, a big screen, darkness, but with the necessary floor lights, ease of exit and working fire alarms. But we must recognize that, for example, the iPod has a versatility that cinemas lack. The iPod allows viewing even in situations where it was previously impossible. In other words, the new conceptualizations of analytic work, and also some of the new communication technologies, enable us to tackle narcissistic disorders and borderline states.

Keeping for a moment to this metaphor, if the container, as Ogden specifies, is identified with the dream itself, binding α-elements/images with the weaving of emotional threads, possible killer contents are all the factors that interrupt the dream, the projection: too much light (too much reality or history), excessively loud noises (overly destructive emotions), smoking in the auditorium (for example, subtle perversions of the relationship that are not recognized), a fire in the auditorium (unmanageable erotic or psychotic transference), and so on. But another possible killer content, especially at the beginning of an analysis, is simply not accepting anything less than an ideal cinema.

However, no exceptions can be made regarding the analyst's internal setting, in other words, the fact that the analyst should be able to listen analytically and to observe the transference. This, if you like, is the film that the analyst has in his mind, the 'second look', or 'third ear', or 'third eye', or 'analytic attitude'. This internal setting must be rigorous, a principle which also includes knowing how to lose it and then how to get it back. Analysis can only proceed under cover of darkness; it needs to project a veneer of darkness on things. The significant facts of the analysis are those that share their material with dreams, and like dreams, they are darkly luminous.

There is yet more to be said about the setting. The setting, even when formal, functions as a third party, as a guarantee for both patient and analyst. I personally think that precisely from the perspective of analytic field theory there is a greater risk of losing contact with the internal setting than by making a fetish of the formal setting of analysis. Obviously the analyst is not transparent to himself, he does not fully control the unconscious context in which his intentions are determined. Basically, I would be cautious about justifying deviations in the formal setting of the analysis on the grounds of an emotional attitude springing from any form of therapeutic zeal, which is the most harmful thing there is in analysis. It may in fact be precisely the ability to register signals from the field, the derivatives of waking dream thought, that provides a mechanism for critically examining the appropriateness of introducing certain 'parameters' of the setting, as they used to be called, and the assessment of their sustainability.

In conclusion, there exist various levels of empathy and attunement, from the more conscious (such as putting oneself in another person's shoes) to the more unconscious (for example, letting oneself be surprised and touched by one's own fantasies, dreams, memories, experiences and insights that can be seen either as field factors or elements of communication from one unconscious to another); this means using one's own subjective experience in analysis (Jacobs, 2007). When this happens, resonance effects are created between patient and analyst and between the experiences that each has of the encounter. The facts of the analysis become a joint creation of two intercommunicating internal worlds. It's like sharing a space of virtual reality or a dream space, or entering into a kind of dance. One needs to be lulled by the more regressive waves of the setting, but then, every time, after allowing oneself to lose the internal setting, one needs to get it back. Indeed, to paraphrase Winnicott, one might say that there is no such thing as a dream, but a dream becomes such only at the moment one wakes up. Otherwise it would be a hallucination, if it were lost in the imaginary, or at most a hallucinosis, if it were stuck to reality. The analyst must function as a sort of amphibious creature, both observer and participant. Immersion and interactivity are two possible terms that help us to conceptualize this key aspect of the analytic device (Civitarese, 2008a).

The best proof that one has correctly grasped something about the history of the patient comes from the emotional truth of the analytic relationship lived in the here-and-now of the session. An intellectual understanding of the patient's past and present is useful, but is not enough. The expression 'internal setting' has this distinctive quality: it implies a concept of space, time and functioning that is lacking in terms like 'evenly suspended attention' or 'free-floating attention', because, although they refer to its components, on the one hand, unlike reverie, they suggest turning attention to the outside in general, and on the other, do not in themselves imply an intersubjective model. What the concept of internal setting does more than this is to constrain the analyst to keep to the dream dimension, the virtual, or 'field' element of the analytic encounter; it commits him to creating a dream space, a stage set or a play area. Compliance with the extreme version of the internal setting would lead the analyst to prepare himself for a mental state whereby each meeting would be like seeing the patient for the first time: as Bion writes, 'If he feels he has [seen the patient before], he is treating the wrong patient' (1992, p. 382).

8

FROM THE MYSTIC WRITING PAD TO THE α FUNCTION

Metaphors of text and translation in Freud and Bion

The metaphor of the text and the related metaphor of translation are absolutely central to both Freud and Bion. For Bion, however, they take on a 'social' dimension that is not so evident in Freud and that reflects the shift from a one-person to an interpersonal psychology. To help me highlight the differences between the two paradigms, in this chapter I shall draw on Derrida's reading of Freud's paper on the mystic writing pad. In Freud the way in which perceptions are inscribed on the wax tablet of the mystic writing pad of memory still suggests a subject that at the beginning of life is a blank slate and that receives its data from the senses. For Bion, on the contrary – and this is also true of Winnicott – from a certain point of view the psychic surface on which the child inscribes the mental data of its experience at birth is the memory of the mother, that is to say, a page that is by no means immaculate but rather is already written.

In suitable lights

The term 'work' is common currency in psychoanalysis. It is found in the definition of drive as a 'demand for work' imposed on the psyche (*Arbeitsanforderung*). We use the expressions 'work of mourning' (*Trauerarbeit*) to indicate the subject's struggle against the depression caused by loss and 'dream work' (*Traumarbeit*) to denote the transformation of dream thoughts into a manifest text. It is contained in the concept of psychic elaboration (*psychische Verarbeitung*), viz. the work of integration performed by the psychic apparatus to tie up pathogenic excitement. There is also the rather 'dark' concept (Laplanche and Pontalis, 1967) of working through/out (*Durcharbeitung*)[1] or 'interpretive elaboration,' a term that refers to the retrieval of repressed items that is promoted by interpretation, even when it at first seems to have no effect. One could also mention Green's 'work of the negative' (1993) and the Botellas' 'work of representability' (2001), and so on. In essence, each of these examples refers to a process that requires an expenditure of energy to overcome resistances and to produce transformations in the psyche.

The expression 'memory work', on the other hand, does not appear in psychoanalytic dictionaries, although it was used by Freud and Breuer ('work of reproduction' or 'work of remembering') in 'Studies on Hysteria' (1892–1895), and is also to be found in Derrida's dazzling and dense commentary, 'Freud and the scene of writing' (1967), on a 1924 text by Freud (1924a) of barely six pages, 'Note upon the "mystic writing pad"'. In this essay, the brilliant French philosopher highlights the shift in the representation of memory from naturalistic models to graphical and mechanical models based on the notions of text and writing.

But what is the work of memory, or rather, what is the business of memory? Traditionally, memory is seen as an archivist, a kind of filing clerk who is always on the go collecting new documents. But, as anyone who has a house full of books knows very well, there's a problem: how can you avoid taking up all available space? How can you arrange things so that there are still enough shelves ready to receive yet more texts? And most importantly, how can you make sure that the most important books or those you use most often are available to take down off the shelf? How can memory retain traces of old perceptions, how can it continue to register ever-new perceptions and thus retain and receive unlimited numbers of stimuli? It is immediately clear just how essential the task that this tireless clerk performs in the psyche is. Indeed, it guarantees the subject the chance to keep its identity and to change; in other words, it ensures the possibility of learning from experience, of adapting to the demands of reality, and of growing. The whole question is, however, by no means simple. Freud struggled for a long time to find a model to represent these two key functions, and he came up with all kinds of metaphors: the telescope, the photographic plate, paper, and so on.

But it is only when he came across the extraordinary device of the *Wunderblock* (the original German term for the mystic writing pad) that he realized with joy he had finally hit upon the solution; what's more, the joy is clearly expressed. Here is how he describes it:

> The Mystic Pad is a slab of dark brown resin or wax with a paper edging; over the slab is laid a thin transparent sheet, the top end of which is firmly secured to the slab while its bottom end rests on it without being fixed to it. This transparent sheet is the more interesting part of the little device. It itself consists of two layers, which can be detached from each other except at their two ends. The upper layer is a transparent piece of celluloid; the lower layer is made of thin translucent waxed paper. When the apparatus is not in use, the lower surface of the waxed paper adheres lightly to the upper surface of the wax slab.
>
> To make use of the Mystic Pad, one writes upon the celluloid portion of the covering sheet which rests on the wax slab. For this purpose no pencil or chalk is necessary, since the writing does not depend on material being deposited on the receptive surface. It is a return to the ancient method of writing on tablets of clay or wax: a pointed stilus scratches the surface, the depressions upon which constitute the 'writing'. In the case of the Mystic Pad this scratching is not effected directly, but through the medium of the covering-sheet. At the points which the stilus touches, it presses the lower surface of the waxed paper on to the wax slab, and the grooves are visible as dark writing upon the otherwise smooth whitish-grey surface of the celluloid.
>
> (Freud, 1924a, p. 229)

To recapitulate: the pad is made up of three layers: (a) a transparent sheet of celluloid is laid upon (b) a second, more fragile sheet of waxed paper by way of protection, and, finally, (c) below this there is a slab of resin. When a stylus is pressed against the top sheet, the other sheet adheres to the wax tablet and makes a mark there. So, between the various components of the writing pad, which Freud describes as a specific medium, what we have is a certain translation or transference of stimuli: a contact or pressure or an im-pression or incision (a certain amount of force is necessary, in fact, to produce the inscription) is transformed on the wax tablet into a sign, *into a system of differences, writing without ink*. Recording is dictated by the functions that are an integral part of the archive system itself, which reflect the spatial and temporal relations among its constituent elements. This is what happens to the perceptual stimuli transmitted by the sense organs, although, plainly speaking, inscription occurs by modulating the genetic expressiveness that regulates protein synthesis at the level of the synapses.

To ensure that the tablet can be written upon again, after writing the top layer has to be erased:

> If one wishes to destroy what has been written, all that is necessary is to raise the double covering-sheet from the wax slab by a light pull, starting from the free lower end. The close contact between the waxed paper and the wax slab at the places which have been scratched (upon which the visibility of the writing depended) is thus brought to an end and it does not recur when the two surfaces come together once more. The Mystic Pad is now clear of writing and ready to receive fresh notes.
>
> (Ibid., p. 229).

In order to describe this process, Freud further develops his metaphor: 'If we imagine one hand writing upon the surface of the Mystic Writing-Pad while another periodically raises its covering-sheet from the wax slab, we shall have a concrete representation of the way in which I tried to picture the functioning of the perceptual apparatus of our mind' (ibid., p. 232). So the writing-pad's readiness to be written on is not total or continuous: the left hand must occasionally lift the sheet while the right hand writes. What one hand does is a precondition for the action of the other. As in Escher's lithograph *Drawing Hands* (1948), a certain paradox is inherent in this activity, namely that there is no memory without cancellation, or in other words, without forgetting.

For Freud the rhythmic process of detaching the two layers which cleans and prepares the surface for a new impression corresponds to the periodic investment from within (*aus dem Inneren*) the perception-consciousness system. From the standpoint of neurophysiology, the Freudian hypothesis seems to foreshadow Edelman's concept (2004) of the periodic discharge, lasting several hundred milliseconds, of the *dynamic core*, that is, the set of interactions that form part of the thalamo-cortical system, a functional aggregate that sends signals mostly to itself and is thought to be at the origin of states of consciousness. This discontinuity is what brings about the representation of Time. At this point, Freud's enthusiasm becomes understandable. The *techno-logy* of the mystic pad provides him with the opportunity to work out a very vivid metaphor of the psychic apparatus. Not even the most cutting-edge computer would have the same potential because its files are fixed and it can run out of memory.

Finally then comes the twist, as it were: 'The surface of the Mystic Pad is clear of writing and once more capable of receiving impressions. But it is easy to discover that the permanent trace of what was written is retained upon the wax slab itself and is legible *in suitable lights*' (ibid., p. 230, emphasis added). The memory traces of wax on the tablet of the unconscious can be read 'in suitable lights' *(bei geeigneter Belichtung lesbar)*. The expression is singularly suggestive. The whole of psychoanalysis can be equated with this beam of light, or rather ray of darkness, that gradually and with due sensitivity brings to light a latent text that could otherwise not be revealed. And of course the suitable lights I am thinking of in this case are the transference, the only lighting capable of bringing forth both repressed and non-repressed memories from the implicit memory of foetal life and the first two years of life. The metaphor of the mystic writing pad also tells us that only what reaches the wax tablet will make sense. Each perception has a meaning only when it enters the differential system or the Saussurean realm of the articulations of the language of memory. The presentation of perception is thus from the very outset representation or symbolization (even at its zero degree);[2] it could also be called a form of experience, a construction, a fiction or an *as if*.

Memory does not give us back copies of the 'real world', of the thing itself, of the real. It is not made up of pure presence. Nothing is perceived and then entered into memory as it is. The process is simultaneous. Meaning is the result of a continuous activity of *après-coup*, deferral, reference. Every perception is from the very beginning a re-transcription or translation, 'saying almost the same thing' (Eco, 2003), a primary transference. As in the theory of Lacan, the subject is constituted in the relationship with alterity; it is not an

> initially closed individuality, which then opens up to external reality and the intersubjective world. Its identity is *relational* from

> the beginning, and what best defines it is non-coincidence. The subject is alienated from the outset, 'thrown into the world' (as Heidegger put it), that is, thrown into relationship, and not defined by its properties.
>
> (Bottiroli, 2006, p. 267)

The identity of the memory trace is entirely relational, that is, it is made up of relationships from the very beginning. It is negative and differential. It is itself only to the extent that it denies all other elements in the system. Memories do not correspond to things, they are not labels for them, nor do they make up a catalogue of objects; and this remains true *even if they are bound to things by belonging, by co-ordination, by relations of meaning.* The logic that applies to writing is the logic of the sign, but also of semiosis in general. It is therefore the same logic as that which applies to the memory trace and to memory.

Let us return briefly to the mystic writing pad. We have seen how inscriptions on the unconscious and cancellations on the layer of the perception-consciousness system that interfaces with external and internal reality function. If we look at what happens on the wax tablet, we realize that in fact the traces become superimpositions and that the different inscriptions will either inevitably cancel each other out to varying degrees or reinforce each other. The structure is like a palimpsest comprising a dynamic set of layers. This is a level of cancellation and oblivion that goes much deeper than the level of the hand that lifts up the sheet (repression). The idea of memory as a process of continuous reshuffling is in fact expressed by the metaphor of the writing pad on two levels: the 'material' level of signs on the wax and their destinies (the letters of the alphabet), and the 'semiotic' level of the metaphor of the text (the level of meanings); which is to say that already in pre-Saussurian times, prior, that is, to the postulate of the arbitrariness of the link between signified and signifier that ushers in structuralism, we find in this extraordinary paper by Freud the principles of a differential economy of meaning. Memory traces, just like the letters of the alphabet, have a meaning only in opposition to each other, and not because they are mimetic of things. There is an irremediable break between words and things.

At last we can now define memory as the device that presides over the continuous re-arrangement and re-transcription, and thus re-signification, of memories. Memory can carry out its work 'cost-effectively' only if the memory traces are not permanent, only if the library is continuously reorganized along functional lines, if there are multiple copies of certain texts etc. In other words, it must work on the principle of *Nachträglichkeit*,[3] a term that has been translated in various ways (deferred action or retrospective attribution, retrospectivity, retroactivity, posteriority) and that not only expresses a sophisticated concept of psychic causality but also reflects how meaning in general is structured – at the same time as reflecting how its own meaning is structured on the basis of a variety of translations.

The signs that are successively added to those already impressed on the wax tablet are *supplementary*. Each time a supplement, addendum or postscript (*Nachtrag* in German) is added, it changes the entire context. The effect of the addition is not limited to itself; it changes the whole text in a continuous play of identity and difference, regularity and variation. Like the *Wunderblock* (in Italian: Notes magico*)*, *Nachträglichkeit* also has something magical about it. It might even be taken to indicate a reversal of the arrow of time and causality (Civitarese, 1996, 2008b). Derrida (1967) and Brooks (1984), respectively, believe that it is a 'discovery' of Freud's and one of his most brilliant feats, because it arrives at a sort of undecidability between reality and fantasy and makes inevitable the influence that psychic reality has on the subject. Derrida writes:

> For repetition does not *happen* to an original impression; its possibility is already there, in the resistance offered the first time by the psychical neurones. Resistance itself is only possible if the opposition of forces lasts and is repeated from the beginning. It is the very idea of a first time that becomes enigmatic. [...] It is non-origin that is originary [...] the concepts of *Nachträglichkeit* and *Verspätung*, concepts which govern the whole of Freud's thought and determine all his other concepts, are already present and named in the *Project* [the work Freud outlined and then abandoned, in which he tried to found a psychology of the neurology of time – 1985]. The irreducibility of the 'effect of deferral' – such, no doubt, is Freud's discovery.
>
> (Derrida, 1967, pp. 253–255)

He goes on: 'Writing supplements perception before perception even appears to itself. "Memory" or writing is the opening of that process of appearance itself. *The "perceived" may be read only in the past, beneath perception and after it*' (ibid., p. 282, italics mine).

But if this is the structure of memory and of the mind that can already be seen at work in the Freudian metaphor of the writing pad, the problem of origin remains because the wax tablet can only be imagined as at one and the same time (and paradoxically) virgin and already with a text that precedes the nascent subject's first inscriptions. Freud was conscious of this. He coins, for example, the concept of primal fantasy. Later, in a passage in 'Formulations on the two principles of mental functioning', he proves that he is well aware of the child's situation of dependency from the mother's care:

> It will rightly be objected that an organization which was a slave to the pleasure principle and neglected the reality of the external world could not maintain itself alive for the shortest time, so that it could not have come into existence at all. The employment of a *fiction* like this is, however, justified when one considers that the infant – *provided one includes with it the care it receives from its mother* – does almost realize a psychical system of this kind.
>
> (Freud, 1911, p. 220, my italics)

However, due to the space given to the drives and the positivistic framework of his psychology, this point was pushed aside in Freud or in some way taken for granted. The 'fiction' has lasted and has shaped an entire psychology (Girard, 2010).

Thinking reveries and sacred conversation

The metaphor of the text and the principle of non-origin that Freud inaugurated implicitly with the mystic writing pad and explicitly with the concept of primal fantasies are even more intrinsic to Bion's theory of thought. Bion, too, sees at the heart of mental life a process of alphabetical transformation/transduction/translation (or rather, in the opposite direction, from β to α), and unlike Freud he immediately makes it into a social and intersubjective phenomenon. But first, to contextualize the paradigm shift from Freud to Bion, let us return for a moment to the mystic writing pad and look at it from another perspective.

On the Internet you can find the video of an installation by Arnold Dreyblatt, a New York artist who lives in Berlin.[4] The work is called *Der Wunderblock* (Berlin 2000) and is obviously inspired by Freud's essay. The merit of the installation lies in the way Dreyblatt effectively depicts the dynamism that characterizes memory, that is, the interaction of the traces as signs of a writing system whose meaning is not given at source (*although it can also not be reinvented every time*!) and is not enclosed in itself, but is defined by the relations of similarity and dissimilarity that each term enjoys with all the other terms. The concrete metaphor of an electronic mystic writing pad[5] readily shows how superimposed traces can reinforce each other, cancel each out or create unexpected effects. The individual letters can form words or entirely original phrases, or they can create drawings, fragments of images and real images. They can then be divided up according to different levels of complexity, and usually the most visible will be the most recent.

The wax tablet could be regarded as being sensitive in the same way as photographic or cinematic film, but it is important that the metaphor of the writing pad puts the emphasis on signs which can then become the letters of the alphabet. Signs suggest in more immediate fashion that there is always a symbolic aspect inherent in perception, even the perception of images. In the film metaphor, which is also in current use, and which in some ways is closer to the truth, the image (representation) is more likely to be seen in a naturalistic sense as a pure reflection of physical reality.

According to Bion's theory of thought (and it is no accident that it features letters), the elementary sensations or proto-emotions constitute β-elements that are constantly being transformed by a mysterious α function into α-elements, primarily (but not only) visual images ready to become dream thoughts and be deposited in the archives of memory. The α-elements then combine to create dream scenes, waking dream thought, and go on to produce more sophisticated forms of thought. We do not know how this function is formed; not even neurobiology can as yet provide explanations of how we move from body to mind, from emotions to thought. The fact remains that perhaps not enough thought has been given to the question of why Bion so closely identified the α element (using a letter from the Greek alphabet) with an image (pictogram). I do not think this is simply a matter of convenience – as we have seen, inherited from Descartes – but it contains, as indeed does maternal reverie, a whole theory of cultural/linguistic/social mediation that is interposed between the thing (*das Ding*)/the real and the subject.

In this same context, one might also think of Bion's famous Grid, the matrix he uses to represent the reversible psychic transformations that lead to more abstract thought. It could be read like the mystic writing pad because it likewise seeks to account for the transition from material to immaterial, from the body to the psyche. The Grid is constructed like a psychical version of Mendeleev's table of elements but, most importantly, it immediately presents itself as a language, as a differential system of signs, as if it were the wax tablet of the mystic writing pad that already had all of its text. It is not only a diagram, then, but a metaphor; like the writing pad, it is a rhetorical device that serves to give an idea of how psychic transformations take place while at the same time helping to structure the field of observation.

Both these metaphors – Freud's mystic writing pad and the Bionian Grid, although one is more concrete and the other more abstract – tell us something important, namely, that *perceptions are endowed with meaning practically from the outset*. There are no perceptions that are, so to speak, pure. No perception is the perfect mirror of nature, of a reality out there captured as it is. It follows that there can be no absolutely 'true' thoughts. But we ask ourselves, where does the psyche at birth take this auroral sense from? How do representations of the world begin to form that possess a sufficient degree of coherence?

And here I propose to look at a third image. This is a work by Sebastiano del Piombo painted at the beginning of the sixteenth century which is now in the Metropolitan Museum of New York and which was exhibited as part of a beautiful exhibition held at Palazzo Venezia in Rome (Strinati, 2008). It is a curious picture. There are a variety of figures arranged in pairs with the exception of a woman standing on the right (also excluding a figure at the woman's side who, although he seems to be involved in the general emotional atmosphere of the painting, has his eyes closed and could also be a representation of death). The action is fragmented. The paired figures seem isolated from each other, each pair caught in a secret and intimate exchange of gazes. The Italian title of the painting is *Sacra Conversazione* (English title: *Madonna and Child with Saints and Donors*). If one wanted to venture a secular and psychological reading, one could say that the painting depicts a clear blending of reveries, a loving conversation. The solitary figure, however, is not reflected in the faces of anyone and it seems consumed with jealousy or envy; it suffers from being excluded from this social network – can this explain the success of Facebook and other online communities? To the left the figures tend to expand, whereas on the right they shrink into a corner. The background is clear on one side, dark on the other. At all events, the real protagonist of the picture is the exchange of gazes. A counterpart to this can be found in scenes in novels where the spark of mutual recognition is ignited – scenes such as those Rousset discussed (1981) in his splendid *Leurs yeux se rencontrèrent*.

A passage from Bachelard comes to mind: 'to conquer a soul is to find one's own soul. In the reveries of a lover, of a being dreaming of another being, the dreamer's *anima* deepens dreaming the *anima* of the dreamed being' (1960, p. 77). Almost in the same year, first Winnicott and then Bion formulated something similar. An example of spirit of the times, perhaps? Winnicott wrote that there is no child without a mother, Bion that the first form of communication is projective identification and the ability of the mother's reveries, an expression of the maturity of her α function. In this way they laid the groundwork for a radically social theory of the birth of the subject. Basically, a mind alone cannot exist. *The psychic can only come from the psychic.* Sebastiano del Piombo's fascinating painting was actually saying something else because it depicts people of various ages: subjectivity is not only born, but it continues throughout life to feed on the 'sacred conversation' embodied in this exchange of reverie.[6]

Coming more specifically to an analytic setting, Ogden (1997) poses the question in paradoxical terms: when an analysand enters analysis he 'loses' his mind. Surprising, isn't it? But this is what he means: a third space will form between the two parties (he calls it the intersubjective third) which persists even outside the analysis (!), and there everything that is part of it belongs at once to each of the two and also to the third. And from the section of Hegel's *Phenomenology of the Spirit* (1807) that talks about the relationship between master and servant he borrows Hegel's concept of dialectics (*Aufhebung*). In essence, self-consciousness can only exist in the recognition of another self-consciousness, only in their mutual negation, only in a dialectical relationship.

The images we call reverie are for Ogden the probe that allows us to explore this common field where two minds come together and in so doing find each other in getting lost and are lost in finding each other. Reveries, like dreams, come to a subject that has a certain relaxed attitude, but they can also emerge in the mind during a concentrated effort of attention. They are the magma from which the mind emerges. Reveries give us the chance to intuit something of the unconscious scenarios of the relationship between two 'lovers' who are dreaming each other. And here I use the word dreaming to refer to the perhaps less ephemeral part of *Traumdeutung*, to the dream-work (*Traumarbeit*) and the primigenial shaping of experiences into images that this work becomes when it is absorbed into the concept of α function. Freud explains more clearly what this means: displacement, condensation, the taking into account of figuration and secondary elaboration (a kind of editing). In particular, figuration means that the dream-work selects elements that may have their origin in visual images. It is also clear that condensation and displacement can be seen as primary cognitive modes and as equivalents of the principal tropes, metaphor and metonymy – and this brings us back once again to the metaphor of writing. The dream images are not thought by the dreamer, who receives them entirely passively, but rather they think for him.

Meanwhile, our theoretical and technical attitude towards reverie has changed. Freud's free-floating attention does not strictly speaking imply an intersubjective theory. The analyst is first and foremost an archaeologist of the psyche. He is guided by an evidential paradigm, not aesthetics. Like Sherlock Holmes or Giovanni Morelli (Ginzburg, 1986), he is looking for the slightest traces that may help him reconstruct a scene from the past, because the very act of reconstruction would have a liberating meaning. It is not a question of listening to one's feelings or a viewing one's own mental images. On the contrary, these are perceived as interferences, and even after the phenomenon of transference has been discovered, it will be interpreted above all in the meaning of false connection and misunderstanding. Compared with reverie, even free association, which Ferro places in the conceptual area of narrative derivatives of waking dream thought, is much less rooted in the terrain of the dream.

Ferro and Ogden, both of whom have contributed original readings of Bion, have a different notion of listening. Reveries are instruments for getting into tune with the patient, being in unison; in short, ways of starting a sacred conversation with the patient. The goal is the development and expansion of his mental container, his psychological growth. In this way analysis becomes an exchange of reveries or the set of transformations that are activated in the emotional field. And *shared emotion* is the factor that lends coherence to perceptions that would otherwise be just a chaotic succession of images. Emotion introduces motive into the story. It is the impulse that organizes the sequence of events and that triggers the narrative function of the mind. It is the essential function that allows human beings to become aware of their existence.

And how can I say the unsayable to you?

If the psyche is a non-original 'text', or in other words, if it lends itself to being represented as the decentred coming forth of language – but in a broader sense, not only in its meaning as a vehicle for concepts, but as form, body, sign, gesture, ideogram – the metaphor that immediately flows from this is the metaphor of translation, already reflected in Freud's famous formula *Wo Es war, soll Ich werden* ('Where id was, there ego shall be').

Overdetermination

According to Lacan's well-known assertion, the unconscious is structured like a language. And in fact, the science of the unconscious came into being, as Derrida points out in his essay on the mystic writing pad, a writing device that translates perceptions into a system of traces, at the moment when Freud abandoned neurophysiological models of the psyche in favour of the metaphor of the text and accounted for the expressiveness of the dream using a rhetoric of tropes. Dreaming is the paradigm of the primary process, of the specific functioning of the unconscious. Using its codes, in dreams the unconscious transforms a latent text into a manifest text. It does this because for Freud every dream has the task of fulfilling in hallucinatory mode the infantile desire which is repressed because it is unacceptable to the civility of the ego. Interpretation is then seen as a backward-moving process that attempts to undo the dream-work.

The Freudian model of the psyche aims at getting to know the other by investigating intrapsychic dynamics: conflicts, drives, the quality of unconscious identifications, etc. The analyst reveals to the patient his unconscious fantasies – for example, his incestuous desire for his mother and his hatred for his father – and relies on the therapeutic value of knowledge. But we must not think that Freud was naive. One of his key principles is the idea of overdetermination

(*Überdeterminiert*; Gabbard, 2007). As a result of the condensation work that makes each representation the point of intersection between multiple chains of association, any formation of the unconscious, symptom, dream, etc., is always determined by multiple causes. And over-interpretation corresponds to multiple determination. There are always several layers of meaning, an obscure point always remains, a navel of the dream that is lost in the intricate web of our mental universe.

Wreader/wrider

In post-Freudian psychoanalysis, however, something important happens: especially from the seventies onwards the relational paradigm starts to take hold. The subject is born, as Hegel would say, from a dialectic of recognition, the desire for the other's desire. For this reason, whatever happens in the session is no longer seen as the product of the unidirectional projection (transference) of aspects of the analysand's infantile neurosis on the white screen of a *neutral* analyst, but rather as something both old and totally new which involves both actors/spectators of the analytic scene, even though there is an obvious asymmetry in their relationship. Translating the unconscious for the purpose of therapy according to a relational or intersubjective model becomes more difficult. The analyst must now take into account his own ineradicable personality and also the contribution he makes to the creation of the facts he observes. In essence, this corresponds to theories that emphasize the subjectivity and the role of the reader in the interpretation of the text as come out in the neologisms *wreader* and *wrider* (*writer* + *reader*; Jennings, 1992). Something similar has occurred in psychoanalysis: the analyst no longer reads/interprets the patient in one direction but is constantly engaged in negotiating with him the significance of what happens.

But then, as if that weren't enough, things get even more difficult. The unconscious may be structured like a language, but we must consider that it is not just a verbal language, because there is an older pre-discursive unconscious that is not a repressed unconscious. It is, instead, an 'unthought known' (Bollas, 1987), made up of memories that keep the bodily impressions of the first object relations, even before the ego is formed, or developed (if we admit that it is already present at birth in a rudimentary form), and which have therefore never passed through consciousness. By shifting the focus of their attention from drives to the relationship, analysts have begun increasingly to realize that much of the pathology they face in clinical practice results from dysfunctions on this level, the level of the 'aesthetics of being' (ibid.).

To get an idea of this we need only think about how Ogden (1994a, p. 174) describes the first psychic birth that starts from the first completely autistic idiosyncratic forms that are created at the cheek–breast interface and give 'the experience of being a place'. At the origin of the child's feeling of existence is no visual perception but 'an area of sensation of a soothing sort'. It is nothing less than the dawn of meaning, the first transference, the first metaphor; what happens when, as Nietzsche would say, the similar is equated with the dissimilar, and what is other than oneself (difference) is experienced in relation to self (identity).[7] We should keep in mind, then, that the whole analytic situation, the so-called setting, can be seen as symbolically equivalent to the mother's body, the first home and world, and that if the first 'words' of the child are tactile, they will keep for ever this sensory quality, in a real sense somato-psychic, even after they have become the expression of symbolic thought.

Saying almost the same thing

Helping the patient to integrate is not so much (not just) a matter of translating contents (meanings) – for example, revealing latent dream thoughts – as avoiding introducing disruptions of meaning (differences) that the ego would find untenable. The promotion of psychic growth is rather a question of keeping time, being in unison, like when people say with a sense of pleasant surprise, 'You have read my thoughts!' (at the same time, one can see how the persecutory note implicit in the moment of fusion might appear on the horizon if a frontier of self is not immediately erected from the absence of the other and the experience of the *no-thing*). That's why translation in analysis now takes the form of saying almost the same thing, and is to be termed weak, unsaturated, narrative etc. interpretation. That is, it is like someone translating from one language to another who introduces tolerable new elements while respecting the need for identity. Identity has to do with the frame of the picture, with the background against which the figure stands out, with the body and its emotions, and is not to be understood in purely logical-rational terms.

The important thing is to help in defining the margins, the frames, the setting within which experience is organized; we must be in tune with the music of what happens, with the inexpressible, with the primitive rhythms of being;[8] we need to restore meaning, which is also tantamount to creating meaning for the first time; for example, I live what you live/what you have experienced and I will translate it into another form which is perhaps better because it helps you reconnect with split-off aspects of yourself. It is something we could see in terms of rhythm, in the sense that rhythm is something you feel and something that contributes to the creation of meaning but cannot be said. Again, this is the reason why the aesthetic experience and the feeling of truth we associate with it eventually become a model for analytic work.

This is why it is so important for the analyst to pay attention to his reveries (including sensory reveries) as reflections of unconscious processes that alphabetize protoemotional and protosensorial elements into images. This is why using the paradigm of the dream in his work allows the analyst to proceed with certainty – because he is sheltered from excessive light, or because he knows how to project a ray of darkness on to things (Freud). Perhaps no one better than Shakespeare has expressed the peculiarity of this look: in one of the sonnets he speaks of eyes which in the darkness of the dream are 'darkly bright', and 'bright in dark directed'. Sanguineti (2006) translates this well into Italian ('oscuramente luminosi, sono luminosamente diretti nell'oscurità') although, of course, the rhythm is completely lost – another self-evident example of impossible translation.

But these are the translations that the analyst is now called upon to carry out – and here the ambiguity is intentional, because it is really a question of learning from the poets, especially when they themselves are translators – also because he sees more seriously ill patients than in the past, patients upon whom the burden of trauma weighs more heavily. Translating an absent text, giving meaning to the 'whiteness' of the trauma, to the memories of the body that are prior to the ego, is the task assigned to him in the most difficult clinical situations (Kluzer, 1996). He has to get in touch with the primitive rhythms upon which the aesthetics of being are founded, to reconstruct the background from which the reflective consciousness emerges, to reconstruct the margins that make possible the experience of the world.

If the essential function of the mind is to write or to film reality, to transform raw emotions and feelings into pictures or pictograms that help us dream and think, what Bion calls the α function, in analysis we see what happens when this function breaks down or is under-developed. And then it is only thanks to the scenic space of the analytic setting, which puts the analyst in a position where he can make up for this deficiency with his capacity for reverie, that a person can once again start to make sense of his life, and perhaps for the first time really begin to dream himself into existence.

'We have often encountered reveries that think,' says Bachelard (1960, p. 211). Here is a point worth reflecting on: reveries, like dream images, are not so much thought as they themselves think; they found the subject, they are like messengers that set out from the emotions and the body, from the intersection with the real, the thing-in-itself, 'O', the Thing (*das Ding*), the 'Tiger' (Bion, 1975). Dreaming, then, is a verb that should only be used in the passive: not 'I dreamed,' but 'it came to me in a dream'. 'Il a été rêvé,' as Valéry would put it. In analysis, in other words, we give ourselves up to a flow of images which through negative capability, somewhat like the experience of being immersed in the darkness of a cinema, help us gain access to aspects of experience that would otherwise be beyond representation. The passivity that allows its reception in some way guarantees its proximity to the real. If it is true that the iconic register is central to the normal functioning of the psyche, this does however presuppose an adequate somatic level of integration of self. It implies that the margins of the ego must first of all be structured, that there is a space or a screen on to which the images can then be projected.

The theoretical framework of Bion's concepts of α function and waking dream thought, as they have been elaborated since by Ferro and others, becomes essential to an understanding of how reverie may become the suitable lights that enabled Freud to read traces that were not visible to the naked eye of memory, or were repressed. For Bion, in fact, we do not dream only at night but also when we are awake (and dreaming, as we can see, is a word that takes on different shades of meaning for analysts depending on the context). Our mind is constantly engaged in transforming *bits* of experience, mixed-up pixels of screen images of the world, protoemotions and protosensations, α-elements, which we then use like Lego bricks to dream and to think. In fact, a true caesura between these two types of psychic functioning is cancelled. In essence, we all film *live*, that is, we dream or rather alphabetize our reality (but we should say 'the real', since what we call reality is already an elaborate and highly personal version), the stimuli of the environment in which we live.

On the stage of the therapy invented by Freud, the analyst's reverie (the images that take him by surprise) and the narrative derivatives of waking dream thought contained in what the patient says, but also in what he himself says, become the access roads to the unconscious communication that takes place between two minds, to the wax tablet which, as should be clear by now, is only a fragment of a much larger writing pad and which corresponds to sociality, culture, the Other.

Notes

Foreword

1 These include Stefano Bolognini, Franco Borgogno, Jacqueline Amati Mehler, Fausto Petrella, Riccardo Lombardi, Domenico Chianese, Vincenzo Bonaminio and, last but not least, Antonino Ferro, Civitarese's 'teacher and friend' and the dedicatee of this book.

2 *The Intimate Room: Theory and Technique of the Analytic Field*. London: Routledge, New Library of Psychoanalysis, 2010; pp. 192.

3 See the recent '"Psychoanalytic Controversy": on the value of "late Bion" to analytic theory and practice'. *International Journal of Psychoanalysis*, 92(5): 1081–1116, 2011.

Introduction

1 See Borges's 'The other tiger' in *Dreamtigers* (trans. Mildred Boyer and Harold Morland), Austin: University of Texas, 1964, p. 71.

1 'Caesura' as Bion's discourse on method

1 This expression is taken from a poem by Valerio Magrelli (2006, p. 75), inspired by the ambiguous or bistable figures studied by Wittgenstein towards the end of his life.

2 Translator's note: the wording in the *Standard Edition* is 'would have us believe'.

3 Translator's note: this sentence appears in E. L. Freud (1961) as 'I had to blind myself artificially to focus all the light on one dark spot …'.

4 *Parergonal* logic (from *parergon*=frame or ornament) refers to the peculiar status, neither outside nor inside, of the frame and hence to the paradoxes of representation (see Derrida, 1978).

5 In linguistics, the contrasting terms *syntagm* and *paradigm* describe the two aspects of language: on the one hand, the syntactic–historical–diachronic–horizontal–developmental–combinatorial–process-related aspect of the sequential disposition of

words, and, on the other, the synchronic–vertical–selective–associative aspect of words as a system of relationships and differences. The methodological primacy of the paradigmatic, which lies at the root of the structuralist revolution, has made it possible to call into question the linearity of the text and the conception of the signified as produced and transmitted by way of a linear development (Bottiroli, 2006).

6 Translator's note: a play on words: in Italian *campo* means 'field'.

7 Translator's note: the original German words were presumably *Zäsur* and *Zensur*. The latter should of course be translated as 'censorship' rather than 'censure'.

2 Under the cover of darkness

1 See Cottingham (1986, p. 136): 'Descartes employs a celebrated simile of a blind man probing the world with a pair of sticks. He is able to differentiate "trees, rocks, water and similar things", but there is no reason to suppose any resemblance between "the idea he forms" and the "resistance or movement of the bodies, which is the sole cause of the sensations he has of them." In the same way, when the ordinary sighted person sees colours and light, "there is no reason to conclude … that there is something in the objects which resembles the ideas we have of them"'.

2 'I know that in writing I have to blind myself artificially in order to focus all the light on one dark spot, renouncing cohesion, harmony, rhetoric and everything which you call symbolic, frightened as I am by the experience that any such claim or expectation involves the danger of distorting the matter under investigation, even though it may embellish it.' (E. L. Freud, 1961, p. 312).

3 The Latin word *intuitio* means 'reflection in the mirror', and the verb *intueor* 'watch', 'stare at', 'contemplate', 'examine carefully' (Calonghi, 1950, p. 1480).

4 By 'dream' Bion means the 'the combination in narrative form of dream thoughts, which thoughts in turn derive from combinations of alpha-elements' (1962, p. 16). The narrativization of dream thoughts is regulated by the mechanisms of dream rhetoric already highlighted by Freud: 'they require no elaboration beyond what they have received in classical psycho-analytical theory' (Bion, 1963, p. 23), that is, condensation, displacement, considerations of representability and secondary elaboration.

5 See Civitarese (2005, 2006a).

6 Bion explains that sometimes the patient is unable to dream because '[…] it is in the dream that the [paranoid-schizoid and depressive] Positions are negotiated' (1992, p. 37). For a comment on this passage, see also Sandler (2005, p. 225).

7 See Bion (1970, p. 41): '[F]orgetting is as bad as remembering. It is necessary to inhibit dwelling on memories and desires'.

8 See also the expressions used by Coleridge: 'positive Negation', which comes at the end of the poem Limbo, and 'willing suspension of disbelief for the moment, which constitutes poetic faith' in *Biographia Literaria* (1817).

9 Bion himself (1975, pp. 70–71) complains about 'the difficulty of the "public" to grasp that an analogy is an attempt to vulgarise a relationship and *not* the objects related. The psychoanalytical approach […] has been vitiated by the failure to understand the practical application of doubt, by the failure to understand the function of "breast", "mouth", "penis", "vagina", "container", "contained", as analogies'.

10 See Bion (1967, p. 157): 'The psycho-analyst's tool is an attitude of philosophical doubt; to preserve such "doubt" is of first importance on which psycho-analysis can be built'.

11 Bion's so-called mysticism could equally well be turned into a metaphor drawn from quantum mechanics; and in fact this has been done (see Godwin, 1991).

12 See Bezoari (1998, pp. 92–93): 'But more recently (1993) M. Baranger has acknowledged that the idea of a bi-personal unconscious phantasy owes much to Bion's work on groups and, in particular to his theory of basic assumptions.'

13 The reference is to a poem by Montale 'Forse una mattina andando', which is very similar to the lines by Coleridge that Bion cites to identify the emotion that accompanies transformations in O, when the analyst achieves the mental state of negative capability: 'Like one that on a lonesome road / Doth walk in fear and dread, / And having once turned round walks on, / And turns no more his head; / Because he knows a frightful fiend / Doth close behind him tread.'

14 See Searles (1965a, p. 486): 'In my experience, any successful, long-range psychoanalysis or psychotherapy comes to involve the patient and the doctor in facing life's most basic issues together, even though the doctor may be participating little in an overt, verbal fashion. Each emerges, when the treatment is over, with a deepened and enriched understanding of life's meaning.'

3 The burning body

1 The concept of subjectification, especially as used in psychoanalysis in the last few years, appears to have filled a theoretical gap. The term was coined by Breton in 1937 and later taken up by Lacan and especially by Foucault, who defined it as unconscious subordination to a symbolic law. But only since Cahn, starting from his paper 'Du sujet' given at the 51° Congrès des Psychoanalystes de Langue Française des Pays Romans in 1991, has it been increasingly identified as the interpersonal process which leads to the development of a subject capable of reflecting on its own actions, constructing a psychic space distinct from external space and creating a Self.

Thus defined, the subject has a twofold paradoxical status: on the one hand, it is bound by an interpsychic law and pattern, to a prior order of discourse, and, on the other, it is an autonomous agent. Hence, in psychoanalysis it is not used to designate the grammatical subject or the classic philosophical subject but rather 'nothing other than the psychic apparatus in its entirety' (Cahn, 1991, p. 8). The term 'subjectification' therefore refers to two things: the possibility of being inside oneself only to the extent that one is (and has been) outside oneself, 'alienated' in the gaze of the other, and the work the individual must necessarily carry out in order to institute symbolic functioning and to acquire one's own thoughts, one's own body and one's own identity: a never-ending, ongoing process of differentiation; a process of 'progressive mentalization' (ibid., p. 13) that is never fully accomplished. To sum up, the distinguishing marks of this process are: processuality, the reference to the global nature of the psyche, and intrinsic paradox.

2 See Butler (1997, p. 84): 'The claim that a discourse "forms" the body is no simple one, and from the start we must distinguish how such "forming" is not the same as "causing" or "determining", still less is it a notion that bodies are somehow made of discourse pure and simple', and elsewhere (Butler, 1990, p. 96): 'Always a cultural sign, the body sets limits to the imaginary meanings that it occasions, but is never free of an imaginary construction.' See also Brusset (1998, p. 121): 'Far from being elementary at an initial stage, sensation, especially when it is cenesthetic, is immediately complex. Several levels are intrinsic to it, relating to emotions, memory, history, categorization and cultural semiotics'.

3 My translation. (Henceforth, unless noted otherwise, all translations from texts not available in English are by the author.)
4 On the felicitous nature of the encounter between psychoanalysis and the theory of performativity, see Felman (2002).
5 See Cahn (1991, p. 1358): 'For the analysand as for the analyst the question that poses itself unceasingly is: who is speaking? who is speaking to whom? in spite of or by means of misunderstandings? And, it follows, who understands what? [...] The analytic device is designed to develop the capacity to receive meaning as it is produced and fostered by thinking about it [...] This is the psychoanalytical process of subjectification, the problem of the subject as a psychoanalytic project'. See also Ogden (2005, p. 110): 'The analytic writer is continually bumping up against a paradoxical truth: analytic experience (which cannot be said or written) must be transformed into "fiction" (an imaginative rendering of an experience in words), if what is true to the experience is to be conveyed to the reader. [...] At the same time, the "fiction" that is created in words must reflect the reality of what occurred.'
6 Translator's note: the word in the original – 'lei' – is ambiguous and can also mean 'you'.
7 See Brusset (1998, p. 101). 'When the interface between the erogenous zone and the complementary object turns to violence, "a complementary object joins with its zone, but the image that comes to mind is that of a scorching fire" [P. Aulagnier].'
8 Note: the idiomatic Italian word in this case is 'campo', which usually translates as 'field'.
9 Fruit-flavoured or liquorice sweets. The word also contains a reference to the word for 'girlfriend/boyfriend'.
10 For a general discussion of the relationship between the interpsychic and intrapsychic points of view, see Bolognini (2008).
11 See Nietzsche (1887, p. 45): 'there is no "being" behind doing, effecting, becoming; the "doer" is merely a fiction added to the deed – the deed is everything.'
12 This is not unlike the meaning of inscriptions on the skin, the 'highly identitary' (Bobbé, 2002) piercings and tattoos which signal a subject's belonging to a given community. Similarly, the discourse of hypochondria is a vindictive and resentful way of bringing attention to one's own body; a manoeuvre for directing the gaze of the other person, a shock tactic to become visible again, to come back to oneself; it is a move to mark one's confines which paradoxically has the structure of retreating into non-differentiation.
13 See Derrida (1967) and, below, Chapter 8.
14 On the theme of exile and the concept of the hypochondria of the dream, see Civitarese and Foresti (2008).
15 This aspect is represented at the highest degree of delusional hypochondria in Judge Schreber (Schreber, 1903).
16 On the transformation of doctors into enemies, see the case-study of the Wolfman (Freud, 1918).
17 The unworked-through grief of melancholia, described by Freud in 1917 (1917a), becomes in 'The ego and the id' (1922) the very model of the construction of the ego. The subject is formed by the successive internalizations of the lost object and by the consequent identification with the critical agency of the Ego ideal.
18 Freud's (1911) famous remark about the existence of a hypochondriac core in paranoia could be reversed. In other words, one could say that there is a basis of paranoia in all manifestations of hypochondria.
19 See Lacan (cit. in Cahn, 1991, p. 1396): 'We need [...] to recognize exile as the very territory of the subject'.

4 The cat's eyes

1 Di Chiara (1997, p. 105) points out, however, that this principle has always come with a special corollary, 'that it was a particular kind of knowledge that had to originate in the field of the experience of the relationship between patient and analyst, and that it could not be replaced by an intellectual act or transferred outside the psychoanalytic field'.
2 See Bion (1975, p. 110): 'Non-artistic methods of communication are less accurate than those used by artists. [...] I can say this with conviction of the psycho-analytical experience also'.
3 In narratology, the term metalepsis is used to denote the transgression of the space-time boundaries of the narrative, for example when a character enters or leaves the pages of a novel or the scene of film, or when he/she addresses the reader (or audience) directly, and so on. The concept was first defined by Genette (2004), but see also Civitarese (2007).
4 *Purgatory*, XXX, l. 48.
5 Torquato Tasso, *Rime*, 'Rime d'amore', Libro IV, 498.
6 Translated by R. C. Trevelyan. London, G. Allen & Unwin Ltd. 1919.
7 In German, transference is *Übertragung*, which also means contagion, transmission, transfer, transcription, conveyance, money transfer, translation. It is significant that one of the translations of this term in Italian is 'traslazione', which is connected to death, moving the relics of a dead body, what happens when a body is brought to its final burial place – perhaps an image of the work of mourning?
8 Translator's note: again, 'lei' can also mean 'you'.
9 Translator's note: 'it' here could also be understood as 'him'.

5 The equation analysis/painting and the aesthetics of the real

1 'Thus a war of principles, grown up from the infinite space of the past, is carried on with equal strife.' (Titus Lucretius Carus, *On the Nature of Things*. Translated by John Selby Watson. New York: Cosimo, Inc., p. 75).
2 On this Lòpez-Corvo (2002) draws attention to the fact that Latin people had already made a connection between mind ('mens') and lying ('mentior'). The Devoto and Oli (1991) dictionary states that 'mentire' (to lie) derives from *mens* (mind), first meaning 'to imagine', then 'to pretend' and then 'to lie'.
3 Psychic growth requires the food of truth, but perhaps, observes Bion, for lack of evidence regarded as scientific 'It may be that the formulation belongs to the domain of Aesthetics' (1965, p. 38).
4 For Bion 'The most, and the least that the individual person can do is to be [O]' (1965, p. 140)
5 See Fachinelli (1989, p. 180): 'Such joy is clearly *beyond pleasure* as commonly understood. It is rather closer to the most disquieting side of pleasure, in Freud. That is to say, at the moment when the reduction of tension, pursued to avoid displeasure, is going down to zero, towards the cessation of all tension, i.e. the ceasing of life itself. In terms of drive, it is the *Todestrieb*, the death drive. In terms of psychic experience, this unbridled joy is close to the fear of annihilation'.
6 Cf. Ferro (2007) and Ferro *et al.* (2007).

7 See Grotstein (2007, p. 249): 'Column 2, to me, constitutes the *dreaming Column – that is*, the α function column – which must aesthetically alter (quasi-falsify) the β–elements… A parallel to this would be a work of art or of fiction, which skilfully alters the initial *presentation* of the truth about reality so that the truth can survive and be transmitted. Thus, from this perspective, Column 2 reveals the activity of the *pleasure principle*'.

8 Abstract painting has the same reductive character. It seems obsessed with reducing reality to its primordial elements, the grain itself of matter, a game of full and empty, a play of light and shadows, cohesion and disconnection of elementary particles. Similarly the derealization of the object in Morandi's paintings or the series of Impressionist pictures by Monet in London, called *Houses of Parliament* serve to approximate reality, to resolve shape into what Cezanne called 'the thrill of duration' (Recalcati, 2007, p. 1985, p. 143).

9 See Bion: 'The sense of well-being engendered by a belief in the existence of the perfectly understanding mother (or analyst) adds force to the fear and hatred of thoughts which are closely associated with, and may therefore be felt to be indistinguishable from, the "no-breast". A painful state of mind is clung to, including depression, because the alternative is felt to be worse, namely that *thought and thinking mean that a near perfect breast has been destroyed*' (1965, p. 63, my italics).

10 Similarly, for Diderot the foundation of beauty is not contemplation of something absolute but the perception of certain relationships (2001).

11 By 'intuition' Bion means *faith* in being able to bind up into a significant network the data provided by experience, if memory and desire are removed from conscious intention and, rather, left free to determine, in the waking state, the dream-work. The negative capacity indicates a disposition of mind, waiting patiently for a selected fact to organise the shapeless chaos of reality. Emphasizing these concepts, Bion accentuates the ecstatic and receptive (affective) side of cognitive experience.

12 See Agamben (1974) for the definition (taken up by Pound) of art as a technique for arousing ecstasy or for producing epiphanies of the divine.

6 Aesthetic conflict and the α function

1 This chapter was originally part of a book edited by Stokes entitled *Painting and the Inner World*, Tavistock, London 1963.

2 See also Capello and Civitarese (2010), Civitarese (2010).

3 See Lemma (2009) on the relationship between body dysmorphic disorder and aesthetic conflict.

4 In a fragment of his juvenilia (Kojève, 1947, p. 636), Hegel talks of the consciousness of death as the only way that lovers can conceive of the possibility of their separation. But the fantasy, which sometimes becomes the act, of double suicide negates this possibility to fulfil oneself as distinct beings, and therefore represents the most extreme defence against the experience of not being recognized. As in Baudelaire's 'The Death of Lovers', double suicide is 'a pure coincidence […] the absolute mirror, the joyful mirror, gratification (intermediate space is cancelled)' (Barthes, 2007, p. 91).

5 By 'dreaming' I mean, following Ogden (2009, p. 104), 'the most free, most inclusive, and most penetrating form of psychological work of which human beings are capable […] the principal medium through which we achieve human consciousness, psychological growth and the capacity to create personal, symbolic meaning from our lived experience'.

6 On the aesthetics of the psychoanalytic process, see Levine (2003).

7 The passage by Ogden (and likewise Bion in *Transformations*) can be read in the light of a passage by Derrida (1972, pp. 41–42) which talks about the Hegelian conception of the dialectical structure of reality:

> how do space, how do nature, in their undifferentiated immediacy, receive difference, determination, quality? Differentiation, determination, qualification can only overtake pure space as the negation of this original purity and of this initial state of abstract indifferentiation which is properly the spatiality of space. Pure spatiality is determined by negating properly the indetermination that constitutes it, that is, by itself negating itself. By *itself* negating itself; this negation has to be a determined negation, a negation *of* space *by* space. The first spatial negation of space is a POINT [...] The point is the space that does not take up space, the place that does not take place; it suppresses and replaces the place, it takes the place of space that it negates and conserves. It spatially negates space. It is the first determination of space. As the first determination and first negation of space, the point spatializes or *spaces* itself. It negates itself by itself in its relation to itself, that is, to another point. The negation of negation, the spatial negation of the point is the LINE. The point negates and retains itself, extends and sustains itself, lifts itself (by *Aufhebung*) into the line, which thus constitutes the *truth* of the point. But secondarily this negation is a negation of *space*, that is, itself is spatial; to the extent that essentially it is this relationship, that is, to the extent that it retains itself by suppressing itself [...] the point is the *line*, the first Being-other, that is, the Being-spatial of the point.

8 See Winnicott (1949b, p. 184, my italics): 'Belonging to this feeling of unhappiness is the intolerable nature of experiencing something without any knowledge whatever of when it will end. It is for this reason fundamentally that form in music is so important. Through form, the end is in sight from the beginning.' On the theme of musicality in analysis, see also Petrella (1996), Di Benedetto (2000), Barale (2008), Barale and Minazzi (2008).

9 Bion's theory is also particularly flexible and exportable because, more than being a direct description of the mother-child relationship, it starts as a collection of metaphors useful for constructing a model of what happens on the unconscious plane in the analytic situation (Ogden, 2005), and this makes it of greater technical and operational value.

10 One Italian translation of *Aufhebung* is 'sublimazione' (*sublimation*).

11 *Iliad*, Book XXII, l. 98–99

12 In a 1924 paper, *The Economic Problem of Masochism*, Freud (1924b) discusses rhythm and sees it as the *qualitative* element that might help us to understand the interplay between pleasure and displeasure, whereas the question does not become any clearer if one considers only the *quantitative* increases in tension provoked by the stimulus.

7 The analyst's internal setting and its discontents

1 See Meltzer (1984, p. 39): 'Melanie Klein's evocation of the mental geography surprisingly revealed what might be called a theological aspect of the personality. Every person has to have a "religion" in which his internal objects perform the function of gods [...] if a person does not put his trust in his internal gods, he must live in a state described so vividly by Kierkegaard as "despair".'

2 See Bion (1997, p. 46): 'the analyst has to be quite clear [...] as to what are the minimum requirements on which he proposes to exist [...] not because you want to stop him from doing anything he likes, but because you understand that he wants an analysis and you know whether or not you can do analysis in the conditions the patient is proposing.'
3 For example, Glover (2005) points out that there is no trace in Ferro's clinical work of any extensive use of self-disclosure, which is the hallmark of North American relational psychoanalysis, and adds that the author takes great care to distinguish between his own model and any concept of corrective emotional experience or interpersonal reciprocity.
4 For Bion the patient is 'the most powerful, knowledgeable collaborator you are ever likely to find' (1997, p. 35).
5 For example, a patient who repeatedly recounted a sado-masochistic fantasy that pre-dated the beginning of the therapy and that nevertheless has to be thought of re-actualized in the transference.

8 From the mystic writing pad to the α function

1 See Di Chiara (2003), pp. 87 ff.
2 Here the term 'representation' is used in the sense of 'correlation or covariance between configurations of neuronal discharges and perceptual signals or states of memory' (Edelman, 2004, p. 88).
3 See Birksted-Breen (2003).
4 Accessibile at: http://dreyblatt.org/video/Wunderblock.mov or http://www.independently.de/2011/07/30/the-wunderblock-an-installation-by-arnold-dreyblatt/
5 The stream of green numbers on a black background which can be seen running across computer screens in the world of *The Matrix* are another possible and fascinating example of a modern depiction of software (that is, symbolic codes) which identifies a human being as a subject, a further variation of the mystic writing pad. See also the figure with which Ferro (2007) shows how scattered signs can be recomposed into a meaningful word, the same process that can be seen in the metaphor of emoticons, the little symbols used in text messages. For example, the punctuation marks [( ) : - can produce :-) (happy) or :-((sad) or :-[(depressed); another sequence could be o : 8 – D, producing :-o (surprised) or 8-] (wow! or in love) or again :-D (laugh), and so on.
6 See Fonagy (2001, p. 9): 'The process of attachment lasts all one's life; it is not confined to the first two years of life. We continue to need attachment relations for self-confirmation and self-recognition'.
7 See Freud (1895, p. 366): at birth '*the information of one's own scream* serves to characterize the object'.
8 See Meschonnic (2000) on the importance of rhythm in translation.

Bibliography

Agamben, G. (1974) La 'notte oscura' di Juan de la Cruz. In *Poesie* (pp. V–XIII). Turin: Einaudi.

Aisenstein, M. and Gibeault, A. (1991) The work of hypochondria – a contribution to the study of the specificity of hypochondria, in particular in relation to hysterical conversion and organic disease. *International Journal of Psychoanalysis*, 72: 669–680.

Andersen, J. (1992) *Missing*. Unpublished paper presented at the International Conference for Tavistock-trained Child Psychotherapists. Larmor Plage, France.

Aron, L. (2006) Analytic impasse and the third: clinical implications of intersubjectivity theory. *International Journal of Psychoanalysis*, 87: 349–368.

Aulagnier, P. (1975) *The Violence of Interpretation: From Pictogram to Statement*. Hove, UK: Brunner-Routledge 2001.

Bachelard, G. (1960) *The Poetics of Reverie*. Boston, MA: Beacon Press 1992.

Barale, F. (2008) Alle origini della psicoanalisi: Freud, Lipps e la questione del «sonoro-musicale». *Rivista di Psicoanalisi*, 54: 129–147.

Barale, F. and Minazzi, V. (2008) Off the beaten track: Freud, sound and music. Statement of a problem and some historico-critical notes. *International Journal of Psychoanalysis*, 89: 937–957.

Baranger, M. (1993) The mind of the analyst: from listening to interpretation. *International Journal of Psychoanalysis*, 74: 15–24.

Baranger, M. and Baranger, W. (2008) The analytic situation as a dynamic field [1961–62]. *International Journal of Psychoanalysis*, 89: 795–826.

Barthes, R. (1973) *The Pleasure of the Text*. New York, NY: Hill & Wang 1980.

Barthes, R. (1977) *A Lover's Discourse*. London: Vintage 2002.

Barthes, R. (2007) *Le discours amoureux. Seminaire à L'École des hautes études*. Paris: Seuil.

Benjamin, W. (1955) *1913–1926 v. 1: Selected Writings*. Boston, MA: Harvard University Press 2004.

Bezoari, M. (1998) Dimensioni della mente nel setting analitico di coppia: tra l'individuale e il gruppale. In P. Bion Talamo, F. Borgogno, S. A. Merciai (eds.) *Lavorare con Bion* (pp. 91–100). Rome: Borla.

Bezoari, M. and Ferro, A. (1989) Listening, interpretations and transformative functions in the analytical dialogue. *Rivista di Psicoanalisi*, 35: 1014–1050.

Bick, E. (1968) The experience of the skin in the early object-relations. *International Journal of Psychoanalysis*, 49: 484–486.

Bion, W. R. (1962) *Learning from Experience*. London: Karnac 1984.

Bion, W. R. (1963) *Elements of Psycho-Analysis*. London: Karnac 1984.

Bion, W. R. (1965) *Transformations: Change from Learning to Growth*. London: Heinemann.

Bion, W. R. (1967) *Second Thoughts: Selected Papers in Psychoanalysis*. London: Karnac 1984.

Bion, W. R. (1970) *Attention and Interpretation. A Scientific Approach to Insight in Psycho-Analysis and Groups*. London: Karnac 1984.

Bion, W. R. (1974a) Bion's Brazilian lectures 1 – São Paulo. In *Brazilian Lectures*. Revised and corrected edn. London: Karnac 1990.

Bion, W. R. (1974b) Bion's Brazilian lectures 2 – Rio de Janeiro/São Paulo. In *Brazilian Lectures*. Revised and corrected edn. London: Karnac 1990.

Bion, W. R. (1975) *A Memoir of the Future. Book 1 – The Dream* (pp. 1–218). London: Karnac 1991.

Bion, W. R. (1976) Evidence. In *Clinical Seminars and Four Papers* (pp. 312–320). Abingdon: Fleetwood 1987.

Bion, W. R. (1977a) Emotional turbulence. In P. Hartocollis (ed.) *Borderline Personality Disorders: The Concept, The Syndrome, The Patient* (pp. 3–13). New York, NY: International UP.

Bion, W. R. (1977b) On a quotation from Freud. In P. Hartocollis (ed.) *Borderline Personality Disorders: The Concept, The Syndrome, The Patient* (pp. 511–517). New York, NY: International UP.

Bion, W. R. (1977c) Caesura. In *Two Papers: The Grid and Caesura* (pp. 35–56). London: Karnac 1989.

Bion, W. R. (1977d) *A Memoir of the Future. Book 2 – The Past Presented* (pp. 219–426). London: Karnac 1991.

Bion, W. R. (1977e) *A Memoir of the Future. Book 3 – The Dawn of Oblivion* (pp. 427–575). London: Karnac 1991.

Bion, W. R. (1978) Four discussions with Bion. In *Clinical Seminars and Four Papers* (pp. 241–292). Abingdon: Fleetwood 1987.

Bion, W. R. (1979) Making the best of a bad job. In *Clinical Seminars and Four Papers* (pp. 321–332). London: Karnac 1994.

Bion, W. R. (1992) *Cogitations*. London: Karnac.

Bion, W. R. (1997) *Taming Wild Thoughts*. London: Karnac.

Bion, W. R. (2005) *The Tavistock Seminars*. London: Karnac.

Birksted-Breen, D. (2003) Time and après coup. *International Journal of Psychoanalysis*, 84: 1501–1515.

Blanchot, M. (1969) *The Infinite Conversation*. Minneapolis, MN: University of Minnesota Press 1993.

Bleger, J. (1967a) Psycho-analysis of the psycho-analytic frame. *International Journal of Psychoanalysis*, 48: 511–519.

Bleger, J. (1967b) *Simbiosis y ambigüedad: Estudio psicoanalítico*. Buenos Aires: Editorial Paidós.

Blin, G. (1989) *Stendhal et les problèmes du Roman*. Paris: José Corti.

Bobbé, S. (2002) Le 'piercing', ou la difficulté d'être soi. *Psychanalyse et Psychose*, 2: 145–156.

Bollas, C. (1987) *The Shadow of the Object: Psychoanalysis of the Unthought Known*. London: Free Association Books.

Bollas, C. (1999) *The Mystery of Things*. London: Routledge.

Bolognini, S. (2008) *Secret Passages: Theory and Technique of Interpsychic Relations*. London: Routledge 2010.

Bonaminio, V. (2009) The psyche in-dwelling in the body: states of integration, un-integration and the primary identification. 13th Frances Tustin Memorial Lecture, Los Angeles, USA, 6–7 November 2009.

Borges, J. L. (1964) *Dreamtigers*. Austin, TX: University of Texas Press 1985.

Borutti, S. (2006) *Filosofia dei sensi: Estetica del pensiero tra filosofia, arte e letteratura*. Milan: Raffaello Cortina.

Botella, C. and Botella, S. (2001) *The Work of Psychic Figurability*. London: Routledge 2004.

Bottiroli, G. (2006) *Che cos'è la teoria della letteratura: Fondamenti e problemi*. Turin: Einaudi.

Brooks, P. (1984) *Reading for the Plot: Design and Intention in Narrative*. New York, NY: A. A. Knopf.

Brusset, B. (1998) *L'hypocondrie*. Paris: PUF.

Brusset, B. (2002) L'hypocondrie: Thématique ou organization spécifique? *Revue Française de Psychosomatique*, 22: 45–64.

Butler, J. (1990) *Gender Trouble: Feminism and the Subversion of Identity*. London: Routledge 2006.

Butler, J. (1997) *The Psychic Life of Power: Theories in Subjection*. Stanford, CA: Stanford University Press.

Butler, J. (1999) Preface. *Gender Trouble: Feminism and the Subversion of Identity* (pp. VII–XXVI). London: Routledge 2006.

Cahn, R. (1991) Du sujet. *Revue Française de Psychanalyse*, 55: 1353–1490.

Calonghi, F. (1950) *Dizionario latino–italiano*. Turin: Rosenberg & Sellier.

Capello, F., Civitarese, G. (2010) Changing styles, affective continuities and psychic containers: Corrado Govoni's early poetry. *Journal of Romance Studies*, 10: 11–25.

Civitarese, G. (1996) Note su memoria e causalità psichica a partire dalla teoria della funzione cerebrale di G. Edelman. *Prospettive psicoanalitiche nel lavoro istituzionale*, 14: 356–369.

Civitarese, G. (2005) Fire at the theatre: (un)reality of/in the transference and interpretation. *International Journal of Psychoanalysis*, 86: 1299–316.

Civitarese, G. (2006a). Dreams that mirror the session. *International Journal of Psychoanalysis*, 87: 703–23.

Civitarese, G. (2006b) Discusiones: 'Vinculo simbiótico y encuadre'. *Revista de Psicoanálisis*, 63: 485–500.

Civitarese, G. (2007) Metalepsis, or the rhetoric of transference interpretation. In *The Intimate Room: Theory and Technique of the Anaytic Field* (pp. 50–71). London: Routledge 2010.

Civitarese, G. (2008a) Immersion versus interactivity and analytic field. *International Journal of Psychoanalysis*, 89: 279–98.

Civitarese, G. (2008b) *The Intimate Room: Theory and Technique of the Analytic Field*. London: Routledge 2010.

Civitarese, G. (2010) Abjection and aesthetic conflict in Boccaccio's *(L)Isabetta*. *Journal of Romance Studies*, 10: 11–25.

Civitarese, G. and Foresti, G. (2008) La fragilità/brutalità del mondo nell'opera di Georg/George Groß/Grosz. In G. Bedoni (ed.) *La lente di Freud* (pp. 292–331). Milan: Mazzotta.

Corrao, F. (1981) Struttura poliadica e funzione gamma. In *Orme*, vol. I (pp. 34–41). Milan: Raffaello Cortina 1998.

Cottingham, J. (1986) *Descartes*. Oxford, UK: Wiley-Blackwell.

De Cesarei, A. O. (2001) *Trauma e violazione del senso di esistere*. Paper delivered to the Milan Centre of Psychoanalysis (CMP) 24 May 2001.

De Toffoli, C. (2001) Psicosoma. Il sapere del corpo nel lavoro psicoanalitico. *Rivista di Psicoanalisi*, 47: 465–486.

Deleuze, G. (1983) *Cinema 1: The Movement Image*. London: Continuum 2005.

Derrida, J. (1967) Freud and the scene of writing. In *Writing and Difference* (pp. 246–291). London: Routledge 2001.

Derrida, J. (1972) *Margins of Philosophy*. Chicago: University of Chicago Press 1985.

Derrida, J. (1978) *The Truth in Painting*. Chicago: University of Chicago Press 1987.

Derrida, J. (1990) *Memoirs of the Blind: The Self-Portrait and Other Ruins*. Chicago: University of Chicago Press 1993.

Descartes, R. (1637) [Internet]. *Discourse on Method* [accessed 19 May 2008]. Online Literature Library. Available from: http://www.literature.org/authors/descartes-rene/reason-discourse/

Devoto, G. and Oli, G. C. (1991) *Nuovo vocabolario illustrato della lingua italiana*. Milano: Selezione Dal Reader's Digest.

Di Benedetto, A. (2000) *Before Words*. London: Free Association Books 2005.

Di Chiara, G. (1997) La formazione e le evoluzioni del campo psicoanalitico. In E. Gaburri (ed.) *Emozione e Interpretazione: psicoanalisi del campo emotivo* (pp. 103–112). Turin: Boringhieri.

Di Chiara, G. (2003) *Curare con la psicoanalisi: Percorsi e strategie*. Milan: Raffaello Cortina.

Diderot, D. (2001) *Traite Du Beau (1772)*. Whitefish, MT: Kessinger 2010.

Eco, U. (2003) *Dire quasi la stessa cosa*. Milan: Bompiani.

Edelman, G.M. (2004) *Wider Than the Sky: A Revolutionary View of Consciousness*. London: Penguin 2005.

Egginton, W. (2003) *How the World Became a Stage*. Albany, NY: State University of New York Press.

Empson, W. (1930) *Seven Types Of Ambiguity*. London: Pimlico 2004.

Fabbri, V. (2000) La danza e l'immagine-tempo: Figure del ritmo nell'opera di G. Deleuze. *Studi di estetica*, 21: 125–148.

Fabbrici, C. (2008) *Il campo. Attrazioni e stagnazioni*. Rome: Borla.

Fachinelli, E. (1989) *La mente estatica*. Milan: Adelphi.

Felman, S. (2002) *The Scandal of the Speaking Body: Don Juan with J. L. Austin, or Seduction in Two Languages*. Stanford, CA: Stanford University Press.

Ferro, A. (1992) *The Bi-Personal Field: Experiencing Child Analysis*. New York: Routledge 1999.

Ferro, A. (1999) *Psychoanalysis as Therapy and Storytelling*. London: Routledge 2006.

Ferro, A. (2002a) *Seeds of Illness, Seeds of Recovery*. London: Routledge 2004.

Ferro, A. (2002b) Some implications of Bion's thought. *International Journal of Psychoanalysis*, 83: 597–607.

Ferro, A. (2002c) Narrative derivatives of alpha elements. *International Forum of Psychoanalysis*, 11: 184–187.

Ferro, A. (2005) Bion: theoretical and clinical observation. *International Journal of Psychoanalysis*, 86: 1535–1542.

Ferro, A. (2006) *Mind Works: Technique and Creativity in Psychoanalysis*. London: Routledge 2008.

Ferro, A. (2007) *Avoiding Emotions, Living Emotions*. London: Routledge 2011.

Ferro, A. (2009) Transformations in dreaming and characters in the psychoanalytic field. *International Journal of Psychoanalysis*, 90: 209–230.

Ferro, A. and Basile, R. (2004) The psychoanalyst as individual: self-analysis and gradients of functioning. *Psychoanalytic Quarterly*, 73: 659–682.

Ferro, A. and Basile, R. (2006) Unity of analysis: similarities and differences in the analysis of children and grown-ups. *Psychoanalytic Quarterly*, 75: 477–500.

Ferro, A. and Basile, R. (eds.) (2009) *The Analytic Field. A Clinical Concept*. Hove: Routledge.

Ferro, A., Civitarese, G., Collovà, M., Foresti, G., Mazzacane, F., Molinari, E. and Politi, P. (2007) *Sognare l'analisi. Sviluppi clinici del pensiero di Wilfred R. Bion*. Turin: Bollati Boringhieri.

Ferruta, A. (2004) Les mouvements paranoïaques qui sont actualisés dans le transfert, 'ou ça existait, J'ai à devenir'. Colloque de Talloires, 13–14 Novembre 2004.

Finotti, F. (2004) *Retorica della diffrazione. Bembo, Aretini, Giulio Romeno e Tasso: Letteratura e scena cortigiana*. Firenze: Olschky.

Fonagy, P. (2001) *The Roots of Violence in the Failure of Mentalization*. Paper delivered to the Milan Centre of Psychoanalysis, 18 May 2001.

Fornaro, M. (1990) *Psicoanalisi tra scienza e mistica: L'opera di Wilfred R. Bion*. Rome: Edizioni Studium.

Foucault, M. (1963) *The Birth of the Clinic: An Archaeology of Medical Perception*. London: Routledge 2003.

Freud, E. L. (ed.) (1961) *Letters of Sigmund Freud 1873–1939*. London: Hogarth.

Freud, S. (1895) A project for a scientific psychology. *SE* 1: 283–397.

Freud, S. (1899) The interpretation of dreams. *SE* 4: 1–338; 5: 339–625.

Freud, S. (1911) Formulations on the two principles of mental functioning. *SE* 12: 215–226.

Freud, S. (1912–1913) Totem and taboo. *SE* 13: 1–161.

Freud, S. (1917a) Mourning and melancholia. *SE* 14: 239–258.

Freud, S. (1917b) A metapsychological supplement to the theory of dreams. *SE* 14: 222–235.

Freud, S. (1918) From the history of an infantile neurosis. *SE* 17: 7–122.

Freud, S. (1920) Beyond the pleasure principle. *SE* 18: 7–64.

Freud, S. (1922) The ego and the id. *SE* 19: 1–86.

Freud, S. (1924a) Note upon the 'mystic writing-pad'. *SE* 19: 226–232.

Freud, S. (1924b) The economic problem of masochism. *SE* 19: 157–170.

Freud, S. (1926) Inhibitions, symptoms and anxiety. *SE* 20: 75–176.

Freud, S. (1930) Civilization and its discontents. *SE* 21: 57–146.

Freud, S. and Breuer, J. (1893–1895) Studies on hysteria. *SE* 2: 1–335.

Gabbard, G.O. (2007) 'Bound in a nutshell': thoughts on complexity, reductionism, and 'infinite space'. *International Journal of Psychoanalysis*, 88: 559–74.

Genette, G. (2004) *Métalepse: De la figure à la fiction*. Paris: Seuil.

Ginzburg, C. (1986) Clues: roots of an evidential paradigm. In *Clues, Myths, and the Historical Method* (pp. 96–125). Baltimore, MA: John Hopkins University Press 1992.

Girard, M. (2010) Winnicott's foundation for the basic concepts of Freud's metapsychology? *International Journal of Psychoanalysis*, 91: 305–324.

Glover, W. (2005) In the analyst's consulting room by Antonino Ferro. *Fort Da – The Journal of the Northern California Society for Psychoanalytic Psychology*, 11: 126–129.

Godfrind, J. (1993) *Les deux courants du transfert*. Paris: Presses Universitaires de France.

Godwin, R. W. (1991) Wilfred Bion and David Bohm: toward a quantum metapsychology. *Psychoanalysis and Contemporary Thought*, 14: 625–654.

Green, A. (1983) The dead mother. In *On Private Madness* (pp. 142–173). London: Hogarth, 1986.

Green, A. (1992) Cogitations. *International Journal of Psychoanalysis*, 73: 585–589.

Green, A. (1993) *The Work of the Negative*. London: Free Association Books 1999.

Green, A. (1998) The primordial mind and the work of the negative. *International Journal of Psychoanalysis*, 79: 649–665.

Grotstein J. S. (ed.) (1981a) *Do I Dare Disturb the Universe? A Memorial to Wilfred R. Bion*. Beverly Hills, CA: Caesura Press.

Grotstein, J. S. (1981b) Who is the dreamer who dreams the dream and who is the dreamer who understands it? In J. Grotstein (ed.) *Do I Dare Disturb the Universe?A Memorial to Wilfred R. Bion* (pp. 357–416). Beverly Hills, CA: Caesura Press.

Grotstein, J. S. (2000) *Who Is the Dreamer Who Dreams the Dream?: A Study of Psychic Presences*. London: Routledge.

Grotstein, J. S. (2006) Letters to the editors: on Whose Bion?. *International Journal of Psychoanalysis*, 87: 577–579.

Grotstein, J. S. (2007) *A Beam of Intense Darkness: Wilfred Bion's Legacy to Psychoanalysis*. London: Karnac Books.

Hamon, P. (1977) Pour un statut sémiologique du personnage. In *Poétique du récit* (pp. 115–180). Paris: Seuil 1977.

Handke, P. (1970) Nauseated by language (interview with Arthur Joseph). *The Drama Review*, 15: 56–61.

Hegel, G. W. F. (1807) *Phenomenology of Spirit*. Oxford, UK: Oxford University Press 1979.

Heidegger, M. (1950) The thing. In *Poetry, Language, Thought* (pp. 161–184). New York, NY: HarperCollins 1976.

Hölderlin, F. (1965 [1979–99]) *Hyperion, or the Hermit in Greece*. Translated by Willard Trask. New York: F. Ungar Pub. Co.

Horovitz, M. (2007) Transfert et verité. In T. Bokanowski, F. Guignard (eds.) *Actualité de la pensée de Bion* (pp. 45–51). Paris: Éditions In Press.

Jacobs, T. J. (2007) [Internet]. *Listening, Dreaming, Sharing: On the Use of the Analyst's Inner Experiences* [accessed 24 June 2010]. Available from: *http://www.ipa.org.uk/Default.aspx?page=27&terms=jacobs*

Jennings, E. M. (1992) The text is dead; long live the techst. *Postmodern Culture*, vol. 2, n. 3.

Kandinsky, W. (1968) *Point and Line to Plane*. Mineola, NY: Dover 1979.

Khan, M. R. (1974) The use and abuse of dreams in psychic experience. In *The Privacy of the Self* (pp. 306–315). London: Karnac.

Kluzer, G. (1996) Nuove ipotesi interpretative del concetto di trauma. *Rivista di Psicoanalisi*, 42: 405–423.

Kojève, A. (1947) *Introduction to the Reading of Hegel: Lectures on the 'Phenomenology of Spirit'*. Ithaca, NY: Cornell University Press 1980.

Kristeva, J. (1974) *Revolution in Poetic Language*. New York, NY: Columbia University Press 1984.

Kristeva, J. (1980) *Powers of Horror: An Essay on Abjection*. New York, NY: Columbia University Press 1984.

Lakoff, G. and Johnson, M. (1980) *Metaphors We Live by*. Chicago, Il: University of Chicago Press 1981.

Laplanche, J. and Pontalis, J.-B. (1967) *The Language of Psychoanalysis*. New York: W. W. Norton 1974.

Lemma, A. (2009) Being seen or being watched? A psychoanalytic perspective on body dysmorphia. *International Journal of Psychoanalysis*, 90: 753–771.

Levine, S. S. (2003) Beauty treatment: the aesthetics of the psychoanalytic process. *Psychoanalytic Quarterly*, 72: 987–1016.

Likierman, M. (1989) Clinical significance of aesthetic experience. *International Review of Psycho-Analysis*, 16: 133–150.

López-Corvo, R. (2002) *The Dictionary of the Work of W. R. Bion*. London: Karnac 2003.

Magrelli, V. (2002) *Vedersi vedersi. Modelli e circuiti visivi nell'opera di Paul Valéry*. Turin: Einaudi.

Magrelli, V. (2006) *Disturbi del sistema binario*. Turin: Einaudi.

Marion, J.-L. (2001) *De surcroît. Études sur les phénomènes saturès*. Paris: PUF.

Massarenti, A. (2006) *Cartesio: vita, pensiero, opere scelte*. Milan: Il Sole 24 Ore.

Matte Blanco, I. (1975) *The Unconscious as Infinite Sets*. London: Karnac 1988.

Matte Blanco, I. (1988) *Thinking, Feeling, and Being*. London: Routledge.

Mazzacane, F. (2007) L'analista e i contenuti killer. In A. Ferro, G. Civitarese, M. Collovà, G. Foresti, F. Mazzacane, E. Molinari, P. Politi, P., *Sognare l'analisi. Sviluppi clinici del pensiero di Wilfred R. Bion* (pp. 109–130). Turin: Bollati Boringhieri.

Meltzer, D. (1973) On the apprehension of beauty. *Contemporary Psychoanalysis*, 9: 224–229.

Meltzer, D. (1976) The delusion of clarity of insight. *International Journal of Psychoanalysis*, 57: 141–146.

Meltzer, D. (1978) *The Clinical Significance of the Work of Bion*. In *The Kleinian Development: Part III* (pp. 270–396). London: Karnac 1998.

Meltzer, D. (1984) *Dream-life: A Re-Examination of the Psycho-analytical Theory and Technique*. London: Karnac.

Meltzer, D. (1986) *Studies in Extended Metapsychology: Clinical Applications of Bion's Ideas*. London: Karnac.

Meltzer, D., Bremner, J., Hoxter, S., Weddell, D. and Wittenberg, I. (1975) *Explorations in Autism*. London: Karnac 2008.

Meltzer, D. and Williams M. H. (1988) *The Apprehension of Beauty: The Role of Aesthetic Conflict in Development, Art and Violence*. London: Karnac 2008.

Merleau-Ponty, M. (1964) *The Visible and the Invisible*. Evanston, IL: Northwestern UP 1969.

Meschonnic, H. (2000) Se cambia una teoria del linguaggio cambia tutto. *Studi di estetica*, 21: 11–30.

Mills, J. (2000) Hegel on projective identification: implications for Klein, Bion, and beyond. *The Psychoanalytic Review*, 87: 841–874.

Mitrani, J. (1998) Unbearable ecstasy, reverence and awe, and the perpetuation of an 'aesthetic conflict'. *Psychoanalytic Quarterly*, 67: 102–127.

Neri, C., Correale, A. and Fadda, P. (eds.) (1987) *Letture bioniane*. Rome: Borla.

Nietzsche, F. (1873) On truth and lie in an extra-moral sense. In C. Cazeaux (ed.), *The Continental Aesthetics Reader* (pp. 53–62). London and New York: Routledge 2000.

Nietzsche, F. (1887) *On the Genealogy of Morals/Ecce Homo*. New York: Vintage Books 1989.

Nietzsche, F. (1999 [1872–1873]) *Unpublished Writings from the Period of 'Unfashionable Observations': Volume 11. The Complete Works of Friedrich Nietzsche*. Stanford, CA: Stanford University Press.

Nobus, D. and Quinn, M. (2005) *Knowing Nothing, Staying Stupid. Elements for a Psychoanalytic Epistemology*. London: Routledge.

O'Shaughnessy, E. (2005) Whose Bion?. *International Journal of Psychoanalysis*, 86: 1523–1528.

Ogden, T. H. (1989) *The Primitive Edge of Experience*. Northvale, NJ: Jason Aronson.

Ogden, T. H. (1994a) *Subjects of Analysis*. London: Karnac.

Ogden, T. H. (1994b) The concept of interpretive action. *Psychoanalytic Quarterly*, 63: 219–245.

Ogden, T. H. (1997) *Reverie and Interpretation: Sensing Something Human*. Northvale, NJ: Jason Aronson.

Ogden, T. H. (2001) *Conversations at the Frontier of Dreaming*. Northvale, NY: Jason Aronson Inc. Publishers/London: Karnac.

Ogden, T. H. (2005) *This Art of Psychoanalysis: Dreaming Undreamt Dreams and Interrupted Cries*. London: Routledge.

Ogden, T. H. (2009) *Rediscovering Psychoanalysis: Thinking and Dreaming, Learning and Forgetting*. London: Routledge.

Petrella, F. (1996) L'ascolto e l'ostacolo: musica, discorso, immaginazione nel lavoro psicoanalitico. *Atque*, 14/15: 155–188.

Petrella, F. (2007) Sublimazione. In F. Barale, M. Bertani, V. Gallese, S. Mistura, A. Zamperini (eds.) *Psiche: Dizionario storico di psicologia, psichiatria, psicoanalisi, neuroscienze* (pp. 1063–1069). Turin: Einaudi.

Pozzi, M. E. (2003) The use of observation in the psychoanalytic treatment of a 12-year-old boy with Asperger's syndrome. *International Journal of Psychoanalysis*, 84: 1333–1349.

Pragier, G. (1995) Enjeux métapsychologiques de l'hypocondrie. In '*L'hypocondrie*', *Monographies de la Revue Française de Psychanalyse* (pp. 73–90). Paris: PUF.

Propp, V. (1928) *Morphology of the Folktale*. Austin, TX: University of Texas Press.

Quinodoz, J.-M. (2001) *Dreams That Turn Over a Page*. London: Routledge 2002.

Recalcati, M. (2007) *Il miracolo della forma: Per un'estetica psicoanalitica*. Carlo Mondadori, Milan.

Reed, G. S. (1994) *Transference Neurosis and Psychoanalytic Experience*. New Haven, CT: Yale University Press.

Resnik, S. (1987) *Theatre of the Dream*. London: Routledge.

Ricoeur, P. (1987) [Internet]. La filosofia di Cartesio [accessed 7 May 2008]. Available from: http://www.emsf.rai.it/interviste/interviste.asp?d=399

Rilke, R. M. (1923) *Duino Elegies and the Sonnets of Orpheus*. Translated by A. Poulin, Jr. New York: Mariner Books.

Robutti, A. (1992) Cassandra: a myth for hypochondria. In L. Nissim Momigliano, A. Robutti (eds.) *The Shared Experience: The Psychoanalytic Dialogue* (pp. 189–211). London: Karnac.

Rousset, J. (1981) *Leurs yeux se rencontrèrent*. Paris: José Corti.

Ruskin, J. (1843) *Modern Painters*. Charleston, SC: BiblioBazaar 2009.

Ryan, M.-L. (2001) *Narrative as Virtual Reality: Immersion and Interactivity in Literature and Electronic Media*. Baltimore: Johns Hopkins University Press.

Sandler, P.C. (2001) Prefazione. In G. Civitarese, *La violenza delle emozioni. Bion e la psicoanalisi postbioniana* (pp. IX–XVI). Milano: Raffaello Cortina.

Sandler, P. C. (2005) *The Language of Bion*. London: Karnac.

Sanguineti, E. (2006) *Quaderno di traduzioni. Lucrezio-Shakespeare-Goethe*. Turin: Einaudi.

Schreber, D. P. (1903) *Memoirs of My Nervous Illness*. New York, NY: The New York Review Books 2000.

Searles, H. F. (1965a) *Collected Papers on Schizophrenia & Related Subjects*. London: Karnac 2005.

Searles, H. F. (1965b) The effort to drive the other person crazy – an element in the aetiology and psychotherapy of schizophrenia. In *Collected Papers on Schizophrenia & Related Subjects* (pp. 254–283). London: Karnac 2005.

Saint John of the Cross (1618) *Dark Night of the Soul*. Mineola, NY: Dover Publications 2003.

Starobinski, J. (1974) *Trois fureurs: Essais*. Paris: Gallimard.

Stern, D. N., Sander, L. W., Nahum, J. P., Harrison, A. M., Lyons-Ruth, K., Morgan, A. C., Bruschweilerstern, N. and Tronick, E. Z. (1998) Non-interpretive mechanism in psychoanalytic therapy: the 'something more' than interpretation. *International Journal of Psychoanalysis*, 79: 903–921.

Stokes, A. (1963) *Painting and the Inner World*. London: Tavistock.

Stolorow, R. D. (1977) Notes on the signal function of hypochondriacal anxiety. *International Journal of Psychoanalysis*, 58: 245–246.

Stolorow, R. D. (1979) Defensive and arrested developmental aspects of death anxiety, hypochondriasis and depersonalization. *International Journal of Psychoanalysis*, 60: 201–213.

Strinati, C. (2008) *Sebastiano del Piombo. 1485–1547*. Milan: Federico Motta.

Sweetnam, A. (2007) 'Are you a woman – or a flower?'. The capacity to experience beauty. *International Journal of Psychoanalysis*, 88: 1491–1506.

Tustin, F. (1986) *Autistic Barriers in Neurotic Patients*. London: Karnac.

Weber, S. (2004) *Theatricality of the Medium*. New York, NY: Fordham University Press.

Winnicott, D. W. (1945) Primitive emotional development. In *Through Paediatrics to Psycho-Analysis* (pp. 145–156). London: Karnac 1975.

Winnicott, D. W. (1947) Hate in the countertransference. In *Through Paediatrics to Psycho-Analysis* (pp. 194–203). London: Karnac 1975.

Winnicott, D. W. (1949a) Mind and its relation to the psyche-soma. In *Through Paediatrics to Psycho-Analysis* (pp. 243–254). London: Karnac 1975.

Winnicott, D. W. (1949b) Birth memories, birth trauma, and anxiety. In *Through Paediatrics to Psycho-Analysis* (pp. 174–193). London: Karnac 1975.

Winnicott, D. W. (1956) On transference. *International Journal of Psychoanalysis*, 37: 386–388.

Winnicott, D. W. (1974) Fear of breakdown. *International Journal of Psychoanalysis*, 1: 103–107.

Wittgenstein, L. (1953) *Philosophical Investigations*. Oxford, UK: Wiley-Blackwell 2009.

Wright, K. (2006) Psychic growth and the search for form: a Winnicottian theory of art. Winnicott Conference. UCL, London 10th June 2006.

Index